James Waring [See

Extracts from Chordal's Letters

James Waring [See

Extracts from Chordal's Letters

ISBN/EAN: 9783744725248

Printed in Europe, USA, Canada, Australia, Japan

Cover: Foto ©ninafisch / pixelio.de

More available books at **www.hansebooks.com**

EXTRACTS

FROM

CHORDAL'S LETTERS.

COMPRISING THE CHOICEST SELECTIONS FROM THE SERIES OF ARTICLES ENTITLED
"EXTRACTS FROM CHORDAL'S LETTERS," WHICH HAVE BEEN APPEARING
FOR THE PAST TWO YEARS IN THE COLUMNS OF
THE AMERICAN MACHINIST.

*WITH STEEL PORTRAIT OF THE AUTHOR; ALSO, ORIGINAL
ILLUSTRATIONS BY CHAS. J. TAYLOR.*

PREFACE BY THE AUTHOR.

NEW AND ENLARGED EDITION, WITH ADDITIONAL PLAT

NEW YORK:
JOHN WILEY & SONS.
1883.

PREFACE.

The letters to the Editor of the AMERICAN MACHINIST. from which he has made so many extracts under the title of "Extracts from Chordal's Letters," were written with pleasure to the author. They were without any continued thought on any one subject, being intended as the presentation of the topic, rather than the thought.

With such intentions, it made little difference which side of a question was taken, or that an opposite side was taken in a succeeding letter.

There is but little need of consistency, where there is no tenacity of view.

A pleasure has also followed the writing of these letters. It has often come to the author's knowledge, that they were read by people who, as a rule, never read anything. It is not known that this proves merit in the letters, but there is a pleasure in knowing that one has in the smallest way, or in any way, been instrumental in getting anybody into the habit of reading anything.

There is plenty of shop in these letters; good shop and bad shop; in fact, they are shop letters, written for shop men, by a shop man, who has as much interest in the people who go into the shops, as in the marvelous products which come out of the shops.

As if there were not enough of the mechanic in these letters, it seems a pity to miss the chance, in a preface, to express the view that we live in a peculiar land, under a peculiar form of government, surrounded by peculiar social conditions.

In other lands, the well-being of all depends on the wisdom of the few who rule. In our land, the well-being of all depends on the wisdom of the mass, who select their rulers. In other lands, the ignorance of the mass will insure the stability of the existing civic form.

In our land, the ignorance of the mass will insure the total destruction of the existing civic form.

The shop men form a large proportion of our civic mass. They must be more than workmen; they must be citizens. They must have more than skill; they must have education.

Education and wise citizenship cost money. The mechanic of the Republic must be better paid than the mechanic of the Monarchy.

Our mechanics are wiser citizens than are the mechanics of any other land, and they are better paid than in other lands.

The Republic owes it to its mechanics, that it pay the hire of good citizens; and the mechanic owes it to the Republic, that he make himself worthy of a citizen's hire, as well as the workman's hire.

JAMES W. SEE.

HAMILTON, OHIO.

CONTENTS.

CHAPTER I.
Mechanics Who Succeed and Those Who Fail.—Reasons Why.—What to do With Money Saved - - - - - - - - 9

CHAPTER II.
Sackett and Wycoff in Missouri.—Saw Mill Emergencies.—Devising Make-Shifts.—Stealing Men and Being Stolen - - - - 16

CHAPTER III.
How the Panic Struck Pete & Cady.—A Yankee Contractor in the Shop - - - - - - - - - - - 25

CHAPTER IV.
Hunter's Troubles with Foremen.—Sackett's Experience - - 36

CHAPTER V.
How Far Should Purchasers' wishes Influence Manufacturers?—What to do with Odd Patterns - - - - - - - 43

CHAPTER VI.
Mrs. Toodles Runs a Machine Shop.—Comparative Cost of Small Tools.—A Machine Screw Missionary.—How a Grindstone was Made to Pay - - - - - - - - - - 51

CHAPTER VII.
History of Two Jours.—Wycoff's Shop Photographed.—Longevity of Shops - - - - - - - - - - - 56

CHAPTER VIII.
Ye Heartsick Tramping Jour.—How to Get Up in the World.—Keeping Mum about Wages.—High Wages vs. High First Cost of Product.—What Constitutes a Good Workman - - - 61

CHAPTER IX.
Extension of Shops.—Developing Into a Stock Company.—A Time-Keeping Machine.—Hunter's Foundry Accounts.—Ownership of Patterns - - - - - - - - - - 72

CHAPTER X.
Altering Details to Suit Customers.—Journal Boxes and How to Place Them.—Fear of Advertising Somebody - - - - - 79

CHAPTER XI.

Emery Wheels in the Shop.—An Emery-Wheel Man Wanted.—Charley as the Champion Oiler.—A Mechanical Time-Keeper - - 86

CHAPTER XII.

Shop Nomenclature. — Sackett's Planer Arrangement. — Milling Machines and Yankee "Trappery."—A Core Device for Foundries 95

CHAPTER XIII.

Taking Things on Trial.—Starting New Shops and Starting New Tools.—Shop Ablutions - - - - - - - - 100

CHAPTER XIV.

Shops in the Sky.—Value of Testimonials.—Location of Factories.—Selling Agencies - - - - - - - - 108

CHAPTER XV.

Tells How Dix and Chordal Established Standard Sizes in Wycoff's Shop - - - - - - - - - - - 118

CHAPTER XVI.

Outwitting the Almanac.—Lighting Shops - - - - - 124

CHAPTER XVII.

The Lightning Machinist.—His Lazy Neighbor.—The Soldier on Duty.—Giving Satisfaction to Purchasers.—Order in Shops - 135

CHAPTER XVIII.

Chordal's Boy Joe.—What Books Shall Machinists Read? - - 143

CHAPTER XIX.

The Traveled Machinist.—Fair Play for Apprentices.—Bright and Black Finish - - - - - - - - - 153

CHAPTER XX.

Sackett's Theories of Wages and Finance.—Systems of Gauges.—Newton's Casting Room.—Who Shall Clean Castings?—Country Moulders - - - - - - - - - - 160

CHAPTER XXI.

Journals and Bearings.—The Younger Sackett in Wycoff's Shop - 172

CHAPTER XXII.

Mr. Huber's New Button Set.—Poor Dan Takes the Floor - - 187

CHAPTER XXIII.

Turning Shafting on the Hotchkiss Plan.—A Simon Pure Machine Shop - - - - - - - - - - - 196

CHAPTER XXIV.

Geography in Machine Building.—Getting Ready for Business.—Two Cases in Point - - - - - - - - - - 203

CHAPTER XXV.

Working for Nothing.—How Chordal Got Ugly.—Sixteen Glasses of Beer.—Money Saved on Mandrels - - - - - - 210

CHAPTER XXVI.

Finding One's Vocation.—How Bob Did It.—Pattern Making in Country Shops.—Devices Born Too Soon - - - - - 222

CHAPTER XXVII.

Coarse-Grained Foremen.—The Chronic Mistaker.—The Blunderer.—The Anxious Man.—The Man Who Knows.—The Mullet-Head.—Cliques in the Shop.—Benches for the North Shop - - - 229

CHAPTER XXVIII.

Procrastination in Shops.—Ingraham's Opening Day.—Making Repairs.—System and Organization.—Sick Lathes, and How to Cure Them.—Short-winded Planers.—A Point in Sackett's System - 236

CHAPTER XXIX.

Paint on Machinery.—Functional Machines.—Shafting and Hangers.—A New Wrinkle in Shafting.—A New Tool Wanted - - 249

CHAPTER XXX.

Elasticity of Workmen.—How Chordal Got Bounced.—A Glorious Mechanical Tramp.—Resurrecting Shops - - - - 258

CHAPTER XXXI.

Successful Things that Won't Do.—Screwing-on versus Casting-on.—The Ten-Year-Old Method of Polishing.—Migrating Westward - 265

CHAPTER XXXII.

Settling Mechanical Disputes.—Advantages of Having no Foundry.—Mechanical Quixotism.—Forges and Shelves for the North Shop.—The Steam Engine Indicator. - - - - - - - 274

CHAPTER XXXIII.

Old Castings in the Shop.—How New Tools are Suggested.—How They Ought To Be.—Combination Machines - - - 282

CHAPTER XXXIV.

Arranging Machine Shop Floors.—Methods of Finishing Work.—Our Artist Sketches a Common Boiler Front - - - 292

CHAPTER XXXV.

Sackett's Experience with a Titled Engineer.—Personal Identity of Bennett, Sackett and Wycoff.—Shop Drawings and Symbolism.—Tramping Jours.—Starting New Shops.—Chordal as a Pilgrim - 302

CHAPTER XXXVI.

The Men who Design Mills and Shops.—Characteristics of Professional and Non-Professional Men.—Architects who Fail in Designing Industrial Works.—Inconveniences in Machine Shops.—The Usual Experience in Building and Extending Them - - - - - - - - - - - - 321

CHAPTER XXXVII.

The Acquisition of Knowledge.—Experience of the Country Banker's Son in a Machine Shop - - - - - - - - 328

CHAPTER XXXVIII.

Shapes and Styles of Chimneys.—Mistakes in Building Chimneys.—How the Ladies Set Out to Improve a Dirty City.—Mr. Sinton's Pride in his Smoke Consumer - - - - - 336

CHAPTER XXXIX.

Mr. Baker Builds a Mill with Doors and a Lean-to.—A Reformed Consumptive Persuades him to Invest in a Hyphen.—How Things Turned Out - - - - - - - - - 345

CHAPTER XL.

Mr. Marling the Moulder.—His Industrial and Social Habits.—His Efforts to Make his Co-workers Miserable.—How they Appreciated his Efforts - - - - - - - - 354

CHAPTER XLI.

Looking for a Coal Vase with Trunnions.—The Confusion Among Catalogues.—A Hardware Clerk's System.—Bennett's System of Keeping Catalogues.—Chordal's Own System - - - 361

CHAPTER XLII.

Altering the Form of a Mechanical Product to Suit Customers.—Some Opinions and Experiences.—How the Public School Principals liked the Ink.—How Machine-Shop Principals may Take a Hint - - - - - - - - - - 370

CHAPTER XLIII.

Personal History of a Young Machinist - - - - - - 375

CHAPTER XLIV.

Different Kinds of Foremen - - - - - - - - - 385

CHAPTER XLV.

A Shop with Servants for the Workmen - - - - - - 395

FULL PAGE ILLUSTRATIONS.

Frontispiece. Steel Portrait of the Author.

The Negro Engineer bores out the Cylinder with a Grate Bar,	17
"There was a Yankee Contractor in Pete & Cady's Shop,"	31
"Excuse Me, Gentlemen,—got to Shrink this Crank on,"	61
Mechanical Time-keeper in Sackett's Shop,	89
"Never a Day Passed but Something Came Tumbling Down,"	109
The Lightning Machinist,	133
"Mind You, I am Going to Make an Example of You,"	161
"Then Poor Dan took the Floor,"	191
"Who should Come with our Beer but the same Chap who had asked for a Job,"	215
"Ingraham Superintended and Smiled Acknowledgments,"	239
"I Saw a Ten-year-old Nigger-boy finishing Flat Irons on an Emery Wheel,"	269
"I wish you would Send an Artist *** to Sketch a common Boiler Front,"	297
"I seek Far and Wide for the Man Who can Measure me for a Shop,"	323
"Mr. Sinton is Very Proud of his Device, and has almost Paralyzed his Forefinger,"	341
"McCann Informs Baker that he is Running on Forty Pounds of Coal to the Barrel of Flour,"	351
"Mr. Marling Takes an Inventory—a Trowel, Two Slicks, and Two Ratty Suits of Clothes,"	357
"Bennett's Office—Indexing Chordal under his Proper Number, and Shoving him into a Pigeon Hole Marked C,"	367
"He Hears the Foreman Talking 'German,' and it Makes him Sick,"	379
"John Paul on the Ladder,"	387
"The Servants of the Machinist,"	393

Extracts from Chordal's Letters.

CHAPTER I.

MECHANICS WHO SUCCEED AND THOSE WHO FAIL.—REASONS WHY.—WHAT TO DO WITH MONEY SAVED.

* * * * There are a lot of mechanics who manage to get into every shop in the land who judge of possibilities entirely by their own weak accomplishments. They are the ones who do the grumbling. Their weak minds never understand the circumstances around them, and they foolishly and blindly give utterance to the stereotyped growl: "There's no show for a mechanic." It is the miserable and contemptible example of such men that keeps boys with stuff in them out of the shop. They sagely tell the inquiring youth not to go into a shop, that there is no decent show in the world, that they have been there and know. Now these men lie. They never have been there; they don't know, and there is a show. The smart mechanic of to-day has before him a possibility of prosperity, of usefulness, of social position, of home comfort and general respect, such as the lords of earlier centuries, with armed retainers, with no forks, and with dogs under the table, never dared to dream of.

No mechanic in this country dares lift his head and say his children must do without education, and go to work at twelve years of age. No mechanic in this country, when he squats in a town, is compelled to hunt up a dirty hut to live in, and pay a premium on it because it fronts on a sloppy alley.

The mechanic in this country cannot lay special claim to a dirty home because he is a workingman. The eggshells thrown into his slop-yard may be filthier and dirtier than those of his decent neighbor, but it is not the result of his being a mechanic, for his neighbor is one also. When his dirty little girl goes to school in the morning, her dirty stocking may slouch down off her leg and upon her miserable shoes, but it can't be explained by saying that these stockings are dirty and slouched down because they are on the legs of the daughter of a workingman. The explanation would fail for the simple reason that two-thirds of this girl's trim and neat companions are daughters of workingmen. The comforts of life and home are within the reach of all American working-men. The best of things that are printed, the finest efforts of the stage, and the best of home comforts, the American workingman may enjoy. There is no social bar whatever to his political distinction. He may choose whether he will frequent the finest homes in the land or the lowest pot houses. If he is a low blackguard, he will be refused decent society, not because he is a workingman, but because he is a blackguard. Every prospect for the future which this wide world holds out for its choicest people, this land holds out for the smart mechanic. Yet the shiftless, ignorant, thoughtless sluggard sees no show for the workingman! There is a show, *all* the show, but maybe none for him. The sensible mechanic don't gauge his own accomplishments by the contemptible lack of effort of the ignorant howler.

* * * * Is there no show for machinists, Mr. Editor? Turn to the last pages of the AMERICAN MACHINIST, and there read the biography of the workingman. The advertising pages tell the tale. Sixty men put their names on those pages. They employ five thousand workmen, and over six million dollars of capital.

Were these sixty men born with these millions in their pockets? Did they fall heir to the cash and the shops at an early age? Not a bit of it. Look here: At the age of eighteen, over forty of these men were working in shops, drilling set screw holes in pulleys, cutting bolts, chipping new holes in old boilers, contriving ways and means to get old broken studs out of old cylinders, forging square keys out of round iron, butt-welding erroneous connecting rods, gouging out core boxes, gluing up segments, spitting white pine dust, cutting up old boilers, building up new boilers, putting in new rivets, cutting out old rivets, bedding floor moulds, ramming copes, filing cores, and doing everything one man does for another man's money. They were not preparing themselves to take charge of probated fortunes. They were working. Of these forty men, thirty did not, at the age of eighteen, have fifty dollars they could call their own. Of the five thousand men they now employ, three thousand were then their shopmates.

Among these sixty men can be found the names of some of the highest social powers in this land of ours. High toned society made no exception among the three thousand and sixty. Society never said to one of the sixty: "We find a birth mark on you; twenty years from now come to us." Society never said anything. The sixty said. Fortune never said: "I see a mark; come to me." Fortune never said anything. The sixty said. The five thousand in the shop never said to the sixty: "We see a mark on you; shoot ahead and we will lag and work for you." The five thousand never said anything. The sixty said. Providence didn't chalk out a future for the sixty. The sixty did their own chalking and left the five thousand to lean on Providence.

Civil law never said, "sixty of you chaps must be smart and prudent—thrifty—and five thousand of you must starve in pot houses after work is over." Law don't push men forward. The sixty did the pushing.

A vile blackguard blows the fumes of cheap whiskey in my face and tells me there is no future for a mechanic. Oh no! of course not. If a man is foolish enough to learn the machine trade, of course he can never hope to call a pane of glass or a rose bush his own! Of course, he can never hope to take a daily paper, nor to own a copy of Comstock's philosophy, nor twenty dollars worth of general books, nor to be called on to rule in public councils, nor to head a public charity, nor to see his children well educated!

There's no show of course! If a man ever touches a chipping hammer, a wise people will never call on him to govern the state. If he ever splits a rail, good-bye to all future prospects.

* * * * Mr. Editor, if you know of a bright sixteen-years-old boy, smart and independent, with snap, pride, poverty, good health, and a common school education, and with a hankering after the mechanical arts, tell him to go into a machine shop and learn the trade. You can appear disinterested, but some day he will be your advertiser.

Tell him, when he earns money, to hunt up some way to spend it all before the next installment is due; tell him to learn only one way of doing things, and to fail when that way won't fit; tell him he is to get rich, not by the amount saved, but by the amount of wages received; tell him never to look into the human nature of his foremen and fellow workmen; tell him always to hunt up the slums to live in when he moves to a new place; tell him to cultivate the habit of playing seven-up in a saloon two hours every night; tell him to buy his groceries by the quarter's worth; tell him when he is dissatisfied with his wages, not to go to the office by himself on his own merits, but to find a dozen other fellows, eight of whom already get more than they are worth, and march into the office and demand a raise or threaten a strike; tell him never to hesitate to spend six months' wages to get a three months' job at ten cents a day more; tell him to associate with machinists only; tell him never to pay six dollars to take his folks to the opera, and never to miss a low performance; tell him never to read anything relating to the past, present or future; tell him never to clean up before he goes home, and never to allow his home and family to be as neat as a millionaire's; tell him to take his children out of school as soon as some one will buy them at a dollar a week; tell him all these things, and see that he lives up to them—and he will never be your advertiser. He will curse you to his dying day, and will tell you a workingman has no show in this country.

* * * * *Norman*, one of your correspondents, states that a late letter of mine provoked discussion. This is gratifying and pleasant. Were I a high and mighty power, able to suggest and dictate plans, I could do much good indeed; but, as it is, the utmost I can expect of myself is the ability to turn thought in some certain direction. Thought resulting in discussion, should result in settled plans. I was in hopes that the very empty termination of my former remarks would lead to suggestions as to failures or successes. Men don't like to talk about such things much, and men like Norman, who will tell of a failure, are rare.

If a man is of a prudent character, he will act like all prudent men, and will succeed and fail as all prudent men do. No bank is sure; but the best business men deposit in them. If a wealthy man loses all by a bank, he suffers indeed, for his living capital was there. He must change his course of life, and commence his life's work anew. The workman's money in bank is strictly a surplus, and its total loss need not affect his life to-day or to-morrow one jot or tittle. But it won't do for a person, who at middle age commences to save, to lose it all. It is apt to stop the thing. Men who have never saved, and who propose to save, should have a sure thing on it. Savings banks are not a sure thing; in no state is a depositor guarded absolutely against discouraging losses. Besides that, there is nothing compulsory about deposits. Building associations are, in many ways, superior, especially in some states. The deposits are compulsory, and the securities excellent, though not absolute. Loans are dangerous, when effected by inexperienced men. Profit on savings is no object to the class I speak of. The saving itself is the main thing. Real estate, bought on small notes, is a good investment, if the land is not a swindle. Owning a lot, whether there is a house on it or not, is not a tie to any workman. If he loses his job, he can go elsewhere and work; his real estate don't need to hold him; he can go, just as though he didn't have any. If he can sell it, or can't sell it, he ought not to sell it; if it can't be rented, don't rent it; if taxes must be paid on idle property, pay them. To the class I speak of, the privilege of owning something is worth paying for. The idea that John Smith can't work in Pennsylvania, because he bought a lot in Michigan, is a shallow idea. If the lot is in a good place, it don't make any difference where the job is; the further off the better. He won't be so apt to sell the lot.

Stock in corporations is dangerous to the class I speak of. Such investments need control. The owner has no chance and no capability. Government bonds are the very best investment; they are as safe as can be; the trouble is in the size of them. The ten dollar certificates were exactly the thing, but they were soon used up. If Mr. Sherman would arrange for an issue of several millions of dollars, in similar certificates, *without* interest, convertible into interest-bearing bonds, in sums of five hundred dollars, the workman would hail the day. Money invested in such things is idle, of course, but idle money beats no money at all. If such certificates should be issued, manufacturers would see that their men got them. To a machinist who has a chronic case of squander on hand, and who wants to get well, I can suggest a plan as sure and certain as the stability of this Government. It is this: Every pay-day go to the post-office and get a money order for your extra cash. Don't try to make the figure even, but for any amount, seven, nine, eleven, or seventeen dollars—anything you can; don't dare to make the order larger. Get the money on pay-day, sure. Have the order made payable to the Treasurer of the United States, and take it home.* This is safe; no one can get any good out of these orders, if they are stolen; if burnt up or lost, you can get duplicates. Do this every pay-day; never miss a single one under any circumstances, and when you get a hundred dollars' worth, take them to any bank, or to the man you work for, and buy a hundred-dollar Government bond. Have that bond registered by all means.

---

* It is best not to hold money-orders longer than one year, as after that time their collection might be attended with some inconvenience.

CHAPTER II.

SACKETT AND WYCOFF IN MISSOURI.—SAW MILL EMERGENCIES.—DEVISING MAKE-SHIFTS.—STEALING MEN AND BEING STOLEN.

It was west of the Mississippi that I first met Sackett and Wycoff, who have now returned to the East. They both started small shops in Missouri, in the same town, just as the war came on. They found they had made a mistake, so they returned before they had run a month. Siegel occupied the town, needed grape-shot, and, finding a hundred St. Louis moulders in his command, he "pressed" the two foundries and set the men at work. The cupolas and moulding floors had been designed for heats of one ton; not a dozen flasks had been made; one hundred and twenty miles to a railroad or river, and no pig iron or coal on hand. Candle and soap boxes from the subsistence department were used for flasks; cook-stoves, flat-irons, and sash-weights impressed for scraps; and charcoal used for fuel. The moulders worked all over the buildings and yards, and the cupolas ran continuously. It took six men to carry up charcoal for each one. The result was tons and tons of grape-shot. Then came a battle, a defeat, and a retreat. The grape-shot had not been cleaned or broken from the gates, so they were all thrown into wells and covered up, to keep them from the enemy. The enemy, however, thought it cheaper to dig up these grape-shot than to make new ones. They were thus well-fixed for grape, but had no iron for horse-shoes, so they commenced on the saw-mills in thirty counties, and used up all wrought-iron parts on hundreds of engines; connecting-rods, piston-rods, mainshafts, bolts, nuts, and cam-rods—all went to heel the rebellious army mule.

Oil gives out and water is used till a hog is killed. * * * *The cylinder gets cut, and the negro engineer bores it out with a grate bar.*—Page 19.

The war ended one day and Sackett and Wyckoff went back and found their tools wrecked. They refitted and began to reap a rich harvest. All the aforesaid engines came in for repairs; one hundren dollars for a single cut through a cylinder, and other work in proportion. The Lehigh coal cost eighty dollars a ton, for it had to be hauled over a hundred miles, but they got twelve and a half cents a pound for the heaviest castings. I need not say they made money, but the game was up when a railroad came and brought competition within reach. They wisely sold out and came East again.

* * * * Among the saw mills in this region could be found many triumphs of unlettered genius. There were few real mechanics in these mills; shops hundreds of miles away by wagon road; and accidents always happening. The stop-valve on the engine gives out, but the mill must run while a new one is coming. A brake is put under the flywheel to slow the engine, and a stick of cord-wood thrown under the connecting rod stops it. Rod boxes and cross-head "brasses" of oak were common. A slide-valve of black-walnut was found once in a while. Oil gives out and water is used till a hog is killed. The saw gets sprung, and the factory wants thirty dollars to exercise the saw maker's magic art upon it, and the mill would stand still three weeks. The backwoods sawyer straightens it in an hour, without knowing just how he did it. The cylinder gets cut, and the negro engineer bores it out with a grate-bar. *I saw him doing it.* Flange joints are made with white sand mixed with the white of an egg, and the main belt is spliced with bark. A boiler wanted new fire-box and tubes. The negro engineer undertook the job. He never saw the inside of a boiler shop, and never saw a piece of machinery outside that mill, but the owner had sent for iron, tubes and rivets, and the man had gone to work in his own way. When I happened in that section, he was boring the tube sheets. His special tools were a four-by-four scantling and a five-eighths bolt. All these mills have a ratchet drill. He laid off and drilled the center holes, put the bolt through the hole and scantling, drove a cutter through a mortise in the scantling, and using the scantling as a lever, walked round and cut the holes, feeding by driving on the cutter. I was interested enough to caliper some holes already done, and found them as good as the ordinary boiler shop job. I am satisfied the fellow finished the thing up in good shape. An educated or skilled mechanic would never have attempted to do this work in the woods.

* * * * Some men seem to be deficient entirely in power for devising make-shifts, or in adaptability to novel circumstances.

I was told of a well-educated engineer who found himself fifty miles from port with a broken vacuum gauge. He showed utter helplessness, and proposed immediate return. His assistant was a shovel engineer. He saw nothing amiss in a broken gauge, or in the absence of one. He traded places with his chief, and made the trip by sense of feeling. When his condenser felt too hot, he gave her more injection.

We are told of a party of royal astronomers who went into the northern regions to make observations. The expedition was an important one, but the weather was so severe that the mercury forming the artificial horizon was frozen, thus rendering their instruments useless. They gave it up and came home without the idea of a lamp under the mercury having occurred to them.

* * * * The business boom has brought to our ears the old charge of stealing men.

As near as I can remember, I have heard of no case, during the last few years, of emissaries slipping around and seducing men away from one shop to work in another for better pay. An owner has been thankful if he could keep his front door open and the line shaft turning around, and the men have been thankful for a job at any pay. The dull times lasted so long that tools were allowed to deteriorate and run down generally, systems flagged, capital was withdrawn, and manufacturing facilities were, in many cases, seriously crippled.

During these times, good workmen in many cases became disgusted with a trade which paid such terribly low wages. They quit the business and went into other things, sometimes more profitable, sometimes less, but they at least succeeded in changing the general current of their lives. Some shops had such a poor lot of men left in them that keen-witted boys would not go among them to learn the trade. The less cultivated boys could not get into the shops, and no boy with wit or no wit could learn much from the lot of men which was left. Such circumstances were exceptional, of course, but there was a tendency that way all over. Many good men fell out of the ranks, and few good boys went into the shops.

Now we find that work is plenty in many sections, and sharp workmen hard to get. There has always been some attention paid to keeping good men. Many owners in the dullest times followed the plan of always letting the poorest workmen go, and even replacing them with better ones. Other shops, on the contrary, kept the poorest men because they were cheaper.

* * * * Now we hear some poor, over-crowded owner, with time contracts on hand, with a shop run down at the heel, and with all the men he can get, saying, "So and So steals my men away from me. He's a low down, contemptible, dirty cur," etc., etc.

* * * * Now, honestly, Mr. Editor, do you think Mr. So and So is a cur? How does he steal men? By offering them more pay. Auction is theft according to the morals of some. Now I, for one, like to see this stealing going on. It's awfully inconvenient sometimes, but it's a mutual privilege, and out of the rivalry the poor machinist manages to get his full value. A machinist is entitled to all the favorable fluctuation in the labor market, and when the bidding is spirited all may laugh, for times are good.

* * * * I have had men stolen from me, and called the stealer a thief. I have stolen men from other folks and have been called a thief. I have been stolen myself, and always had the most respect for the biggest thief. The way to get men is to pay their value, the way to hold them is to pay their value, and the man gets and holds his place by making himself valuable.

There are employers who look upon mechanics as a class to be bargained with like business men, who consider a mechanic as having the business ability and sharpness to look out for his own interest. There are other employers who feel and know that workingmen are not business men, and cannot do well by themselves, that they deal in force rather than in business power, and that they can be imposed on with little effort. They would blush to take advantage of these circumstances, as they would if tempted to bruise the weak. This latter class are not exceptional at all. They are about equal with the first class, and they set the wages of the world with a justice which is certainly admirable under the circumstances.

* * * * If a man is filling a situation he brings down the wrath of his employer if he listens to better offers. I claim that when a man sells his services for the time being to another man, it is his duty to listen carefully to every thing which indicates to him his present or prospective value. A man ought to be ashamed of himself who does not say every day: "I expect to be more valuable some day;" and the employer ought to be ashamed of himself who will dicker with a man for his present services and then assume that the man should turn a deaf ear to every offer. * * * Warwick has a superintendent at eighteen hundred a year. Both were satisfied. The superintendent Byron didn't know his real value, and Warwick didn't care. But Mr. Timmerman comes along. He don't care anything for Byron, but he wants a good superintendent; he wants Byron, and knows his value. He don't propose to pay any more than he can help, but he does propose to pay somewhere between eighteen hundred dollars and the real value of the man, so he goes to Warwick's place and offers Byron twenty-five hundred dollars a year or a third interest in his place. Byron is not on a contract. If he was he would not violate it, and if he was, Timmerman would not be a party to the violation. Byron goes to Warwick and states the case. Warwick talks ugly right away, and accuses Timmerman of dishonorable conduct in coming into his mill on such an errand, and accuses Byron of dishonorable conduct in not kicking him right out. The only questionable feature I can see in the play is Warwick's conduct.

* * * I claim that when one man goes to work for another for the time being, he reserves the right to constantly exert himself to do better, and also the right to invite better offers right on the premises. The idea of presuming that paying a man for present services gives the right to blindfold him and stop up his ears forever!

* * * Into this question of course comes the policy of leaving a permanent place for a temporary place at a higher figure. It is supposed that common sense will cover such cases, and any man will understand that once in a while somebody will offer him more than his value, on account of pressing necessities of service. Wise men never bite at such things. A little judgment will tell if a figure is too high to be permanent.

CHAPTER III.

HOW THE PANIC STRUCK PETE & CADY.—A YANKEE CONTRACTOR IN THE SHOP.

* * * * Pete & Cady have a shop in a town of twenty thousand inhabitants. Years ago their business was general. They did saw and grist-mill work; would contract for the iron work for a jail; receive orders for engines of ten to sixty horse power; kept a big stock of sash weights on hand; could point to many nice jobs of store-front work; had a fair line of patterns for repairing everything used in their section; and they had made money.

They had about fifty thousand dollars invested, and worked about ninety men. They did good work, and got good prices. Pete was a machinist, and a good one. Cady was a millwright, and knew lots of things. They were good men, in every sense of the word; square and honest, no lazy bones in their bodies, and with business faculties superior to the average. You will readily see that they owned a machine shop. They would build an engine, and it would be a good one. It would take them a good while to build one, but, when done, there was a margin.

These folks were not manufacturers, and, more than that, they had never seen any manufacturing done in their lives. Their business was local, with a slight tinge of reputation abroad in connection with their number four circular saw mill. Their work came to them, and they figured on it and did it, if they got the order. If they got a whiff of a possible job, Cady would put on his good clothes, and go, say, fifty miles, and labor with the party. They did work only when they had the order. They had made money and had a surplus. Pete was foreman in the machine shop in particular, and superintendent of the concern in general. Cady was in the pattern shop, when not engaged outside. The shop was located in the Middle States, and was booming when the panic struck the trade.

* * * * The panic made things blue around the establishment of Pete & Cady—few men, little work, contemptible wages, and the shop losing money. Like a thousand other men during the panic, they held a council, and decided that they were engaged in a line of trade greatly overcrowded. They must hunt up something to make, which would keep them busy, and make it pay. They looked around, and struck on the last thing for a panic-stricken shop to engage in, to wit: small semi-portable steam engines.

What led them to it, no man knows. Pete said, in gloomy council, "We have all the tools required in this little engine business; we know all about steam engines; we can make them up without orders and sell from stock—lots of these things sold."

The fact is, these boys were hatching up a manufacturing conspiracy. They thought that manufacturing consisted in simply engaging in a line which would permit a stock to be carried to fill orders from, as distinguished from a line of business dependent on special orders to fill. They looked no deeper; they didn't know it was any deeper, or they wouldn't have gone in.

* * * * After the conception, and a long period of incubation, there stood upon the shop floor an elegant little eight-horse power upright engine, just hatched. It was a machine that the purchaser would be satisfied with, and one that would be a credit to the builders.

* * * * They pitched in and built twenty, following the same plan of "manufacture" that they did with a single engine. They knew just what the engine cost; they advertised far and wide, giving a price, leaving but little margin. A month of advertising and not a sale—not even a real earnest inquiry; nothing but postal cards from triflers.

This worried the boys, for they knew such engines were being sold by hundreds. Some friend told them their price was too high, and scared inquirers away. They answered that their engine was something extra good. Friend said, the distant engine needer didn't get to see the engine; he only saw the price.

* * * * They changed tactics, and advertised larger than ever, but omitted any mention of price. This brought heavy mails, and, in response, they quoted a price ten per cent. off list. They made a few sales out of all proportion to the mails; they cut another ten per cent., and sales slightly increased. Still the business amounted to nothing, and there was nothing in it at twenty off.

* * * * The twenty engines were finally gotten rid of, and the question arose as to the desirability of building a new lot. Cady had charge of the disposal-end of the new scheme, and had got thoroughly worked up. He insisted on the engines being cut down in merit, till they could stand simply even with the others in the markets. "If others use boilers too small for the engine, we must do the same," said he, "and we must overhaul the whole thing on the same plan of economical design."

"Next," said he, "we must have the work done by the piece; that's the way other makers do. Then we must rig up for the work. These things taken together must justify another twenty per cent. cut, and then everything will be lovely. There are lots of these engines sold, and if we can only get our share of the trade, we don't need any other work." Pete coincided in the scheme, and things were pushed. The engines were re-designed; what seemed like marvelously convenient jigs, etc., were got out; the men were put on a piece-work price, which drew the sweat, and a new lot of twenty was begun.

* * * * The castings were out, the boiler iron was on hand, and a piece-work price put on every piece, so that it was known just what these engines would cost. Cady looked at the figures—looked solemn; said it wouldn't do at all. Even at this price, their cost was still slightly above the selling price of some competitors. Said Pete must be handling things wrong, or he could get the thing down lower. Pete flared up, and said the thing couldn't be got any lower. The material would not be much cheaper, if they stole it. Said he knew all about engine work, and knew there were only two ways of cheapening it. Either leave off some of the work, or cut down the men's pay. Said the engine wasn't more than half made now, and that the men would burn the shop, if they were cut another cent. They were working like laborers, and getting about half the pay they had two years before. The married men had come down to corn bread, and the single men had taken to cheap, low boarding houses. The best men had left the shop, and some had quit the trade. It cost five hundred and ten dollars to put an engine in the wareroom, and others were selling the same engine for five hundred. He defied any man to go into the shop and get that ten dollars off the cost without a riot.

* * * * These earnest co-workers were at their wit's ends. Their machine lives had been pleasant. Nice, well-paid men, and living profits on work had been their experience. Now, there was no profit. and there was a constant, bitter antagonism between shop and men. It all came from these engines, this "manufacturing scheme." Pete suggested, as they had not yet fairly started in the business, that they drop it and work on these engines as usual, building only when they got a decent order. This meant to discharge half the men, but it was decided on to take place at the end of the month.

* * * * Next week a man walked into Pete & Cady's office. He didn't have a roll of blue overalls, with a hammer, a square, and two pairs of calipers wrapped up in it, under his arm. He had on nice boots, and nice clothes, and a white shirt, which would do credit to a lobbyist. He wore a plug hat. He looked smart and starchy, and had the manner and approach of a business man. He was not timid or impulsive. This clean looking chap actually asked Pete & Cady if they needed any machinists; and Pete & Cady told this clean looking chap "No." Then conversation commenced. The chap proved to be a Yankee, and the Yankeest kind of a Yank at that. He told where he had been engaged down East; worked in such a shop; foreman in such a shop; contractor in such a shop. Said he had come West to stay. Had sold his house, and had brought his money with him.

Pete smiled. The machinist had brought his money with him. Pete wanted to ask how freights were, but didn't.

* * * Cady had heard a new word drop from this Yankee. What did he mean by saying he was a "contractor" in Summit's shop? Yankee explained what a contractor was. He takes the job from the owners of the shop for so much money, and goes into the shop and sees it executed.

* * * Pete, smiling, remarked that it would be a good joke on the little engine business to try and get a contractor's profit out of it, when the men and the shop were both starving, in trying to sell the engines at cost.

* * * * The Yankee's name was Doolittle, and he was business. In an hour he had pumped the firm dry; found out their history and present troubles with little engines, and, at the end of two hours, he had their permission to stand around the shop a week, to see how they did things.

* * * * At the end of the week, Doolittle tackled the firm. Said he had leased a house for a year, got his wife and babies fixed, had twelve thousand dollars in bonds in the Rhino National Bank, and now he wanted to go to work. The firm smiled. Doolittle opened up in this way: " These engines cost you five hundred and ten dollars. They are a bad job, and you ought to be ashamed of them. I never associated with steam engines, but I know all about machine work. You *must* sell these engines for five hundred to sell any. If you can sell for four-fifty, you can probably sell all you want to, according to your talk. To sell at four-fifty, they must not cost over four hundred. Your men are making about a dollar a day at hard work. You don't know what to do. Well, I *do*. If you will furnish stock at the prices you have mentioned, I will contract to deliver you a hundred engines at four hundred dollars each, better built, in every way, than those you build; and I will give your own Rhino bank as security for the fulfillment of the contract. I'll go at it right away, and furnish engines as fast as you can sell."

* * * * The firm dropped its jaw in amazement at this man's check. Cady, who was of an elastic nature, moved to the new conditions, unfolded. He worked upon the stolid Pete, until the latter changed his views, and a lawyer drew the contracts inside of three hours.

There was a Yankee Contractor inside of Pete & Cady's Shop.—Page 33.

* * * * There was a Yankee "contractor" inside of Pete & Cady's shop.

* * * * Notice is served on the engine gang, and Doolittle sails in. The engine work is in his hands; the men are his. He pays them—there are twenty men. He stops every man of them and sets them at work on tools, fixtures, jigs, etc., etc., and keeps them there for a month.

* * * * Now he picks out Walter and asks him how much he got apiece for the cross heads. Walter says: "Four dollars." Doolittle says: "You must now make them for one dollar." Walter squeals and brings out his time book, showing that he only made a dollar and a quarter a day at four dollars. Doolittle dries him up by guaranteeing him a rate greater than a dollar and a quarter. Walter goes at it, and makes two dollars a day without hard work. Doolittle goes through every piece, and cuts the price down and the men's earnings up, in this proportion, all through the engine.

* * * * Pete & Cady soon became aware of the fact that their engines were well made and interchangeable; that they were enabled to enter the market and sell them largely at a profit; that every man working on them got nearly twice the pay he did under the old plan; and that this starchy Yankee was making money out of his suicidal contract. The whole thing looked paradoxical.

* * * * Pete & Cady were happy in their mystery. They opened out into new lines of manufacture, or intended to, rather. Doolittle had a contract for a thousand engines, to be delivered as wanted, and the whole thing moved swimmingly. Neither of the firm had yet solved the problem of "what was the contractor's office?" They wanted Doolittle to go into partnership. He wouldn't do it. They proposed to contract a thousand corn planters to him. He wouldn't do it. Said he would send down East and get them a contractor.

* * * * Doolittle's offer to send for another contractor to take the corn planters threw light on the whole question. Cady was the first to see the point. Pete was tied to the training of his art, and wasn't much of a man to see things. Cady said: "Pete, I see it all. We have a skilled supervisor over twenty men. He is a superintendent getting big pay. We would think we were going to the dogs, if we paid a full superintendent the money, as salary, which Doolittle gets as profit. When you attended to the engine business, you spread yourself thinly over the whole shop, and depended on the wits of the men to execute your desires. You didn't pay the men for wit, but only for skill and force. Doolittle directs every stroke made by his few men. He furnishes the talent, and asks force only of them.

"Every man gets good pay. But if you would go out in the shop and make them change jobs, they would starve; while Doolittle could keep them there, and raise their earnings as he did before. He knows what conveniences and advantages are. You spent a hundred and fifty dollars on what you called a perfect outfit for 'manufacturing' engines. Doolittle paid twelve hundred dollars out of his own pocket before he commenced on an engine, and he sent East for tools that you acknowledged you never had heard of. He knows how to help a man in his work, and he charges big money for knowing how. I have been studying how we could kick our contract over, so we could pocket Doolittle's profit, but now I believe that if we kick the contract over we kick the profits over too."

* * * * Pete & Cady now have five contractors

in their shop on different classes of work, and they see these contractors making more money than the shop; but they are smart enough to see that the shop and the men make money, too, and that the credit is due entirely and solely to the contractors.

CHAPTER IV.

HUNTER'S TROUBLES WITH FOREMEN.—SACKETT'S EXPERIENCE.

* * * * Hunter's foreman has left him; gone West to start a shop of his own.

Hunter is in real trouble now, and regrets keenly not having taken my advice, given five years ago, to encourage and build up the executive qualities of a workman when they appeared, and thus be at all times supplied with material raised in and familiar with the shop, on which to draw in cases of emergency.

Personally, I question the policy of those business men who make their business dependent entirely upon their own presence.

We find the able and successful dry goods man buying his goods to the best advantage, and selling them to patrons drawn to him by his personal qualities. He watches his markets keenly and takes advantage of every opportunity offering chances for low purchases. He makes his regular trips to his source of supply, and buys promptly by mail and telegraph. But in all these operations is his lieutenant with him? Is he educating another man to relieve him or to take his place? If he gets sick or goes to Paris, is there a man who will do his work as well as himself? If there is such a man in the background, our merchant is a wise man and has a business which will allow him to leave it, and enjoy its fruits once in a while. The average machine-shop proprietor generally carries his business in his head, and for some reason, or lack of reason, he declines engrafting his qualities of success upon a supernumerary who might often be his real salvation.

The really prudent proprietor has in his employ a man *preparing* for every important position. Out of fifty machinists, about two can always be found, who, by proper encouragement, can fit themselves for the higher positions. They are not necessarily the best workmen; in fact, good workmen seldom make good foremen or superintendents.

A man with the mental qualities required for such positions generally finds the acquisition of an art distasteful. It is not always to a man's discredit that he is not a good workman. There are rarer qualities than skill, and there is to-day, dull as the times are, a demand for *mechanics*—men who understand human nature and the quality of metals, men who can put workmen in good places where they can, by reason of adaptability, make their results profitable and their existence pleasant. The eternal fitness of things is the golden key to the placing of men in the shop. A good foreman is the most valuable man in the shop, and earns his pay, not by fooling with chipping chisels and lathes, but by the discretion shown in parceling out his work among the men.

A good foreman can earn his pay by the simple increase in productive power of five men, and he does damage, if he attempts to "make a hand" himself.

The demand to-day is for foremen who can secure a maximum of perfection and economy in a product. The simple or complex power of reducing wages and controlling disaffected men, will not accomplish these results. To my knowledge, many of the most profitable shops are paying the highest wages to the men.

Hunter is really despondent, and gave vent yesterday to more philosophy and profanity than I supposed there was in him. Sackett went over with me, and we listened to Hunter's doleful story. He said to Sackett: "It's all well enough for you to talk about what you have always done about foremen, but what consolation is that to a man who didn't do as you did?

"I never had a foreman who could or would make a foreman for me, except Lambert, and it only took Stebbins a month to undo all of Lambert's work. Lambert did get some men into shape for promotion, but Stebbins came, and, fearing to see his feathers plucked, put them out of the shop. They all have good positions now, and are beyond my reach."

Sackett said he would send him a good man, one of his own raising, and warrant the quality. This put Hunter in good spirits, and he told us more of his experience.

He thinks his foreman ought to be called his *tenman*, because he has had two a year for the last five years. Said he: "I honestly think a foreman ought to have full control of his part of the machine, but somehow I can't let go my grip. You know, Chordal, when you told me to send for DeLow. Well, he came, and we quickly settled on terms. Then he wished me to understand his views, as he called them. You ought to have heard them. It sounded too much like law for me and my government, so I dissented, and he said that was all there was of it. He wanted supreme control in the machine shop, and insisted on my passing all instructions through him. He may have been right, but it was too strong for me.

"Then I got Walker. He was simply a good workman, who had never gotten over it. He had no dignity, and fraternized too much with the men. He became the cause of clannish jealousy, and made the shop disagreeable, so I let him go.

"Then I got Morris. He was the worst man I ever saw, and Wycoff told me he was the best man in the country. He substituted tyranny for dignified discipline, had no good judgment as to real economy, and didn't understand his men. He cut down wages to curry favor with me, and succeeded in raising the cost of my work past all reason. My cost books are well kept, and when Morris had "reduced" every really cheap man out of the shop, and got it full of men who couldn't get work elsewhere, I found things cost more than they sold for. It's hard to see through these things, but I watched the thing for a while in search of information. You know Cook, who ran that thirty-inch lathe? Well, that man didn't seem to amount to Shucks. He was a good workman, and I knew it, but he accomplished nothing, had no gumption or ambition or interest. He didn't steal time or use fine feeds or slow speeds, but he seemed indolently indifferent to everything.

"I knew he was doing more irksome work, than if his ambition had been called into play. He knew how to run a lathe, but seemed to understand that he wasn't paid for knowing how, but simply for running it.

"One day I found Morris blackguarding a man fearfully, so I discharged Morris and the man too; Morris for insulting the fellow, and the fellow for not resenting it. I despise a man who has no self-respect to defend. You can't make the whole of a good machinist out of half of a man, so it was small loss to the shop.

"Then I got Lambert for a foreman. I had just found out his worth when he died. I could afford to give a man like him a half interest in the shop and a salary too, and would make money by it every day.

"He knew the character of every man in a week, and shipped about half of the men, keeping only those he knew to be rough diamonds. He sent one man to another shop, telling him it was impossible for him to earn much here, as there was no work suitable for him. Then he took a bolt-cutter man and put him on the best planer in the shop—just where he belonged.

"The man's pride received a hoist, and he was giving ten times as much for his money as he was before. Then he tackled Cook, for he had seen something in the man. He saw that he was, under the crust, a real good workman, so he withdrew rough work from his lathe and raised his pay. Then he put him on the best lathe in the shop, and gave him the best work and raised his pay again.

"Cook was now fulfilling his mission. He seemed to be perfectly satisfied with his position in life, walked alongside of me on the street, instead of falling about two inches behind, as he used to do. He got twenty per cent. more pay, and gave three times as much value in work as he did under Morris. He wore better clothes, kept a bank account, and used his brains every day, for he had learned from Lambert that a machine shop was a good place to use brains in.

"Lambert worked just such changes all through the shop, and, when he died, I was paying higher wages and getting cheaper work than anyone else in my line.

"Then I got Stebbins, and it took him about a month to knock down Lambert's whole structure. Then I got Morgan. He was neither good, bad, nor indifferent, and the only evidence of his having been here is the vacancy he leaves behind him."

* * * * Sackett gave me a slight insight into his plan of making machinists and foremen as we walked home:

"When I started, I was my own foreman. I kept as many apprentices as I could use, because I could make better workmen of them than I could hire. When a town boy became an annoyance around the shop by his intrusive and impertinent interest in things, I spotted him for an apprentice.

"Lambert served his time with me, and was one of a good lot of boys. I notice that those street boys, who have to be kicked out of shops, are always good boys, and make not only good machinists but good mechanics. Lambert worried me considerably before he came in the shop for good. He loafed around, and if a planer was idle, he would deliberately take possession and work on some tinkering job he had on hand, a little engine or some such nonsense. Finally I set him at work on a three years' apprenticeship. I first set him to chipping castings, and told him he could drop such work forever the minute he could do it well. He seemed to understand my plan, and passed through the bloody ordeal quickly. Then I put him on a bolt cutter with the same understanding. He soon graduated, took a rough lathe, then a better lathe, then a vise, then a floor. *He always did the most valuable work of which he was capable.*

"This was my regular plan in the shop, and secured for every man his proper sphere of action, and I always made some small difference in the pay, so that they could more readily appreciate the matter. I let the boys play midshipman and take charge of the ship week about. They were all sensible, proud, ambitious boys, and I never had any complaint from workmen at being bossed by these youngsters. Many of my boys now have high places, and write me frequently. There are more like them in the shop. I can leave my business a month, or my foreman can leave me forever, and it will not interrupt things at all.

"I work on the artillery plan, and train number Four to number Seven's work, so that firing may be continued in case of accidents."

* * * * If foremanship can be a profession, DeLow was a professional foreman. He is dead now, but I know you would like to hear something of his style, if you are interested in the interior management of the shop. In another letter I will tell you something of this very peculiar man, whose memory is revered by every proprietor or workman with whom he ever came in contact.

CHAPTER V.

HOW FAR SHOULD PURCHASERS' WISHES INFLUENCE MANUFACTURERS?—WHAT TO DO WITH ODD PATTERNS.

* * * * How far should the opinions or desires of a purchaser influence the manufacturer? I do not refer to special jobs for special purposes, but to those articles which, being upon a manufacturer's price list, become a standard with him. Is it wise to humor the whim of every buyer by changing unimportant details at his request?

It seems to me that customers fight shy of a builder who don't seem to know just what he is about, and take rather to those autocrats, who, collecting and refining the experience of many buyers, develop that experience into form, and adhere rigidly to details known to be correct and adequate. A manufacturer with little experience and poor judgment can never be arbitrary, and a weak man can never build up a product to a standard. The unyielding builder must sometimes see a desirable customer depart in a heat, but often the customer will return after many days and bow with respect to a more extensive experience and a firmer judgment.

* * * * Here's a case in point. Sackett builds a wood-working machine, and has sold several hundred of them. He don't build any other wood tool, but has made this a success.

Among other details, this machine contains a cutter shaft running in babbitt boxes. One journal is grooved to prevent end-play, as is commonly done with such shafts. He cuts the grooves in the journal. Some makers turn them upon the journal, which is much more expensive, but does not weaken the shaft.

A gear shaft in the machine runs in a long sleeve

bearing, bored in the main frame. The other day, when I was in Sackett's shop, he showed me about twenty letters regarding this machine, and called my attention to two of them. One party wanted the collar rings mentioned to project from the journal, instead of being cut into it. The other party asked that the aforesaid gear-shaft bearing be capped, so wear could be taken up.

Sackett opened up with : " There's two good cash orders, which I won't take. I won't alter those things, for that shaft business would be a useless and annoying concession, and that gear box is better as it is, a matter which I know a hundred times more about than those men. Its my business to know, not what one of these men thinks, but what is the average or general demand. My self-interest as a manufacturer demands that I should reduce a machine to its mean profitable terms and keep it so. I can't afford to make a bad machine. If anything is really wrong, it will certainly damage me more than the buyer, and I should at once demand the return of the job. How silly I would be to listen to every suggestion ! I made that machine a success, the *purchasers* didn't.

"I didn't guess at the proportions or details of the thing, for I am no designer, but I had it done by a man whose vocation and business is to study the wants of users, develop them into an average, and furnish me with the scheme and drawing, made with the understanding that the machines were to be not only good to the purchaser, but profitable to the manufacturer.

"He didn't do it in a day, but put details side by side, and considered closely the relative utility and cost of each. He knew what he was about, and would not have made grooves instead of rings without reason.

"Of course I accepted his judgment, but that was eight years ago, and I have watched the things closely.

I notice all these little suggestions come from men who intend to buy.

"Why don't those who have the machines complain? Simply because there's nothing to complain about. It's simply a notion of intending purchasers. I know by the experience of six hundred uncomplaining buyers, that things are right.

"That bearing has never in eight years shown shake, and I know that if it was split and capped it would never fit just right, even by chance, and would wear out in a year.

"Why, Chordal, I wish it wasn't too much trouble to get you out the letters I have received from inquirers. If I listened to all, I would not be able to make two machines alike; in fact, I would have no machine that I could call my own, for there isn't a thing that somebody hasn't struck. That machine stands on its reputation. I have no patent on it, and competitors have too much honor to steal my personal thunder, but would bounce my legal patent, quick as thought, if I had one, and they could find a hole in it.

"I make those machines good and all alike, and a man can know just what he's going to get. Why, there's three thousand dollars worth of special tools out in the shop, rigged up to make the machines uniformly good and uniformly cheap. What would become of my jigs, if I listened to Thomas, Richard and Henry? I lose a sale once in a while by being stubborn, but I find in the end that stubbornness wins. I won't change any unimportant detail to suit a buyer's fancy on anything I make. If I find something is really wrong, I change for good; but I don't jump at the first free suggestion made.

"Why, I went up to Backgear last year and ordered a drill press of Coane. I came the same game on him, which my patrons try on me. I wanted changes.

Coane builds tip-top drill presses, and I wanted nothing special, but I wanted little changes made just to suit my whims. I am no tool builder, and Coane would have told me so, if he had done his duty by me, but no—he's one of those men who want to please customers. Now, that drill's a fraud, and its just as I ordered it. I wish I saw some good ground for suing him. He ought to have known better than I did, and ought to have insisted on doing the right thing. Just come out and look at that fine machine, 'altered to suit the purchaser's fancy !' "

* * * * I interviewed Wycoff next day. He builds portable engines:

INTERVIEWER—Do you change things, if purchaser says to?

WYCOFF—Every day in the week. Wouldn't sell anything if I didn't. Guess a man knows what he wants. There's that engine over there. Making it for Pittman. Same as usual, only he wanted that governor. It isn't worth five cents, but that isn't my look out, and he wanted the valve shortened up, and the crank pin smaller, to reduce friction, as he said, and the bearings turned half an inch smaller than the shaft. I am doing it all, of course.

INTERVIEWER—But don't this interfere with regular plans of work, and make work cost more without being right; and don't your name and reputation go out on engines you are ashamed of? Will such a man come to you the second time?

WYCOFF—Oh! the system ain't anything. I never could do anything with system. Machine work is centering and turning and drilling and planing, after all, and when a man comes after some, I, for one, propose to do it to suit him. If he is wrong, I have the satisfaction of one sale, at least. I don't make two engines alike. They all want something different, and I give it to them.

INTERVIEWER—How much respect would you have for a tailor, who, acting on your dictation, would make you ridiculous, and, after finding out your mistake, would you go to him again, or to the arbitrary tailor who refused your absurd order, and which of the two would receive the most orders from you in the next ten years?

WYCOFF—Now you're going round the question. It don't make any difference about the other orders, that ain't what we are talking about, and you can see yourself who got the order in question. You can't stuff me with any such talk. Why, look here. Do you mean to tell me, that, if I order a second machine of a man, I must not tell him, and demand that he should make the bolt heads uniform, and balance the pulleys? Nonsense!

INTERVIEWER—That's just what I say. If you are green enough to order anything from a man who has to be told his business, you should keep up the thing by using his green machine, till you learned that a man who accepts such suggestions needs them, and that if he is open to such criticism, his whole product should be suspected of immaturity and patchwork.

WYCOFF—Now I have a case for you. You see that screw machine? I went out to Ohio and got that from the Niles Works. They made them with a one and five-eighths inch hole through the spindle, so that they would make three-quarter bolts. I wanted a two-inch hole, so I could make inch bolts. Gray said he wouldn't do it. Said they were tool builders, and had designed that machine in proper proportion, hole and all, and that if I wanted to make inch bolts, I ought to get the larger machine, with a two-inch hole in the spindle, and with the other parts in proportion. Says he: Suppose I should do as you ask, and our machine should fail to do what it never was intended to do? What then? Who would lose the most, you or the Niles Works? Then I dried him up by saying, that if he would not make the machine as I wanted it, I did not want it at all, and more than that, I wouldn't take it. He showed his sense by giving in. Do you say he did wrong?

INTERVIEWER—Of course I do. He violated a principle which, strictly adhered to, would, in the end, result in more screw machine sales than the plan followed. If the thing fails and I should notice it, what conclusion would I have to come to, in the absence of knowledge?

WYCOFF—But it didn't fail, and Gray did what any good business man would do under the circumstances. If you want patrons, you must study to please them.

Then I left. Here are two voices from two directions.

* * * * I want to tell you something about Sackett and Wycoff some day. There is something rich in their history.

* * * * Two more cases pertaining to this question. The B——— Locomotive Works ordered planers of a well-known shop. Wanted cross rail changed. Tool men said, No; the rail was right. They wouldn't allow a detail to be questioned after they had satisfied themselves that it was right; claimed superior judgment upon that art, and saw valuable patronage depart apparently for ever. I honor that principle and that concern, for having specific knowledge which they will thus back up. The B——— Works may have taken their trade away, but I believe they left their profound respect, and that trade will, in the end, seek out and find experience and judgment of the positive kind.

* * * * Another case: McGoon, a master mechanic on a Western road, opened negotiations with a concern for a certain machine. Concern sent cut and description and price. McGoon doubted the strength of a certain part. Concern said they had made fifty of them, and knew them to be all right, but "if you desire we can alter in any way you see fit to suggest."

The next day McGoon ordered elsewhere. I don't know why, but have a suspicion.

* * * * Which is the better policy? To make patterns as cheap as possible, or to make them as good as possible? This question is deeper than it looks, and will not answer itself as some might at first suppose. There are two important sides to it, and the subject is worthy of discussion by shop proprietors. If a man does a jobbing business, and needs odd patterns for one casting, there is certainly no doubt that the patterns should be made just as cheaply as possible, durability being no object. What are a lot of such patterns worth, even if made in the best manner? Not one-twentieth of the cost, in nine cases out of ten. I don't consider odd patterns worth saving. It is better to burn such things and make a new one in a hundred years, than to store and insure them that long. Burn such patterns and put the premiums to the credit of pattern expense.

* * * * But all patterns are not odd patterns. Take manufactured machines, gears and other staple articles. Those patterns are of value. But just how much we can afford to pay for them is the question. A good pattern-maker can, if he sees fit, make a pattern which will stand daily use and storage for fifteen years. His work will be solid, wood to wood all over, five coats of varnish, and an exterior impervious to moisture. If he wants to, he could make the pattern in one-sixth the time, and the exterior shape would be the same, the castings from them identical. But things won't stand much knocking around, and time will open the joints and change the shape.

Modern machinery changes its skin every few months, and new patterns must be made.

This must be considered, for if we pay for durability and don't use it, we are buying something we don't need. But of course this is a matter of experience.

* * * * G———— makes his patterns perfect. I don't think they could be better, for he gets the best pattern makers and tells them to do their best.

His patterns never wear out. He simply changes his style, and burns up those splendid old patterns and makes new ones. He sent two wagon loads to my house for kindling, and I judged them to be worth at least six hundred dollars. Don't you think he would have been wiser to have had these patterns made in a less costly style, and spent a trifle, or many trifles, on their repair or maintenance?

* * * * The pattern account is always a big thing in any shop. One trouble in the matter is that, if you want patterns to make good castings true to drawing, you must get a good pattern maker to make them, and he won't make cheap patterns, and a poor or cheap pattern maker won't work close. It is very hard to get a fine pattern maker to make you a pattern just for one casting; he don't seem to know how. If pattern makers would be a little more considerate, and cultivate judgment in this matter, they would greatly increase their own value, and proprietors would soon show their appreciation.

CHAPTER VI.

MRS. TOODLES RUNS A MACHINE SHOP—COMPARATIVE COST OF SMALL TOOLS.—A MACHINE SCREW MISSIONARY.—HOW A GRINDSTONE WAS MADE TO PAY.

* * * Mrs. Toodles still lives among us. She runs a machine shop now, in fact, she runs a great many shops. Her address is on the books of every receiver, assignee, trustee, and bankrupt firm in the country.

They send her lists of tools and general shop plunder, to be sold on such and such a day. She goes and looks around and reasons in this style: "What do I want with that bolt cutter? That's a *good* bolt cutter, the dies are all there, and in good shape. I came to buy a bolt cutter, but don't want such a one as that. And that lathe—I don't see anything the matter with *that*. If the bed ain't sprung, I don't want it. If it is modern, I don't want it. If the change gears are all there, I don't want it. If no teeth are broken out of gears or racks, I don't want it. If it has proper belt power, I don't want it. Don't care if it is only two years old, I don't want it. Fitchburg lathe, is it? Thirty-inch swing, twelve-foot bed? And you bought it for $400! Well, I don't want that lathe. Why, I run this big lathe forty years ago, when I was a girl. I know it's a good lathe, and its better than it was then, for it's been blocked up twice. You take your Fitchburg lathe, this one suits me. Now, you see, I've got it—only $300. What's that going now? Babbitt metal? Let's see, I don't want that, that ain't old metal. There's a lot of twist drills, four old drills and forty old shanks—I want them and that vise."

* * * It is the experience of machine auctioneers, that old worthless plunder brings half the market price, while it is difficult to get bids on things of real value. Mrs. Toodles' auction bill would buy a sensible person one good lathe, instead of two good-for-nothing ones. Her twist drills cost her exactly twice the list price, and when she gets home, she will find they don't fit her drill sockets; she will alter the sockets, and then her other drills won't fit. The plan of breaking a twist drill in two and calling it two twist drills suits her.

* * * * It won't do to jump at the cost of small tools in the shop. Figures printed on a manufacturer's price-list often look big, but if accurate cost of small home-made shop tools is kept, something will be found out. What shop can make an inch tap as cheap as one can be bought? When a concern fits up specially for a certain class of tools, it is safe to say that their price-list is about fifty per cent. under the cost of home-made tools. A one-inch solid, double-ended caliper for the tool room can be bought for a dollar and a half. Leaving out any consideration of accuracy, how much would it cost if a three dollar man made it with the ordinary facilities? Gear cutting cutters, so near absolute perfection as to be unquestionable, can be bought for about six dollars each. It looks like a great deal of money for very little steel, but have one made in the shop, and watch it. A steel forging of unreasonable size keeps a blacksmith and helper busy an hour; your draughtsman spends an hour drawing a shape on tin; your best paid lathesman works a full day turning the cutter, if he don't make a special tool for it, and he works a day on the tool, if he does make it; then half a day goes in toothing it, and you may put in proper wages and figure up the cost. When it comes to tempering it, it may be done, or it may be done for; it depends on luck, and if tempered without cracking, the thing may be true and may not be; and if it isn't true, it won't cut a space anything like the draughtman's tin drawing, which may have been a good shape and may not have been. Price-lists are often condemned prematurely.

* * * * In a late letter to you, I was guilty of an injustice to the manufacturers of machine screws. I stated that their threads were proper pitch and interchanged nicely. I must apologize for this misstatement, and can only explain it on the ground that the awkward variety of sizes of heads had caused so much trouble in the shops, that I had forgotten entirely the ordinary nuisance of half-inch screws with a variety of threads. There is but one standard thread for half-inch work, and that standard is thirteen threads per inch. If I order screws or taps from half the screw shops, I never know what I am going to get, but I am certain there will be two chances to one against my getting the standard thing, for many of the unconverted send out their lists and work as follows: one-half inch, 12, 13 or 14 threads. The average looks all right, but it won't fit all right. If tap and screw makers would go to a little righteous trouble to discourage the purchase of 12 and 14 thread half-inch taps, they could, in a year, completely stop the unholy traffic. The very life of the machine-screw business rests on the general suitability of the product to general circumstances.

I have, as a missionary, talked to many machine-shop owners, with tears in my eyes, seeking to convert them to a sense of the propriety of buying screws and taps, and have made many converts. Aside from a few sad experiences of my own, I am often called on, by some skeptical convert, to defend the sins of some screw-maker who should and could keep his art above attack.

* * * * I made money by reorganizing my grindstone arrangements. I have been using three foot stones, running slowly in wooden frames, and have depended on almost anybody in the shop to keep them true. By the way, did you ever notice that there was a charm in turning off a grindstone? It's so! This dirty job has positive attractions. The skillful manipulation of the "tool," the caution required, the constant muscular and mental strain, all make the job really unpleasantly pleasant, after it is started. But about my grindstones. They were most always out of true; men put off grinding tools as long as possible, worked with dull tools, and, of course, did poor work and wasted lots of time. Let a man be working on a nice lathe job, the tool gets dull; he thinks of the awful grindstone, postpones grinding till he gets real mad, then does it and gets nervous and unfit for the work in hand.

I pro'd and conn'd over the thing in this way:

These stones are out of true, because they gouge easily. They gouge easily, because they run slow. They run slow for convenience in trueing up. They don't get trued up, because the shaft is loose in the shackly frame. A quick-running stone cuts fast and nice, and a slow-running stone gets cut fast and awfully. I'll change the whole thing.

* * * * I bought three solid metal frames, paid thirty dollars each for them; I think my old wooden ones have indirectly cost me a thousand dollars a piece. These frames are troughs, have heavy shafts, good solid boxes, convenient rests, a wonderful contrivance for holding a tank above them, and the whole establishment is on wheels.

I rigged a pulley out doors, and run the stones out there at slow speed, and had them turned up nicely. I, of course, had to go and turn one myself. Then I wheeled them back in the shop, and run them at very high speed, and fixed pulleys so the speed could be increased as the stone got smaller. The frames had a self-trueing apparatus on them, which will true the stone while it runs wet at high speed, so I don't get any dust in the shop. I appointed Charley a committee of one to see that these stones were always true, not pretty near true, but perfectly true all the time, without regard to the number of stones used up in a year. He is also superintendent of the water works, and sees that no lathesmen have to run after water for these stones, or to grind dry.

* * * * Between you and me, those things were paid for in a month. The men work with sharp tools and neat tools; they pile great clean chips under the lathes, and don't require one-quarter the tool-dressing they did before. Charley keeps the grindstone machinery swept nice and clean, and it is no longer the repulsive servant it used to be.

CHAPTER VII.

HISTORY OF TWO JOURS.—WYCOFF'S SHOP PHOTOGRAPHED.—LONGEVITY OF SHOPS.

* * * * I promised you a story with figures in it. Here it is: Twenty-two years ago, Sherman Sackett and William Wycoff completed their apprenticeships at the Novelty Works. They worked on three months as journeymen, and then, as journeymen, they tramped. They were both, in the ordinary sense of the word, good workmen, and both stood equal on the pay books. They tramped at the same time and with equal resources, viz: valise full of clothes for outfit, and ball pein hammer for plant. They passed through the vicissitudes usual in the life of tramping jours: job after job, shop after shop, year after year. When this stopped, I do not know, but Sackett is now the mayor of a town, the owner of a shop, and the employer of sixty men. Wycoff also has a shop and employs fifty men. They seem to have prospered. The fact is, they struck rich veins of work, of which, more anon; they entered untouched ripened fields as reapers, when almost tired with seeking.

* * * * Two years ago a certain patentee, acting on my valuable advice, took both Sackett and Wycoff a sample of his machine. I say machine, but the following figures will show that it was a very trifling affair, but of such products is the kingdom of industry. He gave each an order for three machines, with no stipulations as to price, his object being to secure samples of their work, and to ultimately solicit propositions to build the machines in quantities. This intention was understood all around. The machines were built, the quality being about equal, and to sample. Wycoff's bill was for three machines, at $40 each; Sackett's bill was for three machines at $67 each. Wycoff had given Mr. Patentee an "estimate" of $40 each, and Sackett's estimate had been $70 each.

It will be noticed that there is considerable difference in these bills, but Mr. Patentee knew something about the machine business and was not disposed to find fault. He knew Sackett's bill was based on cost, plus profit, and that it would not be lowered, and there was no pressing desire to have Wycoff raise his bill.

* * * * He now invited proposals for 5,000 machines. Wycoff bid as follows: "Will make 5,000 machines for $24 each, 100 machines per week, payments weekly." Here is Sackett's bid: "Will make 5,000 machines for $8 each, 1,000 machines per week, payment on completion of order."

If there was anything strange about the bills, there is something stranger about these bids. The two men have about the same capital invested in exactly the same line of business, and their tools are nearly identical, and their shops are not a mile apart.

Wycoff's wanting money weekly is accounted for by the fact that he had no loose capital and could not carry the job. But what caused the difference between 100 machines per week and 1,000 machines per week, and what caused the difference of 200 per cent. in price? I will say, right here, that Sackett got the order and filled it, and has filled several more like it since.

* * * * Knowing the men as I do, I can give the reasons for their great difference in bills and bids. The fact is there is over 200 per cent. difference in the men as manufacturers. Wycoff, in the first place, didn't know, when he "estimated" on the samples, what it would cost to build the three machines; he guessed at it. He didn't know what they did cost after he did build them; he guessed at that. Guessed he had made money on them, and guessed he could afford to shorten up on the profit on a large order. It happened, however, that the larger order "guessed not." My own opinion is that if he had received the job at $24 each he would have lost money. Around his entire premises there is nothing to show what anything ever did cost, except raw material. It is a good thing he saves old bills. He keeps books, of course, and knows all about his debits and credits, but nought else.

Now it happens that Sackett, our successful bidder and successful manufacturer, carries in his hat the brains of a systematic manager. His estimate on the first three machines was not guessed at, but was carefully calculated from the nearest parallel cases he could find in his prime cost books. When the machines were done, he found things about as he had expected, and by carefully watching details, had already mapped out a plan of operations and system of production, which would enable him to make these machines in great quantities and at a low price. There was nothing surprising to him in the difference between the first three machines, and those he subsequently made; while in Wycoff's case, I do not think there would have been much difference.

* * * * The difference between Sackett and Wycoff, as manufacturers, crops out all over. Sackett employs good men at good wages and keeps them. Wycoff employs good men at good wages and can't keep them. There is something in the atmosphere of Wycoff's shop that seems to deprive a man of his self-respect, which is, in reality, the main-stay, sheet-anchor, and only hope of the workingman. Wycoff puts much trust in rules and regulations. You will see a string of them, as long as your arm, as soon as you enter the shop. They are frequent on the walls, supplemented, occasionally, by an enlarged edition of some particular one thought worthy of a separate frame. One may be noticed with the attractive and endearing legend, "We expect a day's work for a day's pay." Wycoff stole this thing somewhere, for there is no "We" in his concern.

* * * I once saw a body of men on a strike. They had been getting $4 for six hours' work, and demanded $6 for four hours' work. This was many feet below the bottom of the Mississippi river, where the air was compressed so much that the workmen who were at all damaged by it were thrown into what the bridge hands called the "Grecian bend." When the bent ones straightened out, it was often permanently. But of course, this is not appropriate. Wycoff's men didn't have to work in a compressed atmosphere. Oh no!

* * * Take a trip through his shop. The tools are generally modern and good, but wretchedly kept, and we see no waste that looks as if it would clean anything. Yonder's a chap turning what appears to be a throttle-stem, for it has an elliptic button on one end. He is taking a water-cut over it, and that white lead keg blocked up on the lathe carriage bears a striking resemblance to the one we saw over the north grindstone. Those earmarks of grindstone grit make the matter certain. Here's a bench or counter in the middle of the shop, and on it some finished work, a chuck or two, an island of horrible looking waste, half a dozen flat drills and a piece of twist drill, and here lies a tap, clean and nice, and we pick it up and examine it. We see at once that it is home-made, but it is a beauty, clean cut and neat. You find it impossible to help admiring this simple tool, for you have made a tap or two yourself, but none so perfect as this. You lay it down and go on through the shop. Next week you may see the dismembered fragments of our tap in place of its present misplaced perfection.

Here we find Wycoff, coat off and honestly greasy. Yes, he does keep a foreman, or tries to, rather; kings without thrones. "Ah! Mr. Chordal, how do you do? Happy to meet you, Mr. Miller, and you, Mr. Bailey, and Mr. Moore; excuse my gloves—belong to the laboring classes, you see. Look busy, eh? should think I was; got enough work to—excuse me, gentlemen, got to shrink this crank on."

* * * * We notice that just in front of us, on trestles, lies a six inch shaft, with an end projecting. And now, upon the scene, through the blacksmith-shop door come four men, whom I know to be the best paid machinists in the shop, bearing a thirty-inch crank-plate, glowing hot. They quickly place it in position to start on the shaft, and proceed to urge it. From the time Wycoff left us, he has not ceased to speak or excitedly yell over this job. We know a single yell will spoil a shrinking fit, but Wycoff, probably, don't know it. Now an excited order to one man to go for that block; to this man to raise up; and to that one to let down; now a snub to the man who is really responsible for the job; now he frantically grabs a sledge and strikes a lick or two; now at something else. Every word spoken seems to be immature, every action a false one. We walk on. You remark that Wycoff don't seem to be a cool man, and that if you had any money invested in that crank, you would prefer to entrust the job to the jour. whom W. just snubbed, and who seems to have lost all interest in the proceeding, simply looking on with servile disgust.

It's a habit of Wycoff's to take all such jobs into his own hands, generally nipping them in their fruition.

"Excuse me, gentlemen, got to shrink this crank on."—Page 60.

The crank was all right, but it is now stuck half way, and to-morrow they will try to get it off again.

* * * * We go over towards a new engine on the floor, when in come four men with a twelve-foot shaft, red hot. They go over to the long lathe. Up goes the shaft on the blocks; now upon the centers; now it is revolved and gets chalked; and now it comes out and gets pounded and dented, and in two hours it will get straightened. Two hours of what? Lathesmen, 60 cents; two blacksmiths, $1.20; one helper, 20 cents; total, $2.00, plus two fires and a lathe standing still, and—those hammer marks.

We go on over to the beforementioned engine; it's about half done. You ask if Trumbull didn't furnish the castings. No; but he furnished the design. Wycoff's pattern maker measured one of Trumbull's engines and made these patterns from those measurements. There is no drawing in the shop for any part of it, not a memorandum even. The "copy" is in a mill about a mile from here, and Wycoff's foreman has made over thirty trips, so far, to take a look at details. Nobody knows how many trips it will take to finish it, but we know that it will take just as many for the next engine, and the next. We know what a set of drawings would cost, but no man knows what this engine will cost, or will not cost. We leave it.

* * * * Here's a planer, splendid tool! Bement's; but Bement wouldn't recognize it. The table don't look like a planer table at all. Seems as if the prismatic rays from a spectroscope had fallen on this table lengthwise, and on these rays have fallen crosswise—hammer marks, and chisel marks, and sand marks, and water, and oil, and soap, and chips, and dirt.

It is not so all over, however, for there a small place has been cleaned, and that new job will soon be fastened there, if Gus can find suitable bolts up among the lathes.

You knew Gus when he worked at the Empire Works. He was not such a miserable slouch then; he was a good workman, and you wonder if his skill is not endangered by his present habits. I can tell you, his skill is now a total wreck. He worked for me long ago, and left another man once and came to work for me again. I sent him back. He seemed to be two different men. He gets good pay and will as long as he stays here, but his pride of skill and his self-respect have gone forever.

You have an eye for the tool holders or clamps on this planer. Three nuts of one size, and one nut of three other sizes. You look to see what manner of universal wrench Gus uses for a tool wrench. Finally, you spy it; a monkey wrench. Strange, but you hadn't thought of that. Now we go into the foundry. Notice that the only way to get into the foundry is through the machine shop, and the only way for the castings to get out of the foundry is through the machine shop, which we find littered up with lamp posts, grate bars, sash weights, spout guards, in fact, an index to the foundry order book.

* * * * Here we are in the foundry. Here's a facing mill, and a blower, and a rattler within six feet of it, showing little regard for the lungs of the workmen or the journals of the blower. There's a man cleaning off a sugar mill roller. Know him, do you? No, he is not a cleaner, but a well paid machinist. We see they intend to run off a heat soon; let's go. We don't want to see Wycoff at work in here. He will come in when the iron comes down, will bring the best men out of the machine shop with him, will tap out, and skim, and riotously work mud on the end of the plugging stick, and yell and swear and superintend generally. His foreman is a well-paid man, but helpless. If Wycoff kept cost books he should *credit* the foundry with his services at five dollars per hour.

* * * * We go out—past the planers, past the Wycoff engine, past the whole committee on mean ways of straightening shafting, past the half-way crank and its ponderous factors, past our beautiful tap—out from under the garish rules and into the street.

We will see Sackett's shop some time and many times. His interior, his processes, his men, his management, will all furnish material for instructive mention in these letters some day.

* * * * Did it ever occur to you that the republican idea could have an effect upon the tenure of life of productive concerns? In the old countries it takes two generations to get an establishment under headway, and then future generations follow the business up as long as one of the family name lives, and when all are dead, others continue it under the old name. Very many foreign shops are run under names having no real representative on earth. The English shops, especially, are noticeable for this. These old shops don't progress any, and, as the people are conservative, everything is lovely. Extinction is to be tolerated, but progress or variation never. Old and well-established firms have a name as an asset. How is it in this country? What man starting business as a manufacturer seeks an old house to follow? Where is there a case of an old house even with the times? Our old shops don't retrograde at all; they simply remain, and our republic marches on and leaves them behind. We are nationally progressive, and enterprises in this country must be ever in moving order. Conservative nations don't move, so there is no danger of shops being left behind. In our country an old shop cannot be sold. No keen man builds a shop on the ground where one of the old shops stood. An old name is a damage. There is a limitation to the life of all manufacturing concerns here. They start even with the times; they prosper; they make money; while they settle into habit, the world moves. They slumber and make less money. They wake, and see what's up. Too late! All their former earnings are lavishly expended in attempts to regain their old place. It is a waste of money and against the national nature of things. "Last scene of all;" Advertisement —"An old established business for sale." The wise man don't buy it, and don't steal their name, and don't build next door, and don't copy their product. Not much! He goes where their smoke cannot reach his roof; he builds new, makes his bow, shows goods adapted to the day—and prospers, and falls into habit and slumbers, and wakes, and expends, and advertises "An old established business," etc.

Men, as they leave middle age, become averse to changes of their customers, and will not yield to them; they cannot yield and they must fall. It is human nature against climate, government, youth, growth and human nature combined. The conflict is inevitable, the result certain. To the old something, "Strike while the iron is hot," let me append, "Heat the iron while the fires burn, and then quit and live on the result." Cold iron will never relight dead fires.

CHAPTER VIII.

YE HEARTSICK TRAMPING JOUR.—HOW TO GET UP IN THE WORLD.—KEEPING MUM ABOUT WAGES.—HIGH WAGES VS. HIGH FIRST COST OF PRODUCT.—WHAT CONSTITUTES A GOOD WORKMAN.

* * * There certainly can be no better or surer sign of returning prosperity to the trade than the growing scarcity of craftsmen. Three years ago ye heartsick tramping jour. greeted us daily in search of work at a dollar and a-half a day. He was hard up and hard looking. He had no tools, not even the inevitable twisted scriber. His breeches were patched in the seat, and the patches were worn out. He was really out of work and in search of work.

Now he don't come at all. He has work at wages ranging from $1.75 to $3.00 per day, and receives letters daily asking him if he wants work. He has had a hard time of it, and will welcome a new order of things. He has always made one mistake, and the sooner he finds it out the better. The average machinist considers all machinists the same, and thinks they should all receive the same pay. He has a certain amount of bigotry about him, and cannot be convinced that he is not as valuable a man as there is on earth. You find it hard to convince him that he is worth more or less than others. He will kick, if he gets less wages than others, and others will kick if he gets more. I have worked as journeyman in forty different machine shops, and I give it as my solemn conviction, that my prosperity has been more retarded by the narrow-mindedness of my fellow workmen, than by the greed of my employers. The most uncomfortable shops I have ever worked in, have been those where I was best paid. I never failed in making satisfactory terms with employers, but I never could make any terms with shop mates. I never yet knew of a case of one workman lending a helping hand to another, if that help had a tendency to raise the helpee above the helper's pay. There's a good time coming, boys, and a better time to start new in this thing will never occur. Make yourself as skillful as your talents will permit. Insist on working in places and on work where your skill can be best applied, and insist on receiving market value for the grade of skill you sell.

Study the thing well and grade yourself. You know very well of workmen who are worse workmen than yourselves—men who, if you or I had the say so about it, would quit the bench and go to cleaning castings or pounding sand. You know they are not valuable men at the same work you are on. You know they are not worth the money to the shop that you are. You think the employer a fool for paying them the wages he does, when many better men could be had at the same pay. You and I know this mighty well. But we also know that there are men far more valuable than we; men who do twice the work without sweating half so hard; men who do nice work which we never dared to attempt; men who can do work without tools, and are never helpless. They are mighty workmen whose skill we should envy. We know such a man is worth more money than we are, and that we are doing ourselves injustice, when we make things warm for him because he gets a quarter a day more than we do. It is honest truth, that most employers treat men with more consideration than the men treat each other.

* * * * I have raised my pay several times, and feel justified in giving machinists a little advice on the subject, and unhesitatingly say, that if you will follow what I say in the next few lines, you will get good wages in the next six months. First and foremost, settle with yourself what you are good for, and what you are best for. If you are a lightning man on fine close work, don't go to a threshing machine shop for a profitable job. You will be worthless there. If you are a tip-top lathesman, don't go to botching work at the vise. Good vise hands are in demand to-day at fair wages. So are good lathesmen on good work, and so are crack lathesmen on rough work. Bad ones can't get jobs at any wages, and all are bad, if working on something they can't do satisfactorily. If you are a good and valuable workman in any branch of the regular machine trade, you can get work in that branch, if you will use good sense in determining your proper grade.

Don't haggle about wages, and don't ask for some other man's wages, till you know that that man is as valuable a man as yourself.

Prove your worth in the shop, and you will get your money, and, when you prove more valuable, you will get more. Now comes the golden rule: Keep your mouth shut and don't tell any man, woman or child on the face of the earth what wages you do get, unless you don't get what you are worth, in which case go to the office *alone* and fix it at once. Remember that. Don't brag about your wages to any soul as long as you live. If you get a raise and blab it, the bosses will kick you out for your lack of sense, or the other boys will freeze you out for your good luck.

No man under heaven could carry on business successfully, if he told his competitors all about his business, and kept his books open for inspection. Keep mum about your wages. If some bank cashier asks you how much pay you get, ask him how much he gets before you answer.

Good workmen are not only getting scarce, but they have been scarce for some time. The good workman is generally a good common-sense sort of a man in every way, and when the panic struck the trade, he showed his sense by making other arrangements. The consequence is, that to-day an increased business finds that the only source of special supply is a mass of material first discarded from the shops, on account of being the least valuable. Those who have served their apprenticeship during the dull times have become discouraged at the small wages they were to receive as jours., and, if they were ambitious, they quit and abandon the trade. This left the slouchy cubs in the shop. Those short-sighted employers who think they can make money out of the machine business, if they can only get men at low enough wages, have had their chance. It will be long before they will have another such chance, and I now make all such employers an offer. I will bet a fifty cent summer hat with each of them, that there is more profit in a job done by three-dollar men, than there is in the same job done by one-dollar men, other things being equal. Low wages means a low grade of workmen, and that means a high first cost of product. I speak of comparative wages, of course, comparative with reference to the grade of work.

* * * * Some machinists, when they speak of a good workman, mean a man who is fine, close and accurate. This is not correct one-half the time. There are just as good men working on rough portable engines as you can find in the shops. They are skillful men. But put them into shops building tools, and they are gone; fact is, they should not have come. In the same way, the tool man isn't worth his salt on portable engines. He accomplishes nothing, and is hard at work all the time. Some folks think a job can't be done too well. Nonsense! There's more work done too well than too bad. It is no trouble to go and contract for good work and get it; but it is hard to get rough work properly done. Some one has said that dirt is simply matter misplaced, and I say that bad work is simply labor misplaced. If I saw a man painting a sewing machine shuttle with coal tar, I would say he was botching the job, and if I saw him putting a crocus finish on a hand-car crank, I would say the same thing.

If a man grinds up a sugar mill roll on a Morton Pool machine, he makes no better job of it than if he had taken a single roughing cut over it. A skilled workman is one understanding the tricks and arts of his trade. If he has the judgment and common sense which tells him how and where to apply his skill, he is a good and valuable workman. If he does not know how and where to apply his skill, he is not a good and valuable workman. There are more bad skillful workmen than good ones, and the thing must be equalized by supervision. The foreman is to supply the judgment, and the workman the skill. A skillful foreman is generally a bad foreman, for he has judgment mixed up with his skill, and supposes that every other skilled workman has judgment also. He will give a man a job and leave him to his own devices, and if the job is badly done, he will lay it to the man because he knows he could have done it properly himself. Such a foreman often says it is more trouble to instruct a workman than to do the work. A foreman with more judgment and less skill would advise such a workman to quit the machine trade and go into the post-hole business, on account of its being less abstruse.

CHAPTER IX.

EXTENSION OF SHOPS.—DEVELOPING INTO A STOCK COMPANY.—A TIME-KEEPING MACHINE.—HUNTER'S FOUNDRY ACCOUNTS.—OWNERSHIP OF PATTERNS.

* * * * You honored a former letter by copiously extracting remarks relative to the length of time manufacturing establishments hold their places in this country. I often wonder if any one looks at "extension" in the same light that I do. By extension, I do not refer to the legitimate outgrowth of a business, but rather to the uncalled for spread which elated manufacturers are prone to indulge in.

Can you not call to mind a dozen or a hundred men who, either alone or in association with a single partner, have built up their business from nothing to a decided success, making money and decidedly prosperous? Follow them and ask yourselves: Shall we do as they do?

* * * * Their course is, too often, after this manner. They find their business an unaccountable and overwhelming success. Their money is all invested, their room crowded, their energies and capacity fully taxed, *and they are making money*. So far, so good. But with the expansive desire which leads on to ruin, they look for outside capital, to admit into their own well-feathered nest. The modern stock company suggests itself. They form, incorporate, print stock, sell it, leave the old shop, move to some high-bidding town, build new and large, and strike out with a spoon entirely out of proportion to the sugar. The first election of officers puts the originators at the head, of course. Things prosper, and before another election the new stock-holders get some experience in the business rubbed off on them by contact, and begin to have an idea or two. The new election changes affairs. One of the charter members finds himself out. Next election the other goes. They hold their stock, of course, and share the profits, but what are profits, compared with the privilege of having a hand in the control of a business, whose creation and growth are due entirely to your own fostering care and years of labor?

The new management is often better than the old, but oftener worse; and the "original two" wish they were back in their old concern under the old firm name, with the blessed privilege of occupation in well-known channels.

* * * * I can mention a case in my own little State. Three men, whom I will name after their respective trades, F., B. and M., as Foundry-man, Blacksmith, and Machinist, combined their small capital and went into business with firm name as above. They all worked every day in the year, and they all grew rich. Notwithstanding the increase in wealth they still, through long years, gave their whole time to the business—not as workmen, of course, but as skilled business managers, for their years of successful experience had given them great ability as business men. Each had his department:—production, finance, sales. From young mechanics they had grown to gray-headed business men, powers in their community, loved and respected by all. The legitimate growth of their establishment they were able to foster and father, and their prosperity was such as is due to unflagging attention and honest motive.

But the demon came, and taking them upon the pinacle of their highest chimney, seductively charmed them with visions of further extension, extensions beyond their own means, but extensions warranted by the growing condition of the business. Say the word, and unlimited capital would aid them, and unlimited scope of action could be given to their concern. They hesitated and were lost. They said the word, and the tempter himself took to the capital city the death warrant which made the *F., B. and M. Machine Company* an incorporated concern, as provided for by the act, etc. The tempter brought back the document with the secretary's sign-manual and the State's great seal attached. This was the document destined to destroy the bonds which bound the three creators to their life's creation.

The certificates of stock, with a soaring eagle in the center flanked by portable engines and threshing machines, were engraved, engrossed and eagerly purchased by friends. At the election we find *F.*, President, *B.*, Secretary, and *M.*, Treasurer. They manage the business as usual and see no darkness. The business prospers and election day returns, and *B.* finds himself an outside stock holder, with profits and no duties. The new man becomes an honest element of dissension and makes honest trouble, so the stockholders elect another president from without to aid him. There is less dissension now, and a new election makes *M.* vice-president, with a salary of $3,000 and no duties. The by-laws gives him no voice in the management. His old colleagues are worse off than himself, but are stronger men and can stand it. All the old avenues of his life are closed, and he finds that he has not been working all these years for money, but for occupation. That occupation is gone. He must not open his head on the premises of the incorporated company. He prays for duties and occupation and is told to have recourse to the elegant leisure of the rich.

The leopard cannot change his spots, nor can the working man of years throw off the active, interested habits of a life. He tries to be an idle wealthy citizen and fails. He broods and tosses in his sleep during all his waking hours. One sunshiny day the incorporated company found the body of their vice-president in their pattern loft with a bullet through his brain, and in his private drawer in the safe they find this scrawl, "My usefulness and occupation in life are gone."

There are no such words in the act providing for the incorporation of stock companies under the laws of the State.

* * * * You remember that I showed you, not long ago, a machine in Sackett's office, a mechanical time-keeper of men's work. This machine keeps the time of 200 men, shows when they went to work, and when they quit; and, by the way, if I can find time soon, I will send you a full description of this thing with illustrations. Well, this machine was gotten up by Quirk, who is one of those masterly designers who has all of the orthodox mechanical movements at his fingers' ends. He governs himself by the ethics of design, and deals only in pure mechanurgy. He wrestled with this machine many a long month, and succeeded famously.

When a workman bows before the machine it must record his name or number, the hour of his appearance, the day, the month, the year, and this it must do with accuracy.

Quirk got along all right till he came to the devices for dealing with the days in the month. Thirty days in one month, thirty-one in another, and twenty-eight in another, with a variation of a day every few years. He worried over the thing, piled detail on detail, and complicated movement on complicated movement, till the desired result was accomplished.

When completed, the movement was a thing to

stand before, with awe and wonder at the immense amount of skill and judgment which had been used up in its design, and the vast sums of money expended in its construction.

* * * * Quirk did this awe-and-wonder business for a time, and then it occurred to him that a common calendar clock had to do just what this exasperating part of his machine had to do, and that it would be a good idea to look inside of one. He did so, and wished he hadn't. A single little insignificant piece of brass, not worth ten cents, did the whole thing. In meek humility, he bought a clock for ten dollars, and with it replaced hundreds of dollars worth of his tangled complex machinery.

* * * * Here is a sum in arithmetic for you. The case actually presented itself in Hunter's shop, and was the cause of much contention. Hunter's foundry accounts are kept by themselves; debit everything in the way of stock, sand, coal, labor, power, insurance, &c., which goes into the foundry, and credit it by the number of pounds of castings coming out. At the end of a year, the book showed that the castings cost $3\frac{1}{2}$ cents per pound. At that price the foundry made no money and lost none. In short, Hunter's castings cost $3\frac{1}{2}$ cents. His foundry pays one cent for heavy scrap. He got a piece weighing 4,000 pounds into the machine shop, found it was wrong and had to be broken up, and a new one made in its place. Question: What was Hunter's loss on the blunder? Sackett, whose shop is just across the street, sells heavy castings at $2\frac{3}{4}$ cents. You will find knots in this thing.

* * * * I have a legal question to put, and hope shop owners will feel called upon to express themselves, and cite some case in court which might settle the question. A man came to Hunter to have a machine built, and asked Hunter what he would do it for. Hunter said he would not contract for the machine, and would only do it by the day. Five dollars per day for the work, and four cents a pound for all material. The man said he didn't object, but he wanted to know approximately what the thing would cost, so as to know whether he could ever pay for it or not. He only had so much money at his disposal. Hunter figured the thing up, and wrote that he thought it would come to somewhere in the neighborhood of one hundred and twenty dollars. The man said "Go ahead on $5 per day and 4 cents per pound." When the machine was done, Hunter sent in an itemized bill for seven hundred dollars. Man kicked, they quarreled and kicked over the thing, and finally came together in my place. They asked my advice. I told Hunter to sue the man for the amount of the bill, and told the man to get somebody else to build a machine, and to sue Hunter for damages caused by delay. I am a peacemaker, you know, and try to straighten everything left to me.

But, honestly, what effect is a man's preliminary estimate and representation to have on his bill? This question comes up frequently, and there should be something known about the legal status of the matter. A customer frequently orders a thing on the supposition that his party can figure somewhere near the cost of the job. In the above case Hunter was a little "off," and the man would never have gone into the thing at any such figures as the actual time brought out.

* * * * Another question: When Smith orders a job of Hunter, and Hunter charges Smith with the cost of the patterns, who is the owner of the patterns? It's a common question.

You get a photographer to make a negative of a machine, pay his expenses, and pay him ten dollars for making the negative, and he says the negative belongs to him. He will let you have prints at a certain price, but will not deliver the negative. There is no known way of getting a negative out of a photographer, except with a club. Bone had over a hundred negatives of woodworking machinery, or thought he had, but when he tried to change printers, the music began. If I remember rightly, the law failed to bring the negatives and the matter had to be compromised.

Pope had a similar experience. He thought he owned fifty negatives of steam pumps, but, the first thing he knew, his artist had sold the things, and the purchaser was soliciting his orders for prints from them. If an artist would make no charge for negatives, I do not think the ownership would be a matter to question; but when the thing is ordered and paid for, and nothing said about prints, it seems to me they should belong to the man who pays for them.

* * * * I never saw a man who had taken a degree seeking information from another man. He always wishes to impart. The master mechanic keeps mum, and is always looking for the man who knows.

CHAPTER X.

ALTERING DETAILS TO SUIT CUSTOMERS.—JOURNAL BOXES AND HOW TO PLACE THEM.—FEAR OF ADVERTISING SOMEBODY.

* * * * I once gave you a single strain from Sackett's song about the man who wanted changes made in a machine which Sackett had made for years, and which the man had never seen. Dividing boxes of running journals was the burden of the song. Now I am made to sing myself. I designed an iron-working machine for the Tubal works some years ago. They sold a hundred of them, and this week they send me a letter from a prospective purchaser who is horrified to find, by inspecting one in a neighboring city, that sundry shafts of the machine run in boxes bored from the solid, and having no caps to take up wear. My only reply to my old patrons is to clip Sackett's music from an old AMERICAN MACHINIST, and enclose it to them.

* * * * I am now disposed to express my views on the box question. I will illustrate my sermon by assuming that I am called upon to design and construct a grindstone frame, and that circumstances, over which I have no control, force me to construct the frame of green timber. While scheming upon the parts, I arrive at the journal boxes. What shall they be made of, and shall they have adjustable caps? First, as to the material. I know that a cast iron box bored out is the cheapest, and I know that the steel shaft will run in the cast iron box, and outwear ten babbitted ones.

But I know the latter to hold good only so long as the shaft has a fair bearing in the box, and I know that Hank, or Chris, or Jim, or Bill, in building the rig, will not get the boxes in line, but will quit the job as soon as he can turn the shaft in the boxes; and I also know, that if the boxes were in perfect line they would only stay so as long as the green wood frame allowed them to. Furthermore, I know that a cat-a-cornered cast iron box will cut the shaft and ruin it. If there is going to be any damage done I want it done to the boxes, because they are cheaper to replace than the shaft. I am constrained to abandon cast iron for the boxes and substitute a babbitted box. I now say that, under equally favorable circumstances, the babbitt boxes will have to be rebuilt ten times as often as the cast iron, but that under unfavorable circumstances, known to exist, the shaft will last longer than with cast iron boxes, and that the boxes stand an equal chance of life. I am forced by circumstances to use babbitt on account of its yielding, accommodating nature. Having decided upon babbitting the boxes, I quickly decide to put caps to the boxes for two reasons. First, they are easier to babbitt; and, second, they allow the stone to be lifted out. I never dream of using these caps to make the boxes wear longer.

My grindstone has thus got babbitted boxes with caps and, as in the present case, fitly associated with a green oak frame.

So much for circumstances beyond my control. But suppose I am at liberty to control these circumstances myself, or that a cast iron frame in one piece is called for. I see fit to bolt the boxes down to seats on the frame casting. Shall I use the same boxes I used on the oak frame? I study over it. I went to the expense of babbitt boxes on the oak frame, in order to guard against bad setting and inevitable shrinking. On account of this durability I want the cast iron boxes if they are equal in other particulars.

First, I will see about the setting. If I leave the work to Hank's judgment he will choose between two plans.

He will bore the cast iron boxes and accurately dress their bottoms, then he will dress the seats and line up the boxes, only he won't. He will do just as he did with the oak frame, and leave the boxes as soon as he can turn the shaft; then they will not be in good trim, and will cut the shaft, and my reputation as a designer of grindstone mountings will collapse. Hank has a second chance. He will bolt the boxes down haphazard, but rigidly, and bore them together. By the other plan, he did two accurate or nice pieces of work, and made a bad job, while this way he does no skillful work and makes a good job. Of the two plans, the last is fully fifty per cent. cheaper, and my reputation still stands a chance. Desiring cast iron boxes, can I object to them now? They are in line, for they were bored at once, and they can't get out of line, for they can't be bolted down out of line; they are not only in line but awkwardness cannot get them out of line. I feel satisfied that all objections existing against iron boxes on the oak frame disappear in the present case. I have a shaft with a good bearing in iron boxes, and the bearing will remain good, and the boxes will remain cast iron. In the case of babbitt boxes, the babbitt soon wore down, and exposed the cast iron ledges at the ends of the boxes. These soon cut into the shaft, unfit it for a new babbitt box, or any other kind of a box.

I am satisfied that in the present case the material of my boxes is all right.

In the oak frame case there were bad conditions, and babbitt had to be used with regret. In the present case, the conditions are happy ones, and cast iron is to be used with satisfaction.

Now about the caps. Caps or no caps, that is the question. Why did I cap the other boxes? To take up wear? Not a bit of it. Why not? Simply because I don't care to take up the wear. The stone would run all right in half boxes if the half always came in the right place. The weight of the stone is down, and the pull of the belt is, or may be, up, and the belt-pull may preponderate over the weight, so I desire the shaft to find a bearing, whichever way it may go. The grindstone isn't a reciprocating machine, and slack in the box is a benefit rather than a damage, for it is evidence that the cap is not acting as a friction brake to consume power and wear the shaft. I capped the other boxes for convenience in babbitting and in lifting the stone out. I don't babbitt these boxes so that part of the "why" is settled. As for lifting the stone out, the boxes may come with the shaft. With the old rig this would not have been permissible, because the boxes were delicately located in place, and if removed would have to be skillfully replaced. Now, however, I find that the boxes cannot be placed wrong, and that they may come off with the shaft. This looks as though I desired boxes without caps, and that I was not seeking reasons for and against them. This is true. When discussing the material of the box, I was urged to use cast iron on account of its durability, and was compelled to forego it for other reasons. Now I desire to have the box without caps for the sake of durability, and will certainly forego solid boxes if reason dictates the use of caps. Solid boxes are more durable than capped boxes, for the simple reason that if made to fit, they will stay fit, while if caps are used, some smart Aleck will be forever and eternally adjusting them, and they will never, by any circumstance of good luck, fit right. He will screw the caps down and wear my boxes out in a year. I want them to last, and I insure their doing so, by simply putting it out of the power of officiousness to defeat me.

Some men have a passion for putting a cap on a box

without regard to whether the box is subjected to jumping wear or to steady, uniform, rotary wear.

This is my law based on experience :

For simple revolving journals on light or heavy work, a box without a cap will outwear six boxes with caps. This outwear assertion refers to shaft and box alike. Memorandum : There are a hundred geniuses in the country trying to invent a loose pulley adjustable for wear. When they succeed in doing so, loose pulleys with proper length of hub will wear out, and not till then. There is a difference between "cut" and "wear." Tightening a cut journal will ruin it. No man ever saw a cone fit on a lathe worn out during the lifetime of a lathe. Fortunately there is no way of taking up wear on them. No man ever saw a lead screw bearing on a lathe worn out unless it had caps, in which case he never saw it in shape. An upright drill spindle running in a something which can be tightened is never in good trim—it's always tight or loose. If the same spindle runs in a solid something, it is never tight or loose. It is just right, and will stay so as long as the other organs of the machine last.

One more reference as to adjustability. I will make lathe boxes the subject of a homily some day, but I wish now to call attention to the well-known fact that if a lathesman is silly enough to have filed his boxes open, he will be screwing at them twenty times a day, and his boxes are never right. If he has the joint come metal to metal, he never gives them a thought from week to week, and they are always right. If his work chatters, he never grabs his tool wrench and goes fooling round the spindle boxes, for he knows the trouble is somewhere else.

* * * * Have you ever noticed how tenderly you have to handle mechanical subjects to avoid advertising somebody? Did it ever occur to you, that every step which the world has lately taken in adding to its wealth and happiness is generally traceable to the systematic efforts of individuals? Of late years, the whole world has organized a system of recognition of its benefactors. This recognition has taken the form of a limited monopoly for the inventor, and a monopoly governed by the law of the survival of the fittest for the producer. How can progress be hinted at in the mechanical arts, if the mention of names is improper? Must a man blush because, inadvertently, he intimates the existence of a benefactor when he descants on a benefit? Surely we may talk of work done, and not blush that the worker gains by it. We may do this without sinking to the low vulgarity of the finer arts, in which the merit of the product becomes of less significance than the name of the producer.

The most excellent book I have ever seen on valve motions contains hardly a word regarding those motions which form the basis of the commendable systems. With the utmost respect for the author, I wish to enter my earnest protest against mistaken delicacy of this kind.

* * * * Some man makes money out of every changing emotion of his fellow man. There is no vocation on earth, which is not founded on the tastes and opinions and requirements of men. How idle, then, to withhold information, because somebody will make by it. The managing editor of one of the most enterprising daily papers in the country said to one of his reporters last week: "That thing would be an appreciative piece of news, but I don't see how to counteract the gratuitous advertising it would result in."

* * * * Many of our standard works on mechanical subjects seem to have been based on the intention of pointing out progress in the arts, without touching on anything under seventeen years old, which is the term of life of an American patent.

* * * * This reminds me of the fact that Fetlock, a builder of machinists' tools from other people's patterns, lately laid down a copy of the AMERICAN MACHINIST, and asked: "Who is the Chordal who is always advertising Brown & Sharpe and those other men?" And this again reminds me that Chordal is a machinist keenly appreciative of all that is better and more useful in connection with his craft; a machinist who, as long as he lives, will be alive to the importance and position of such leaders as by their skill and energy develop products which help us forward in the age, and which give us the second blade of grass; and a machinist who will be the first to observe and the first to welcome the tenderest shoot which may spring from a seed planted and nourished by Fetlock.

CHAPTER XI.

EMERY WHEELS IN THE SHOP.—AN EMERY-WHEEL MAN WANTED.—CHARLEY AS THE CHAMPION OILER.—A MECHANICAL TIME-KEEPER.

* * * Emery wheels do not get justice in the shop. The common plan is to rig up some outlandish kitchen-table affair with an illy-proportioned arbor, and to put an emery wheel on it and say the shop is fixed for grinding. The whole arrangement is put off in some place where castings get piled in front of it, and where no man is going to climb if he can help it. Keeping the thing in order is nobody's business, and soon the affair falls into disrepute. So does any other machine treated in the same way. Let a planer be a public tool and soon it will be a wretched tool, and be shunned as the emery wheels are. But the worst is not told. The truth is, nobody in the shop knows how to get good results out of the thing, and it is looked upon as simply one kind of a grindstone, which don't throw mud and water, and is nice to touch a piece of iron on once in a while. There is no little arrangement in the shop which will so well repay investment, and which will so well justify care in selecting both the machine and its operator. There are a thousand-and-one little things turning up every day which a keen-eyed foreman will see are fit subjects for emery-wheel operations. I don't mean in a manufacturing business, but in a simon-pure machine shop, where you don't know what's coming next. Vise work can often be surfaced all over to remove scale. Often it can be surfaced and polished and the vise work left off. Often it can follow vise work, and do the polishing, and often it can be used simply to remove metal and change the shape or dimensions of a piece. All of these things, it will be seen, are common operations performed in a manner not usual in the shop. But one thing must be remembered. A machinist cannot do this work on emery wheels. That is, he cannot take a job from his vise and finish it on an emery wheel. Why? First, because, as before mentioned, the emery rig being everybody's care is nobody's care and isn't in order; and, second, the machinist never gets the swing of emery wheels. He will file up a hex nut all right, but will ruin it on an emery wheel. He can chip scale off work and file it afterwards, but if he tries to scale it on a wheel he gets it hot, burns his fingers, ruins a wheel, and glazes his work so a file won't touch it.

As far as shaping a piece of curved work on an emery wheel is concerned, he might as well try to fly. He will put a thousand cat faces on it, and take away all the delicacy of shape the thing ever had. He tries to shape up a cutting tool; he turns it blue and wears it out in filaments which, when removed by some other process, show that the apparent form was decidedly deceptive. Don't try to mix machinists and emery wheels; they will ruin and corrupt each other. But they can get along splendidly if they are not mixed. Step into a hardware factory. Notice a man finishing a common carpenter's brace. Take one of the rough braces home and set your best vise-man to finishing it. Note the time, and the shape he leaves, and the thing he calls polish.

The man we are watching has a couple of emery belts and a couple of wheels, may be a hundred and fifty dollars' worth of tools altogether. With these and his skill he works on any shape you bring him. If a drop-forging, like the braces, he roughs and finishes and polishes and loses no little detail of the original nicely rounded and purely outlined form. If he finds a bad spot he goes deeper, but blends the flat till it is invisible. His polish is real polish, whatever may be said against it, and is the same all over, while a vise-man's polish is o. k. where it is easy to get at it and do it, but slouchy where the kinks' are. The emery-wheel man can't file a finish on a job. Why? Because he don't know how; he never learned; has a trade of his own. Same with the vise-man. What does this lead to? This: Look around the shop and see how much of your work is similar in shape to what you see in the market, but far inferior in character of surface and superior in cost, and ask yourself if there isn't some art which is not represented in the shop, and which should be represented. If you find considerable such work, and if you have thirty hands in the shop, you certainly will send to some good emery-wheel concern, and either buy from them or get drawings for the proper rigs adapted to your work. Let them send you a man at ten per-cent less wages than you pay the general run of lathesmen. This man will tell you more about the wheels and belts you want than your judgment could tell in a year. Set him to work the same as you would a lathesman, and in a short time you will find that you pile an immense quantity of work around him which you wonder how you ever got done before. Watch the man. First, there is his skill, about which nothing can be said, except that it is skill. He knows how. But you can see that he keeps a different sort of an establishment from the old one. The wheels are always in good face, and they run true, and the arbors are heavy, and stiff, and steady, and the speeds are right, and a wheel is always ready for business. You know very well that bad as the old rig was, its very viciousness was often inaccessible, because the belt was on a strike, or off the pulley, or because the oiler didn't see fit to keep the countershaft oiled.

Mechanical Time-Keeper in Sackett's Shop.

＊　＊　＊　＊　Honestly and truly, do you have an oiler? I don't mean a special dignitary with a sinecure, *vulgo*, soft thing, but some man, high or low in position, who is responsible for every squeak six feet from the floor? If you have such a functionary, does he oil countershafts, etc., over machines having a tender? Some shops give a certain laborer the oiling job, but expect countershafts to be oiled by the man who runs the machine below them. This is a bad plan. It's a nasty job that a lathesman don't like, so he puts it off as long as things will run. When he does it, he must skirmish around for ladders and things, and all the time a valuable man and machine are idle. Then there are always a lot of machines around a shop which are not run regularly by one man. They are run by everybody, and it is a notorious fact, that everybody won't oil anything he can't reach. If he finds something high up on a drill-press stuck for lack of oil, he jumps the job if he can, and waits for somebody else to fix things up. It is a much better plan to make Charlie oil up everything in the shop which is higher than his ear.

　　＊　＊　＊　＊　I send an illustration of the time-keeping machine which I showed you in Sackett's shop. Whether the thing is to be recommended or not, it is certainly an excellent illustration of one way of doing things. The machine is intended to save labor in time-keeping, but has no reference to detail time-keeping on work. As shown in the illustration, it consists of a time-keeper's desk, and furnishes him a place for the performance of his work, and for the deposit of his pay-books, etc. It is placed against the wall, past which all workmen must go as they arrive and depart. There is a hole in the wall exposing two slots in the deck of the machine. Underneath this deck is a compartment box intermittently revolved by clock-work. One of the slots in the deck is called the commencing slot, and the other the quitting slot. When a workman is hired, he is given a number of brass checks, all having the same number stamped upon them. This number is the book number of that man as long as he stays in the shop. By this number he is carried on all the books, and by this number he gives tool-room receipts, &c.

The time book to be used with this machine is gotten up as follows, the first vertical column being for the workman's number:

No.	M.	T.	W.	T.	F.	S.	Total.
	11	5					
13	7	2					
	4	3					7
	13						
14	8						
	4						4
	11	5					
15	7	2					
	4	3					7

Without entering into any description of the mechanical details of the device, we will simply refer to its plan of operations, and to the plan of booking its work.

We will assume that the machine is being used in a shop working ten hours, and keeping time by the hour. The cylinder shown in the illustration has twelve compartments, or pockets, near the outer edge, and twelve more just inside the circle of the first twelve. The deck covers all these pockets, and the commencing slot is always over one outside pocket, and the quitting slot over one inside pocket; there is a coiled spring under the desk, which tends to revolve the cylinder. A pawl hooking into notches upon the cylinder prevents rotation. This pawl is attached to the works of a calendar clock in such a manner that every hour the pawl will lift and allow the cylinder to turn one notch.

At six in the morning the cylinder is in such a position that checks dropped into the commencing slot will fall into what we may call the seven o'clock pocket. The cylinder stands this way for an hour, or till two minutes after seven, at which time the cylinder brings the eight o'clock pocket under the commencing slot, and the seven o'clock pocket under the quitting slot. In an hour it changes again. The slots thus remain an hour over each pocket. A workman may deposit his commencing check any time within the hour before going to work, and has two minutes margin to go on after time is up, and he has an hour in which to deposit quitting checks. The machine has adjustments which allow the intervals to be set to suit the rules of the shop.

The time-keeper, when he gets down to work, revolves the cylinder by hand, and pulls drawers out of the bottom, showing the checks in the properly-labeled pockets. He takes the checks from the eleven o'clock quitting pocket, for instance, and finds checks Nos. 13 and 15. It is Monday, and he finds his time-book, as shown above, ruled for morning and afternoon of each day. He jots down 11 for Nos. 13 and 15, and so on.

When he empties the seven o'clock commencing pocket, he finds No. 13 and 15 there. He puts seven under the quitting figure already noted. Afternoon the same. He subtracts commencing figures from quitting and gets the hour's time. The horizontal row of remainders at the week's end gives the week's time.

* * * * Several shops have these machines, and all have the same experience with them. The men think it part of a deep laid plan to get a full day's work out of them, and kick accordingly. It is sometimes very hard to explain away, but the fact is, the machine is not calculated in any way to correct evil habits, its object being solely to lighten the time-clerk's work, and to make the workman understand that he is paid from a time-book of his own posting.

Herron, working four hundred men, got one of these things, and the men were in arms at once. They wouldn't have it, and Herron could not make them see the thing in the right light, so out it came. It is a good thing, in a way, for the men and for the proprietors.

It will be noticed, in the illustration, that all the men are of one kind, and it may be a matter of justice to state, that if one of these chaps happened to have side-whiskers or even no whiskers at all, the machine would record his time all the same.

CHAPTER XII.

SHOP NOMENCLATURE.—SACKETT'S PLANER ARRANGEMENT.—MILLING MACHINES AND YANKEE "TRAPPERY."—A CORE DEVICE FOR FOUNDRIES.

* * * * If a German in an American shop asks in German for an oil-can, he won't be apt to get it, and we can understand why; but if an Englishman asks in English shop-lingo for a monkey-wrench, two things bother us, first, what he wants, and second, why he don't ask for what he wants, instead of talking about slide-spanners and screw-keys.

We would be bothered still more, and lose a little of our conceit if we were set down in Crewe or Manchester shops. There is really something comical in the difference in nomenclature in the two countries. With the English, our steady-rest is a catch-plate, and our follow-rest, a back-stay. Our engine lathe is their self-acting lathe. Wm. Sellers & Company have absorbed the words self-acting and back-stay into their work, but the words won't stick, after the machines are out of the shop. Our 24-inch swing-lathe is in mother English a 12-inch centers lathe. The word "swing" is certainly wrong, as it is too suggestive of radius, while we apply it to diameter.

Our belt is with them a strap; our shipper, a strap-shifting apparatus, and our counter-shaft, an overhead driving apparatus, and so on, forever. Special trades in our own country vary about as much. Men brought up in railroad shops always call a shaper a compound planer, and engine-slides, of any description, guide-bars. But the worst thing the railroad machinist is guilty of is bringing into shops such words as "six square nuts," "three square files, etc." He has often sent cubs running around among the round-house men after circular squares, and straight hooks, and wondered at the greenness of the boy in supposing for an instant that there are such things, when he himself daily uses such outrageous words as "bevel square," "four-square file," etc.

We have in this country four names for a connecting-rod: main rod, connecting-rod, pitman, and rod. Eccentric-rods are often called cam-rods; cross-heads tee-heads; and safety-valve weights are often called Pees, from $P =$ weight in the equations, I suppose. The crank-pin with some becomes a wrist. Of course there is no bigotry in the use of any of these terms, unless they are unyieldingly adhered to.

* * * * Sackett has got a planer arrangement which it would pay any one to see and copy. He had a good forty-inch planer, and, by a slight additional investment, he has arranged the thing to do work of any size whatever. The plan is well known in large shops, but the smaller shops, which need such things the most, will do well to listen. A heavy, slotted plate is planted under the planer, about four feet ahead of the housings. The plate is about five by fifteen feet, and sits across the planer, connecting equally on each side. It is truly planed on top, and is set true with the planer table, and bolted to the planer by short legs reaching up. It is simply a slotted floor, true with the planer table. He has a heavy knee with a broad base to bolt to this plate. The knee is practically a planer rail set upright and having a saddle, etc., the same as a planer. A job too large to go through the housings may be bolted to the table as usual, and operated on by the tool in this knee; and, in case of extra large work, the job may be bolted to the plate, and the knee bolted to the planer table. The knee has hand-feeds in all directions, and in connection with this planer will do the best of work on any sized piece which can be got into a shop. There is nothing shaky or temporary about the affair, and, to all intents and purposes, it is as good as a planer which will take in a cathedral.

* * * * If there is any one shop tool to which we owe the national pre-eminence in manufacture, which we brag so much about, more than to any other, it is, beyond doubt, the milling machine.

The universality of this machine has been developed entirely in this country, and from that development have sprung manufacturing possibilities before undreamed of. But there is no machine whose virtues are so little understood outside of its New England home. It is usual for all large shops to have one milling machine, and if you ask any one around the premises, from the owner down to the oiler, what that machine is, you will be told that it is a milling machine, and that it is used for fluting taps, and reamers, and such things. How little they know of the latent power of this machine to produce any sort of an effect on any metal, and to reproduce this effect with marvelous uniformity! As a jobbing machine, its virtue lies mostly in its universal adaptation, but in manufacturing, it is found to be an unvarying power for good. It is nothing but a circular saw mill, when you come to look at it, but if there is any one thing in the shop which don't get its deserts, it is the circular saw, or many-toothed cutter. You may file up a nice shape for a special lathe tool, but you will find it dull in a short time, and grinding will invariably alter the shape. Not so with the milling tool. Its sixty teeth distribute the work between them, not all doing the same work, because we find human skill fails to make the teeth all bear alike, but some teeth will cut deeper than others and put the finishing touch on the job. A cutter with sixty teeth, cutting at the same velocity as a common tool, will generally outwear three hundred single tools. An attempt to cut gearing in a planer will generally let light in on the real merits of milling operations.

* * * * New England is not only the home of the milling machine, but it is the national source of real happy ingenuity. There is a current belief that Yankee design runs to complexity and "trappery"—a belief not having the least foundation, in fact. When the New Englander takes it into his head to revise the work of mechanics from other sections, he starts new, discards every functional device, and produces the identical result with much simpler mechanism.

A marvelous gear cutter is brought to our notice, and, upon analyzing the machine, we must admire the perfection of every detail, the life-like action of its automatic devices, the absolute certainty of its operations, and the masterly manner in which the whole is constructed. But we look in vain for original detail, or novel devices. We find only an aggregation of well-known elements and movements, skillfully combined, so as to produce a novel and original whole. We are impressed with the idea that this excellent machine is, in reality, a combination of many familiar machines which retain their personality, even in their novel position. Our New England mechanic desires the functions of this machine, but does not take to the means. He designs a new one, discarding every element of the old one, and produces a machine which does not suggest anything we have ever seen before. His machine is *one* machine, and so perplexingly simple at that, that we wonder where the devices are. We hunt them up, and find that each movement is effected by entirely original devices of extreme simplicity and perfect action.

* * * * One peculiarity of New England design, or construction rather, is the apparent complexity, which results from dividing things up into small pieces. Massachusetts planes up two surfaces and bolts pieces together, while Pennsylvania casts them together, and produces a smoother exterior and greater appearance of general simplicity.

* * * * Sackett has a little arrangement in the foundry which captured me on sight. It is a device for making common round cores, from one-half inch to three inches in diameter. Instead of making a carload of core boxes every year, he made a set of common boxes, all eighteen inches long, and for all diameters up to three inches. They were of uniform size outside. Each core box has an iron plug sliding within it. This plug is cored in one end the shape of the core prints, and, by the way, all his core prints are of uniform length and taper, and the other end has a three-eighths hole in it. The core bench is provided with a socket in which any of the core boxes will stand upright and solid. In the center of the socket slides a graduated rod, on the upper end of which the plugs will fit. If his coreman wants a two-inch core, ten inches long, he sets the rod at the figure ten, puts the two-inch plug on its upper end, and sets the two-inch core box in the socket, and then makes the core as usual.

CHAPTER XIII.

TAKING THINGS ON TRIAL.—STARTING NEW SHOPS AND STARTING NEW TOOLS.—SHOP ABLUTIONS.

* * * * What is to be done with customers who want things on trial, and what is to be done with parties who want to sell us stuff on trial? Some classes of trade have arrived at that stage where all sales are subject to trial. Printers not only don't pay for their machines, but they don't order them till they have tried them a month.

The whole thing is wrong. It has its base in the fact that Tom or Dick, after getting up some new and really valuable machine, goes to making it instead of putting it into the hands of some reputable manufacturers already established. As a consequence, purchasers are met by a hundred irresponsible manufacturers offering their wares. The wares are what is wanted, if they will act as represented; but the trouble is that no confidence can be placed in the representation. If a man gets up a good machine, and takes it to a concern engaged in the manufacture of that line of machines, he can almost always receive fair treatment. If the machine is apparently good and wanted, the manufacturers will work it up to a success as a machine, and will put it on the market as a first-class rig, with their name on it. Ten per cent. on the gross receipts is a fair and proper royalty on machines, and as far as the manufacturer's profit, which these mushrooms ache over, is concerned, bless them, there isn't any. I can go to five hundred premature manufacturing shops in the country, contract to deliver their machines five per cent. less, and 20 per cent. better than they are building them; can go and sublet the job to real manufacturers, and pocket more money than twenty of the small concerns make. And more than that, not a miller, or printer, or thresher, or book-binder will ever dare to ask for thirty days or thirty minutes trial before ordering. Imagine Wm. Sellers & Co.; the Pratt & Whitney Co.; John T. Noye & Son, or George H. Corliss, shipping stuff subject to order, if satisfactory after trial! Such men don't experiment at the cost of the customer, and don't put their names on machines not known to be about what is required. The customer is thus protected against good things put upon the market prematurely. Another feature is that trial machines never get a trial. A man without money-interest in a machine will not investigate enough to develop the good there is in a thing. The first mishap condemns the whole thing, and it is returned as a failure, while real money-interest would refuse to believe that a machine was not capable of doing what it was designed for.

* * * Wycoff had a dozen governors sent on trial. They came. He unboxed one, and told the boys to put her on and see about it. They did, and saw that the pulley came out too far to be in line with the pulley on the engine shaft. They took the governor off and threw it under a bench. The maker of these governors can correspond with W. till doomsday, and never get any satisfaction. When he orders the governors returned he will get them, and will wonder what kind of a governor trial that is which never lets steam into the governor. If W. had money in those governors, it would have been on judgment, and they would have had a fair show.

If the governors had had a responsible man's name on them, W. would not have abused an offer, for he would not have had it. Inventors should be protected as well as purchasers.

* * * * There's no joke about a good many machine men paying themselves more for their product than others would charge.

If the future of a product is established, and if the projector has plenty of money, there is no doubt but that prudence would suggest the starting of a factory arranged expressly for the specialty in hand. He has but ten or fifteen thousand dollars in the world, and is a man whose services are in demand in certain branches. What shall he do with his immortal invention? He can take it into certain localities where manufacture has run in that line, and can contract to have the thing built in shops equipped with a world of special tools adapted to the line, with corps of workmen skilled in that line; and with market facilities of years of growth. He gets his machines without investing a cent in manufacturing facilities. He gets them made to specification, and runs no risk. If he sees fit to work the market himself, he has his whole means as a working capital, and when his device gives way to something newer or better he quits, with his profits in cash, and his manufacturers are where they started ; that is, they have made a profit, and have the same plant they commenced with.

The other way for our man to go at the thing is to start a shop. Work close financially, and work like a major every day, and use up three years' time getting his system of manufacture reduced to a science, and then his money is gone, and he is ready for the market, and some later thing has been in the market six months. It is certainly a fact that it takes three years to organize a factory, so a thing can be made as economically as a well-organized concern already existing can make it. Our man's small pile of money won't touch such a thing, and he has to let outsiders in to share the profits which he might have had himself, if he had let the factory project alone. He can contract for his stuff, go into the market at once, and come out winner, and quit long before a factory can get ready to build a thing not wanted when it is ready. The factory project must certainly start from a desire to get the manufacturer's as well as the factor's profit; but I think, that in a great many cases, the enormous expense of organization will by far overbalance that little thing we call manufacturer's profit, a thing that in many cases you can stick in your eye without damage to the eye. And besides that, the manufacturer involves a host of officers to share the profit if it ever comes. The question is: Is the real party's net gain as much under a manufacturing system as under a contract system? It's a big lot of work which he must do for nothing, and in a few short years there is one more idle concern, and a hundred employes idle, who have been seduced into a shop which never ought to have been started.

* * * With all the originality of the machine trade in this country, it must be acknowledged that too often the inventor finds manufacturers indifferent, and is forced to work the market on his own account. His trifle is not enough to justify him, but would be an important element in the catalogue of an old concern. I do not mean to charge indifference upon manufacturers generally, but I do mean to say that in many cases, manufacturers are loth to touch a thing which originates outside their own premises. I think I am justified in saying that those contrivances of the Gentiles, which by their apparent merit lead disinterested manufacturers to espouse them, are almost always successes, and that home-devised arrangements can never be freed from an appearance of selfish prejudice, which detracts from the force of every argument advanced in their favor. I never mind setting up my own awkward experiences for the benefit of others, and am willing to stand for an illustration of my text.

Years ago I was out continually as a journeyman erecting new work, in most cases steam machinery in mills, factories, and lead mines. Two systems of pipes in such jobs are always the same, to wit: the supply pipe from well to supply pump, thence to tank; and the feed pipe from tank to feed pump, thence to boiler. These jobs were often hundreds of miles from a shop, and the outfit of tools taken along was often taxed to form novel combinations of original tools. As a matter of course, a great deal of judgment had to be used so as to take along as much suitably connected piping as possible. The exit valve for the tank connection of the feed pipe was one of those pieces always taken. Every country machinist knows that valve, if it can be called a valve. It must be built up out of a piece of pipe having a long thread, a tin-shop strainer soldered to a coupling screwed upon one end; a globe-valve and elbow and nipples screwed to the other end; and thick rubber gaskets and specially forged lock nuts run upon the body. With such a rig one may feel prepared to meet a tank made of sheet iron, or six-inch wooden staves. But what a thing that is to have to build up in that manner, and how ugly and inefficient it is when done! The valve freezes four times per winter, and a new one must be put on, and for that reason an elbow is used instead of an angle valve, angle valves being hard to pick up in a hurry. An attempt to put the valve inside the tank involves trappy and unreliable rods to work it. I made such things as this till I got sick of it. I found them entirely too expensive and defective, so I got up a new article of manufacture in which the whole thing was got in good shape, with the valve inside the tank and the hand wheel outside.

It had a downward outlet and a malleable strainer—the body malleable, the valve brass, and long brass nuts. The thing could be sold for the price of a globe valve. No such thing could be made in a machine shop, so I opened up on supply manufacturers. I tackled the best men in the country with my sketch and long letters detailing its merits. They all thought it very nice and so on, but did not remember ever having had a call for one. A fine idea! Who ever had a call for *anything* of that character before he put it on the market? Besides that, engine men know what these supply men make just as well as they do themselves, and are too smart to order a thing they know isn't made. I don't put in any tank valves to speak of now, and, of course, dropped the matter when I could not help myself. I might have done as the subjects of my discourse do, and gone into their manufacture. I would have found that that would not pay alone, so I would have been forced into staple work. My capital, barely sufficient for the tank-valve business, would hardly stand the stretch, and, as a consequence, I would soon have found myself trying to get bread and butter out of an imprudent and uncalled-for competition. In such a business, I could continue to vitiate prices without vivifying my own trade in the least. I would be simply an excrescence upon the trade and my best friends, who, if they cared for the greatest good to the greatest number, would, in such case, do themselves credit by giving me the *coup de grace*.

* * * * There are certain lines of trade in which a demand is always in existence without finding expression. Known requirements or needs are as good as imperative demands to a manufacturer. That inventor is the wisest whose invention is based upon known defects in present systems; and the progressive manufacturer is the one who keeps his eyes open to the needs as well as the wants of his customers. There are limits past which prudence dictates we should not go. We may be aware of the need, but may find that a missionary bureau is required to apprise the public of its necessities. Such cases always connect themselves with inventions of a radical character. We see many things upon the market, meritorious within themselves, which purchasers never would have dreamed of asking for, but long-headed manufacturers, being aware of actual or easily-made apparent needs, have entered into projects with an assurance based on good judgment, and have almost always succeeded. A manufacturer will often spend years in trying to put some device of his own upon the market, when his judgment should tell him that his views are bound to be prejudiced, which could not be the case with the purchased invention of another.

* * * * If a machinist has no more pride about him than to leave the shop and go home without washing or taking his over-alls off, how much pride can he have about his work? Sackett picks a man up every once in a while, as he starts home, and tells him there is water on tap in the washroom. If a proprietor is smart, he will provide good washing facilities, and will have them kept clean by a laborer. Some of these things are disgusting, and a man with decent tendencies finds himself compelled to furnish a bucket for his own individual use. If discipline is loose, these pails will gradually find their way all over the shop, and every man will wash where he chooses, and throw his water over all the bright work in the neighborhood. It is not expecting too much of an owner, that he should keep a decent washroom while he is keeping one. I question whether in all England one can find a shop with washing facilities in it, and it is rarely that men wash before leaving the shop. Such a plan may work over there, but in a republic, where the masses form the power of the land, the decency and intelligence of the masses must be provided for, and are worth ten thousand times what they cost. As a general rule, American workmen never go home before cleaning up, and foreign workmen never clean up before going home. A workman who is dirty and slouchy and down-at-the-heel all over as he leaves the shop, is the same while in the shop, and the stuff he sells for the price of labor is not generally extra super. The finest and cheapest work done in this country is done by high-priced men, who know a cuff from a collar; and the coarsest and most expensive work is done by men who have no soul above clothes which won't show dirt. I can take you into sections of the United States where the shops work full gangs of dirty men, and you will call the products of that section crude or rough, and you will find the work comparatively expensive. I can take you to sections where the hands are neat in appearance, where you can always distinguish between a workman and a blue post in the shop, and their work has astonished the world by its marvelous refinement of accuracy and unaccountable cheapness. I could send you photographs of typical shops in these two sections, with the men massed in front, one crowd of eighty men, with six white shirts in the crowd, and one crowd of four hundred men and twenty dark shirts, and with the photos I could send the heaven-bound oaths of the shop-owners, that the men in either picture didn't have their Sunday clothes on.

CHAPTER XIV.

SHOPS IN THE SKY.—VALUE OF TESTIMONIALS.—LOCATION OF FACTORIES.—SELLING AGENCIES.

Many heavy old concerns have died the natural death of American shops, and, in many cases, I find some short-sighted men trying to do business on one of these old reputations; when the short cut would be to drop the name, and move to the other end of the city. The old Niles Works in Cincinnati has been dead and gone for years, and a railroad necessity has compelled the condemnation and conversion of the old premises. The Niles Tool Works, which, in reality, first started business right under the nose of the Niles Works, is an entirely different concern, and has a good shop at Hamilton, a few miles out. When I saw the old Niles Works building, I prayed that more railroads might some day cut into the city.

* * * * Property and taxes are high there, and, as in all other such places, shops move upward instead of moving outward. At J. A. Fay & Co.'s they have very heavy planers running in the high stories of a high shop. Post & Co.'s shops were in the sky, and one day the sky part got afire. They poured on water till the fire was out, but the water staid on the top floors. The firemen went home, and men commenced to straighten things up. They moved the machinery to the center of the upper floor, and found that the floor would not hold everything up at once. The floor gave way, and the heavy stuff went down to the next floor, then through that, and so on clear to the cellar. I don't know how many men were killed by the accident, but it was a great many. The value of a single one of these lives would have put up clean,

I once worked in a shop having open hatchways through the center of the building. * * * * Never a day passed but something came tumbling down.—Page 111.

roomy works outside of the town, where men would not have to work on ladders.

* * * * I once worked in a shop having open hatchways through the center of the building, no elevator, mind you, but simply a lot of holes and a hoisting rope. I worked on the engine floor on the lowest story, nearly under the hatchway, and never a day passed but something came tumbling down into the space supposed to be reserved for my operations. To-day it would be a monkey-wrench, to-morrow an oil-can, or a dinner bucket, or a lathe chuck, or a portable engine cylinder, or an apprentice, or most anything. One day the whole back wall of the shop fell in, and the shop quit business forever. I have always been thankful, and hope all the walls will fall in in every shop having hatchways in the middle of the building.

* * * * I believe that the Western folks are right about testimonials. They mean nothing whatever, and, in most cases, are a fraud. I can mention one case as a sample of a dozen within my knowledge. Horace owned the Valley Works, and Bill worked for him. Bill was a good workman, and was one of these men who were good in a pinch. If a line-shaft twisted off, or if a gate broke in the water wheel, or if a crane broke down, or if a cylinder-head got knocked out, Bill was the man who would take hold and put forth extraordinary energies till the shop got going again. He was a valuable man. But in his regular work, when work piled up and things got in a rush, he would get on a drunk, and, aside from that, he was the meanest and most contemptible whelp that ever annoyed a lot of workmen by his presence. Horace put up with it for years, but one day discharged Bill, and told him to go to the devil! He went, but one day came back and told a pitiful story about home matters and low funds, etc., saying that some little letter, you know, would get him a good place; of course it would. Anything from Horace would do anything, and he had a soft side, so he wrote the stereotyped letter, bearing testimony to Bill's *good* qualities. With this he went off and imposed himself on somebody, who soon found that Bill was a fraud and Horace a soft cheat.

* * * * How often do we find a foreman who is laboring under the belief that the shop will break up if he don't continue to submit to some evil presence in the shop? It almost always takes the shape of some man, who has been in the shop so long that he thinks, as the foreman does, that the shop can't exist without him; so he gets ugly and "sassy," and has his regular drunk weeks and his irregular sober ones. His work is always important, and a foreman should never delude himself into the belief that there is only one man of a kind made. Barney worked for George, running gear cutters for ten years. He knew every little trick of the machines, knew every cutter which was a little off and not to be used on nice work, etc. He had his whiskey weeks and the gear cutters had their idle weeks. George was tender to all men, but after ten years' cooking he boiled over and kicked Barney out of the shop, and the next day he had a better man on the gear cutters. It always happens that way. Wallace's slotter hand thought he was King of the Cannibal Islands, and Wallace thought so too, for it isn't easy to pick up a good slotter hand; but one day, after a couple of years' of weak suffering, he let him go, and found a better man right in the shop. Babbitt had a man who could run a nice cut right over a six-inch shaft, and get nice work out in a hurry. Man was always ugly, and Babbitt always afraid, for he had seen men fail on that lathe. He screwed up his courage one day and let the man go, and put a smart cub in his place, and found he had been submitting to an unnecessary evil.

* * * * If a man is engaged in the manufacture of spool thread, or nails, or hinges, or licorice drops, it don't seem to make much difference where he carries on his business. He never sees the consumer and never sells to him. His product is sold through numerous middle men, and probably he only needs two or three customers, anyhow. His goods are staple and are ordered by name and grade. A man wanting a dime's worth of lemon drops don't question into the manufacturing facilities of the several manufacturers before he places his order. He don't have to go to the factory to confer as to the advisability of the adaptation of certain lemon drops to his special maw. He don't do anything, but go and buy from a dealer, who bought from a dealer, who bought from a dealer, etc.

The manufacturer of lemon drops finds that he can go off into the woods and squat by a cheap water-power, and a sugar mine, and a coal mine, and engage in business, and actually have a hundred economic advantages over his competitors in metropolitan centers. His freights are a trifle more, but his cheap water, coal, and sugar, will far overbalance the account. His traveler takes a full line of samples in a grip-sack, and the cost of selling is no greater than if he were in a city. He must, of necessity, under all circumstances, sell through representatives or factors.

* * * Suppose I take a notion to envy the man, who is situated among the hills with a coal mine in his front yard, and a water-power in his back yard, and a neighbor's iron pile handy. Suppose I manufacture wood-working machinery, and suppose I sit down and figure up how much I can save on power, fuel, and material in a year. Suppose these figures show a tip-top income in themselves—should I pack up and move into this district myself? Would I make any money by it? Would I lose any by it?

* * * * As a builder of machinery, I would find it necessary to confer with at least one-third of my customers. They want to see what they are going to buy; they want to see the shop, and they want to see me. I travel around, and find men have bought of others, when the order would naturally have come to me. On inquiry and protest, I am told that "We didn't have time to go away up there. We can't step out of the business-world to buy things," etc., etc.

* * * * Manufacturing economies may sometimes be purchased at the expense of business. Go where orders can be filled cheaply, and the orders won't come—not always, of course, but often. A man who wants to buy a three-hundred-dollar machine is willing to go into a certain district and investigate, but he is unwilling and unable to go all over the country, or into inaccessible neighborhoods.

* * * * If a man has a factory in Boston, he is not moving out of reach when he goes to Chelsea. If in New York, Newark and such places are all right. Chester and Wilmington are the same to Philadelphia; Hamilton and Dayton the same to Cincinnati. But when a man moves from a metropolis off to Smith's side track, a thousand miles from anywhere, and away beyond the jumping-off place, he will find that he makes a mistake, unless he is engaged in a business which does not require contact between producer and consumer. Customers don't know where the place is, don't know how to get there, haven't time to go there, and don't want to go there anyhow. Special friends will take the short cut and buy elsewhere. If a man is engaged in making things worth over a hundred dollars apiece, he had better "stay around" if he wants to sell them.

* * * * If a machine builder is unfortunate enough to find himself off somewhere where his customers can't and won't get at him, he must, of necessity, find some way to get at his customers. He finds, by fine calculation, that, by going to a tank station to start business, he saved thirty-five hundred dollars a year, and now he finds he must incur an expense of about five thousand dollars per year on account of extra "traveling and advertising." No matter where a man hangs his shingle, he must travel and advertise, of course. If ten customers run up against his premises accidentally, he can bring ninety more by a judicious investment in printers' ink and railroad tickets. If he lives in the woods, he must sell every cent's worth by appeal.

Another way out of the difficulty is to sell through warehouses; and here I wish to express my earnest sympathy with a machine builder, who depends on a metropolitan agency for business, unless he happens to own the agency himself. In the latter case, he is o. k., and if a business can be made extensive enough, it looks like the right way to do it. Have the "concern" with a full stock in the city, and do the work anywhere. The disadvantage in this is, that freights are crossing and adding, and that the expense of down-town warerooms and offices, and the expense of carrying complete stocks, and the expense of eternally running and telegraphing between office and works, four hundred miles distant, will often exceed the extra expense of having the whole business, shop and all, up town, or in an accessible suburb.

* * * * When you depend on a general machinery agent for sales, you knock off a discount, but this is less than the cost of the sale, if you made it yourself. Your agent's salesmen may, and may not, be good. They may lie for, or against, your product.

Your factor may, or may not, keep your goods in good, attractive condition. He may, or may not, possess the special knowledge required in suiting customers. He may treat you squarely, and he may hold your goods to keep them from other factors, while he throws his influence in other directions where better discounts may be had. Machinery agents have got as much human nature in them as other men. A man is wise to deal through them, but, I think, is unwise and unlucky, if his sole dependence is upon them. I apply this particularly to wood-working and iron-working machinery.

* * * * For ready sales of machinery in these lines, there is nothing like having a good stock on hand. When a man takes a notion to buy a thing, he is much like a woman with a letter to mail. She may have put off writing the letter for several months, but when it is written, it must go into the mail *instanter*. If some man won't get out of bed to mail it, she will go through snow or rain herself. A man has decided to buy a tool. He has the money in his pocket, and starts for head-quarters. If he don't find what he goes after, he gets on his ear. He can't and won't wait. He never dreamed of buying but from one builder, but if he fails there, he will go where he can get instant satisfaction. He is bound to spend that money before he gets home. He won't be satisfied to leave an order. I have known a man to go nine hundred miles to buy a lathe, exactly twenty-four inches swing, and exactly twelve feet between centers; and with a certain kind of cross-feed and certain other things to a dot. He wants this lathe and must have it right away. He didn't find the lathe in stock, and came back with a little planer that he had no more use for than a diamond-pointed tool has for a side-pocket. He is just as well satisfied, however, for the money is gone. It's a good plan to keep something to sell to every man who comes after anything else.

* * * * There are certain classes of machines which are universally disposed of through factors. Among these are farm engines, and agricultural implements generally. I don't believe the shop sales to the consumer, under the most lavish system of traveling and advertising, can be brought to equal ten per cent. of the trade to be had through resident district factors. Farmers never have money or confidence enough to go far from home, and they don't understand the process of doing business by mail.

CHAPTER XV.

TELLS HOW DIX AND CHORDAL ESTABLISHED STANDARD SIZES IN WYCOFF'S SHOP.

* * * * Carr had his mill work done by Wycoff. Lots of inch-and-three-quarter and two-inch shafting, lots of pulleys, lots of spur and bevel gears, lots of gudgeons, and lots of babbitted boxes. Such is the character of most orders for mill gearing. There were probably thirty pieces of two-inch shafting, short and long. By two-inch shafting, I mean two-inch iron turned down a sixteenth, and there were probably fifty pulleys to go on these shafts, many of the pulleys the same size. I watched Wycoff's foreman giving orders in the shop while this work was being done. He would go to Joe with a piece of iron about a yard long, and say: "Turn this up to fit that pulley and that bevel wheel, and turn a journal on each end, so we can babbitt those boxes on them." Joe went at it, but ran against a snag the first thing. The pulley and the bevel gear had not been bored the same size. Joe tells the foreman so. Foreman says: "It's strange; I told Charley to bore it to one and fifteen-sixteenths." Joe says he can't help that; that pulley won't go on any shaft which the bevel gear will fit. Foreman takes the calipers and investigates. Yes! that's so. Well, you fit this shaft to the bevel, and I'll have Gus *file* the pulley out.

* * * * He does have it filed out, and he has something of the kind filed out every day the shop runs. Furthermore, about every hole bored in the shop is tapering; and furthermore, his one and fifteen-sixteenths don't mean anything. Charley does his best, sets his calipers as close as he can to that size, but bless him, he can't set them the same size to-morrow.

If he bores a pulley one and fifteen-sixteenths every day he will have six different sized holes Saturday night. This is the best Charley, or any other lathesman, can do. The fault is Wycoff's. The foreman knows the Monday and Tuesday sizes are not the same, and he is smart enough to have the hole around for the shaft man to measure when he fits a shaft.

* * * Carr comes into Wycoff's office in a few months and orders a fourteen-inch pulley to go on the long two-inch shaft down at the mill. Wycoff says he must send a man down to get the size of the shaft. Carr says, "Why, you made the shaft yourself. Bore the pulley to fit your two-inch shafting and it will be all right." Wycoff says, "It won't be all right; for no two pieces of my two-inch shafting are the same size." Carr says they ought to be, and wonders what will happen if he wants to transpose anything around the mill. Wycoff tells him he can't do it; tells him if he left his mill and worked at the machine business thirty years he would find out that machinists never measured alike, and that every pulley must be fitted where it belongs. Carr is bold enough to think there ought to be some way to keep things decently uniform, and Wycoff is ignorant enough to say there is no way in which it can be done.

* * * * There are a lot of nice machine men in the country who will congratulate us on there being but one Wycoff. There's where they make their mistake. Wycoff is ubiquitous: he outvotes finer owners; he "raises" the most mechanics, he does most of the work.

* * * Carr's old mill-gearing was made by Sackett. Carr never happened to know it, but any two-inch shaft in the mill would fit any two-inch pulley, and if a short two-inch shaft has shouldered journals, those journals will fit any similar boxes in the mill. Carr can go to Sackett's in three years from now and order a box, or a pulley, or a shaft, and the only size wanted is the nominal diameter.

* * * * There is no shouldered shaft in Carr's new mill which will allow itself to be turned end for end. The journals are not the same diameter on each end. Every babbitt box is run on the shaft it is intended for. Sackett's boxes are run on shafts kept in the shop for that special purpose. They are always uniform. His pulleys he reams out; he did just as good work before he got his reamers, but it cost him a great deal more money. Why? Because it took a more expensive man more time to do the work.

* * * * Dix and I both worked for Wycoff at the same time. We tried to get Wycoff to do something to keep sizes uniform. We were simply journeymen, but we claimed some sense. We were working as closely as we could, and as close as any other workmen in the world could, I guess. That is, we set calipers to marks on scales and turned to the calipers. The mortal don't live who could keep sizes uniform with these facilities, and this is all a workman is supposed to have.

We knew if we had some better way of getting a size than by picking it off a scale, we could do more satisfactory work, and by "satisfactory" we meant better work and more of it. We wanted some record, some monument, some standard of sizes. Something we could copy every time. Wycoff didn't know of any such thing; and more than that, he didn't care. He had for thirty years, etc. But Dix and I did care. We decided that if Wycoff would not have good standard sizes, he should have bad standard sizes—some standard we *would* have. We two held a meeting, and, on motion, it was resolved that we would watch our chances and steal the time and bore out collars to one and seven-sixteenths, one and eleven-sixteenths, one and fifteen-sixteenths, and two and three-sixteenths. These collars we would bore as nicely and to as accurate a size as we knew how. These collars we would hide away somewhere, and when we or the other boys wanted a size, we would set inside calipers to these holes, and for shaft work we would try the collars on. We chose the sizes named, because they were the sizes in most common use in the shop.

Well, we made the collars and piled them nicely in a cupboard. We used them all the time, and the other men appreciated the thing. But one day a collar was gone, and soon another was gone. When we came to snort around some, we found Wycoff had found them, and supposed they were simply extra collars; so he had used two of them—had had them set-screwed and sent out with work. Our collars were simply common cast-iron collars, mind you.

* * * * We held another meeting, and, as a result, we invented a collar which Wycoff couldn't-get-a-set-screw-into. We replaced the two lost ones and turned a deep groove in each; that is, we run down with a cutting-off tool till the collar was nearly cut in two. No man on earth could get a half-inch set-screw into such collars, for they were only about an inch and a half wide anyhow, and the cut came right in the middle. Our collars worked very well. We soon added short, wrought-iron plugs, which fit the collars nicely. These plugs we could try in holes. We used calipers, just as usual, but we tested everything by these plugs and rings. Soon we actually had a set of mandrels, which we could go and get, and know they would fit a job without being fooled with. However, we soon found we couldn't go and get them, because somebody else had gone and turned them down to fit something else. We never were able to contrive any plan or plot by which we could keep these mandrels. Remember, Dix and I were jours., not bosses or owners. Had we been bosses, there would have been bloodshed in Wycoff's shop. For a whole long year, Wycoff's work of these sizes was uniform, and there was no fussing over sizes, and many, and many, and many an hour's time was saved to the shop. If we could have mastered the mandrel problem we would have been the means of saving Wycoff hundreds of dollars a year.

* * * * Our fancy gauges had their demerits. They would wear out of size. They were heavy and clumsy. The collars could not be got on work without losing the job, and even then they would not go up close to a tool. If a shaft began to work large, the collar could not be got over the big place so as to try new parts. They were not what we wanted, but they beat "nothing" all to pieces. Dix struck the keynote when he said we never ought to use the gauges at all, except to set calipers by. Then the gauges would never wear out, and we would still have just as uniform sizes.

* * * * We debated on the question of letting Wycoff into the thing. He had several times expressed wonder at a piece fitting in two or three places, and had remarked at our luck in picking up a mandrel which would fit a job. Dix opposed exposure—said the inelastic Wycoff would snub the idea of there being better ways of doing things; that he had for thirty years, etc. We never did tell him. We one day left Mr. W.'s shop, and, since that, it has been the good fortune of both Dix and myself to have a hand in regulating things—in putting into practical use those sundry little rigs which count in economy. We have found out how poor our sly standards really were, and we have found that there are much better ways of doing the thing.

* * * * When a shop contemplates getting a new thing, there is one infallible test to apply. Is the thing an element of economy? Will it reduce the cost of bad work? Will it improve bad work? Will it improve good work? Will it reduce the cost of good work? Will it save the parties money, work, reputation, or time? If all the answers are "no," say we can't afford to get it. If *any* answer is "yes," say we can't afford to do without it.

In ninety-nine machine shops in a hundred there are no provisions made for uniformity of sizes. Not even the poor rigs Dix and I got up on the sly. When a new tap is made it is not the size of the old one. Nothing can be uniform under such circumstances; nothing can be cheap. If you have a machine shop, Mr. Editor, or if you have any authority in a father-in-law's shop, study well into the subject of standard tools. Get decent workmen, pay them decent wages, give them decent facilities, expect decent work, and you can make a decent price list. Standard tools you can't afford to do without.

CHAPTER XVI.

OUTWITTING THE ALMANAC.—LIGHTING SHOPS.

* * * The boom has struck us and so has the evening darkness. As luck will have it, hurried orders almost always come in just when the days get short. You can't always make hay while the sun shines in the machine business. If business moves along at an easy jog, never slack and never overflowing and rushed, the change in the length of days is not of so much importance.

The men can be put on short hours, but this is wrong, for it reduces their pay just when most of them need the most money. The men understand full well that the work done on winter mornings and evenings is of small value, even under the best advantage, and putting a shop on short hours in the winter is a fair transaction. If machinists would work at plastering or bricklaying, trades which must save up money enough in summer to keep them over winter, they would learn a trick or two which might be of use in their own trade.

* * * Instead of cutting down the working hours and the pay, there is another way of outwitting the almanac. That is to cut down the hours and leave the pay as it is, and bring the thing all square by utilizing the long days of summer. I know of many shops working that way. I have worked that way myself in every position about a shop, from cub to super., and found it more satisfactory than any other plan.

There is considerable science required in regulating and arranging the hours on this plan.

I give here a table of hours, calculated by Mr. Chas. A. Bauer, Superintendent of the Champion Bar and Knife Works at Springfield, Ohio.

TIME TABLE.   AVERAGE 10 HOURS.

Date.	Go to work a. m.	Be gone to Dinner.	Go home p. m.
Jan. 1............	7.15	1 hour	5.
" 8............	"	"	5.15
" 29	7.	"	5.30
Feb. 12............	7.	"	5.45
" 19............	6.45	"	6.
Mar. 18............	"	"	6.15
Sept. 16............	"	"	6.
Oct. 7............	"	"	5.45
" 14............	"	"	5.30
Nov. 11............	7.	"	5.15
Dec. 2............	7.	"	5.
" 9............	7.15	"	5.
" 16............	"	"	4.50

This table is to be hung up in the shop for the guidance of the men and the genius who attends to the bell or whistle. By carefully going over this table it will be found that it is made to conform to daylight, and that it gives the men ten hours pay, and the shop ten hours work the year round. The pay of the men is never changed. They get ten hours pay every day. It will be seen that the longest shop days, by this table, are from March 18th to September 11th, during which time the days are ten and a half hours long, and that the shortest are from December 16th to January 1st, during which time they are eight hours and thirty-five minutes long.

This arrangement need not complicate cost accounts, for it need not enter into them.

The more you look into this thing the more you will see what you don't see about the cost matter.

It is giving the men the cream off the milk, for they

get full wages in the winter, while the shop makes no money in the winter, and has to run the risk on summer work. But all's well that ends well.

* * * * There are vicious sides to this time-table plan when taken advantage of by unscrupulous men, both owners and workmen. I have heard workmen kicking against the plan, because some rogueish owner had paid them wages during the summer and then put them on starvation piece-work in the winter; and I have seen owners the victims of sharp workmen who drew wages during the winter and went to other shops in the summer. This table is a good gauge for morals. In smooth-working shops I have seen men growling in the summer over the long hours. These men were invariably big fools who knew nothing of the laws of compensation or the rules of average.

* * * * But when the boom comes and you can't get men enough to fill up the shop, compensating laws and average time tables won't save you. The shop must not only run ten hours per day, but it must run twenty-four hours per day sometimes.

The machine business is nice, it's interesting, it's vocative and intellectual, and all that, but the only way to get any money out of it is to have plenty of work and crowd things. Money can't be made deliberately in any machine shop. When I say plenty of work, I mean all the shop can take care of. A shop a mile long with self-winders, and self-setting attachments, and all the modern improvements, is tip top so long as the shop is full of work. But it takes lots of work to make it full. When half full, the work costs much more than if the shop was only half as big. The big shops have been envying the little ones for several years, and I know of one large concern who, having looked into the matters deeply and seriously, thought of locking up the place and renting a small concern.

The word "elephant" simply means big, and don't refer to material or direction.

* * * * Night work must be done, and some provision for light must be made. In many shops the rule is to pay fifty per cent. additional for night work. This is all right on job work, for the job can be charged with it if the party is over anxious. But when it comes to contract or staple work, fetched deep from bids on an open market, the thing is different.

Here we find that, even with an hour's pay the same, an hour's work isn't the same. If you know of a shop doing regular machine work, which can get forty minutes' work done in an hour after night, I wish you would tell me how they do it. This reduction of the value of an hour adds a big percentage to the cost of work, without the necessity of adding another fifty per cent. to the cost of the labor.

* * * * Men can't do much work after night. If you go into a shop at night, you see a black immensity with little spots of light in it. In the middle of each of these little light spots you will find a little machinist trying to do a little work. Gaslight is used, we will assume. The bracket pipes have half a dozen elbows, and can be crooked around in every direction, and they have six-foot burners with lava tips. You may put more joints in the brackets, you may put on ten-foot burners with salamander tips, till you can't rest, but still your light will come from one direction. Even a vise-man must be forever pulling his light around, trying to get it into useful positions. The planer-men are happy while a cut lasts, but when it comes to setting work or doing any nice measuring or gauging, trouble begins. Lathesmen ditto, except that this work calls for light projected into deep holes. The men working on the floor are at a fearful disadvantage. They always want something. They can't see it and don't know what direction to go in to look for it. They have burners on the ends of hose, but they don't know where to take the thing next. The same happens when any machinist wants any tool or any piece. Gas can't be carried around nicely, after a man does make up his mind where to search for a thing.

* * * * Bad as it looks, it is better to use the gas for fixed lights and give the men candles. A candle is a supple affair. You can stick it anywhere. You may devise and construct ingenious candlesticks, but they will finally yield to a hot-pressed nut. If a man leaves a lathe, he leaves the gas burning; he takes his candle with him, and when he comes back his gaslight acts as a beacon, and enables him to find his lathe again—if he don't break his neck in the meantime.

* * * * Once on a time, when I was using candles for movable lights, a silver-tongued pedlar came along with a gay and festive hand lamp for coal oil. He talked and exhibited. It was small and light in weight, and brilliant and cheap. He couldn't blow it out and I couldn't. He convinced me that it couldn't explode, and gave me testimonials from many shops which *had* been using them. I bought fifty and started the thing up. As was usual with me, I did not deal them out to the boys as supplies, but I presented one to each hand. They were charmed with the taking affairs, and proceeded to do the usual elegant engraving of names, etc. The plan was well introduced, but within a week every lamp had been smashed flat against the only spot of dead wall in the shop. I said nothing, for they were not my lamps. The men might use candles, if they preferred them, but I had my own elegant name on one lamp, and I used the lamp, too. One night my own lamp flattened itself against that same wall, and that was the end of coal oil as a portable light for me.

* * * * After being cured of coal oil as a portable light, I gave still further attention to the subject. I saw that all lights were defective for machine work on account of the light coming so decidedly from one direction. This I thought it idle to grumble about, as it couldn't be helped. But I looked deep into the matter of candles. I had been paying eighteen cents a pound for star candles by the box. They gave good light, and were the best I knew of. They dripped all over the tools, and the men, and the work, and the shop, but that was a feature of all candles. One box I got was clear and transparent. They didn't look like the other candles, and, after the box was about half gone, a bill of correction came from the dealers. The candles had been sent by mistake. They were thirty-five cents a pound, and they wanted the difference or the candles. They didn't get either. Something came of this. I noticed that the drip from these candles didn't stick to anything whatever; that is, it would fall off, or could be picked off clean, while, with the star candles, the stuff had to be scraped off. This was a feature on bright work, and I soon found that these candles dripped but very little anyhow, and they didn't gutter any. I then inaugurated a test, and found that a star candle burned two inches, nearly, while the others burned an inch. This accounted for their cleanliness. The material was only melted as fast as needed by the wick, and it was all used. This put a new face on the thing, and I figured some. As a result of the figuring, I used these candles, thereafter, at thirty-five cents, as being cheaper than the star at eighteen. I forget the brand of these candles, but I think they were paraffine. They were elegant looking, and I found the men got into the habit of chewing them like-gum, and soon I got into it myself. This ought to be considered in the calcu-

lations, for, unless you can confine the chewing to the fag-ends, it will count up.

* * * * I thought the candle business as good as it could be, but still I was trying to get lots of work out of a dark shop. I saw that unless the shop, as a shop, was made fairly light, the night work never could be brought anywhere near the day work. I tried to fix things. I gave each man a gas jet, as usual, and a candle, as usual. Then I put in wall-brackets everywhere, and put chandeliers with four lights in every important neighborhood. This did the business. Men could see each other's noses, and a man could go and get what he wanted without sneaking all over the shop, like Judas Iscariot looking down a rat-hole for eighteen pence.

* * * * The men were now doing lots of work o'nights, and so was that gas-meter. I kept time and watch, closely, and found the thing didn't pay. I must let my pipe-fitter cut the gas-meter's part entirely out of the play, or else the play must stop. Gas cost three dollars. I thought of using coal oil for the side-lights and chandeliers, and then I thought of the chimneys and wondered how they would stand the racket. I decided they would not do at all. I could not use coal oil. Then a happy thought struck me. I brought the secretary of the gas company around to the shop, and had everything prepared for him. Every burner was doing its loudest, and I told him to look at that. I showed him last month's big bill, and told him to look at that. He was pleased. Then I told him how much we increased the value of the workmen by the plan, and he was still further pleased. Then I told him if he didn't give us gas at one-fifty, I would stop it to-morrow, and put in coal-oil. His jaw fell, and then rose in high and mighty argument. I won, and the gas staid in till we joined a couple of neighbors on the same block, and put in a gas machine of our own.

* * * * My experience then and since, has confirmed me in the opinion that night work can never approach day work in cheapness, unless the atmosphere can be made light, as I did it, or otherwise. Of late years the electric light *furore* has opened up something new in this line. Some time ago, I looked into the electric question as applied to shops, and finally opened up on the Brush Company. They sent estimates under guarantee of satisfaction. The outfit, complete, giving lights for each shop, the office, etc., would cost only twenty-seven hundred and eighty dollars. This staggered me. We couldn't spare the money, and so I came to the conclusion that the electric light hadn't got completed yet, anyhow. Last winter, Bennett found his shop running every night, and he took up the subject of electric lights. He has a long shop, splendidly suited for it. We conferred together, and went out to Cleveland. We found the handsomest man I ever saw, shut up in a darkened room, with eighteen lights on a single circuit. It was Mr. Brush. For the first time in my life, I had the satisfaction of seeing a regular machine shop really lighted up at night, and doing effective business. There was no impediment to travel, no wondering if a certain thing was in a certain place. The inside of the shop was light. The keen satisfaction we both had was all that came of the trip. Bennett could not stand the price, and the company had the good sense to stick to the price while they were full of orders.

* * * * Talk about illumination in the shop! I saw a rig in Bennett's foundry the other night, which was not a bad idea. A heat was being run, and, of course, it was long after dark. Otto had thrown a bushel of soft coal on the floor, stuck a six-foot piece of inch-and-a-half gas pipe down into the pile of coal, poured a little melted iron on the coal, thrown on some sand, and lighted the top of the pipe. Here was the biggest kind of a gas works gotten up on the shortest notice. Be it old or new, this hint may be of value in many a foundry and elsewhere.

The Lightning Machinist.—Page 135.

CHAPTER XVII.

THE LIGHTNING MACHINIST.—HIS LAZY NEIGHBOR.—THE SOLDIER ON DUTY.—GIVING SATISFACTION TO PURCHASERS.—ORDER IN SHOPS.

* * * * Did you ever have a lightning machinist to work for you—one of those quick-blooded fellows, all energy and activity? When you walk out into the shop, you see him going into things for all that's out. When he strikes with a hammer, he strikes quick. When he starts for a thing, he starts with a flash, as though he had been shot out of a gun. When he lifts a thing, he simply jerks it up. When he lets it down, he drops it. When he goes to another part of the shop, he goes on a run. When he goes to the grindstone, he rushes there, and rushes back. It is worth the price of admission to a trapeze performance to watch him at a lathe. He wants to change his belt, and he snaps at it like a flash. He knocks his shifter instead of shoving it. When he puts a three-foot shaft in his lathe, he grabs it from the floor, snaps a dog on it, fixes one end on the live center, and lunges out after the tail wheel like a zouave on fancy drill. This genius not only does this when you happen to walk into the shop, but he does it all the time. All day long he jumps, and hops, and snatches, and strains, and blows, and sweats, and works hard and energetically generally, and when night comes he hasn't got any work done. That is the case; for this fellow is the biggest kind of a humbug. This energy of his is not execution. When you come to look into the chap, you generally find he hasn't got sense enough to do anything, even if he took time for it. He is a born fool, or he wouldn't jump around so. He rushes a diamond point tool into the tool post, and screws down on it with a spin. Then he finds it wrong and unscrews it, and does it all over, and so on, half a dozen times. He gets everything he does right by a succession of nervous twitches. He is chock full of vim, and has no lazy bones in his body. He generally wins the approval of short-sighted bosses. He is known to be an honest, hard-working man, but he's a fraud of the grossest order, and isn't worth shop-room.

* * * * Did you ever watch a barber who took nervous, short strokes with the razor? Every second his razor flies like lightning from your face to the paper on your shoulder. He reaches for brushes and things with vehement energy. My! but isn't he a quick barber! You watch him in the glass as he shaves you, but he don't seem to get any beard off your face, and don't seem to get much lather on the paper. The lazy chap "running" the next chair, has taken slow, broad swipes, with a clean precision, from the faces of three customers since you submitted yourself to your quick man.

* * * * If you want to be shaved in time for a train, don't get under an energetic barber: and if you want to get a lathe job done in a hurry, don't go near one of these quick-moving machinists. And if you should take your lathe job to such a one, don't tell him to rush it. If you do, you are gone sure. He can't rush anything. If you crowd him, he will set his tools that much more ineffectively; he will recklessly grind his tools, so they won't cut at all; he will recklessly belt to speeds so fast as to prohibit any iron being removed; and then will get back to the proper speed. If he wants to put a file finish on his horrible job, he can't find time to change to a high speed, so he goes hammering the job with a mill file, while the surface of the work moves at eighteen feet a minute. Every machinist of any sense soon finds out that filing lathe work at a slow speed is not the way to hurry a thing, but this energetic dolt never took time to find out anything. Better put him out in the yard, and let him practise ground and lofty tumbling in breaking scrap iron. His useless gymnastics have no place in a machine shop. Put such a fellow on piecework prices, which make a lazy man rich, and he will starve to death. There is something winning about the fellow's motions, but there is no good in them.

* * * * If you want something done in a hurry, your lazy man is the one to do it. It isn't often he hurries, but when he does do it he enjoys it. A hurry once in two or three months is his recreation. Hurry this man for half a day, and he will be prepared to recommence his old lazy way with renewed vigor. This lazy fellow is susceptible of being hurried. You can't demoralize him by rushing him, because he won't hurry that much. He will slouch over to a grindstone, and fix a diamond point tool as he seldom fixes one. He will patiently grind the face down nicely, and give the edge a keener angle than he usually takes the time to grind to, and he is careful to grind the back of the cutting edge a little the lowest. When he gets back to the lathe after a while, he engineers that tool into its most effective position, and then he screws down on it. He starts up at a speed he knows won't glaze that elegant tool, and he shoves it into a cut as deep as the job will stand. Soon he will be piling great chips under his lathe, and your job is under the best possible headway. This elegant machinist will be sitting down on his tool board. He's tired, poor man!

* * * * I don't want to defend the lazy machinist, but when you want something in a special rush, you will find that he won't do any reckless fussing. He won't make any false strokes for fear it will make too much work. He remembers every little thing in the past, which, by some miscarriage, caused trouble, and now he takes the sure and certain and effective path. If you are in a hurry for the job, he is particularly anxious that you shall have it as soon as possible. He is a man who don't like to have hurried jobs on his hands any longer than possible. The other kind suits him best, and he will get back to them as quickly as he can.

Another good thing about this lazy chap is, that he never soldiers. He don't need to.

* * * * There is a certain kind of machinists who seem always to feel guilty of something underhand. When the boss comes around, they will antic about, and you would think they would work their skins off. This imposition succeeds only with that class of foremen who take considerable stock in the energetic fellow we first talked of.

Every smart foreman knows very well that during this effervescence the men are not doing anything at all. They are making unusual, idle, quick motions for a few minutes, just as our energetic chap does all day long. If they kept on they would get nothing done, and it is only when they quit this momentary make-believe, and go to work, that they commence to accomplish anything. If you see a man reaching out lively when a boss comes around, you can make up your mind that that chap has been soldiering. Such a man generally has no honor that you can depend on. You must watch him. There are two kinds of machinists that I hate above all men. One is represented by the man who works furiously in another man's service, and has nothing at home to show for it, except the sweat wrung from his dirty shirts by his slouchy family, and the other kind is represented by the man whose general actions would lead one to suppose he had some honor, but who, whenever there is a tip-top chance, will be found comfortably fixed in some out-of-the-way place, knocking his heels together, and finding true delight in the hard task of trying to enjoy himself, while he is battling with conscience and keeping a good lookout for the boss. This is the soldier on duty. There are three ways to get along with him. First, kick him out of the shop for keeps; second, watch him all the time; thirdly, if your work will permit it, have a distinct understanding with him that he is to work for you five days a week for pay, and soldier one day at his own expense. I have tried this latter plan, and if the man don't drink, it works first rate. One week-day idle in a busy man's life will make him feel glad to get into the shop for five days of occupation. In about a year you can give the man six days work a week with perfect satisfaction all around.

* * * * If it was not for the two classes of workmen I have mentioned, there would be but few misunderstandings between the two parties mutually interested in manufacturing, namely, the men who do the work and the men who hunt up the work and furnish the facilities for doing it.

* * * * I am half convinced that some manufacturers look upon the ill-will, or dissatisfaction rather, of a customer as simply a matter of annoyance. If Wycoff sells half a dozen nail machines to Woods, and the machines don't act just right, Mr. Wycoff will be pretty apt to hear from Mr. Woods. He will keep on hearing from him, and notwithstanding the fact that he has got his money for them, he will finally fix the machines up and make them work right. He don't do it because he has any particular interest in the nail machines, but simply because Woods won't let him alone till the machines do act right. Wycoff don't seem to say to himself: "Now, here goes half a dozen nail machines. If they give good satisfaction, I will sell lots more of them, and if they don't I won't."

Apparently the only view he takes of the thing is to fill the order and wait for the next thing to come along.

It seems to me there is something more than this in such transactions. It don't pay in the machine business to wait too long for the next thing to come. A certain amount of force must be put into the thing, and it strikes me that the satisfactory operation of something already delivered is sure to result in future orders.

Of course most manufacturers act on this principle, but Wycoff don't. I know some manufacturers who look entirely to the satisfaction of customers, and give no thought to the real merit of the product. This may look unreasonable, but merit will not always insure satisfaction. The notion of a large class, the habits or customs of a section, the ignorance of the mass, the conservatism of a class, the prestige of some old and played-out plan, all these things have a bearing on the question of satisfaction, while they all may be directly against merit.

* * * * It is astonishing how much ship-shapeness and order will tend to economy.

An orderly system and strict discipline in the shop is not hard on men. It is just the other thing. It prescribes duties within the power of each man, and thus really lightens the labor of each man. Go-as-you-please work is the hardest kind of work, and the rigid lines of duty, if prudently laid, are always easy to follow.

The opposite of order is disorder and shiftlessness. Shiftlessness in all things results in an accumulation of things out of place. The replacing of these things forms the hard work of life.

* * * * I know of no more terrifying job than cleaning up a machine shop which is only cleaned when it gets too dirty to work in. One or two such jobs is enough, and generally will be so vast and unpleasant as to put a stop to all future cleaning operations. The red rust of an hour's production is easy to remove, but the black rust resulting from two days' existence of red dust calls for a re-surfacing of metal work. It is not hard to clean up a clean shop, but it seems impossible to clean a dirty one. Lack of neatness in one place will demoralize all places. This demoralization will show in everything. Tidy machine work cannot be got out of an untidy machine shop. Those shops which let things go by the board for weeks and months, and then have what they call a grand cleaning up, are never clean, not even the day after they are cleaned. The job is too great to be well done.

* * * Sometimes you will see a planer hand wearing himself out on a cleaning job. He will run the table off the bed and shovel chips out of the inside, and will dig out old oil thick and stiff with cuttings. He takes down bottom boxes and cracks gum off the journals, and bores out the oil holes. He pulls down the saddle work and wrestles with the down-feed miters. His planer is too black to clean decently, and when half done he begins to slouch the big undertaking. When he gets things in shape again, he does nice planing for three days, and then the oil holes get plugged up again and chips accumulate, and the miters get on a strike and won't work smooth, and Mr. Planerman begins to get down at the heel all over, and don't pretend to work closer than a thirty-second. Maybe the man right next to him never takes a cleaning fit, and always has a nice, clean, tidy planer. This cleaning is really so small a job, when done regularly and well, that you can never catch him at it.

* * * * The dirty machine shop is always complaining of the lack of room. Such shops will continually buy in real estate, and cover it over with a heterogeneous mass of stuff, which, if sorted out and put in proper place, would not be in the way at all. I always notice that those shops which are always crying for room to stretch their neglect in, have ten times more room than common, and are occupying the biggest part of one or two blocks of streets and alleys.

Room isn't the thing needed at all. Order is wanted. Make the decks and hold tidy, and there will be no complaint of lack of room.

* * * * If no men were shiftless, some men would starve. I know many men who grow rich in setting to rights the disorders of careless men.

CHAPTER XVIII.

CHORDAL'S BOY JOE.—WHAT BOOKS SHALL MACHINISTS READ?

* * * * Something must be done with my oldest boy, Joe. He has been knocking around the shop during his idle hours, and has developed a certain amount of original talent. He has never worked in the shop, but has wanted to very much. His originality takes a critical turn as well as a constructive one. He got into the true inwardness of one of my mechanical schemes, and I caught him expressing his opinions of the machine in a way which filled me with pride and mortification. Some of his remarks were not very complimentary to the skill and good judgment of the elder Chordal. I had to find my consolation in the critical ability displayed by the young man. Joe's future is a mechanical one. I have never let my investigations into the boy's character take a suggestive turn, and for this reason I can speak with some certainty of the real bent of his mind. What I am studying on is how to arrange matters to the best advantage; how to start Joe in the best channel. This is a subject which interests other people with other brilliant Joes on their hands, otherwise I would not broach the subject.

When I say Joe's future is a mechanical one, what do I mean? Is he to be a master mechanic of railroads, or is he to have M. E. on the end of his name, and do the scheming and general talent business for large concerns? Is he to be interested solely in construction and become a capable superintendent? Is he to be a managing proprietor, or is he to become a power to appeal to in matters mechanical, and be the consultee of all who see fit to come?

I don't know which of these specific niches Joe will stand himself in, and more than that, I don't care. I only know that whichever way his lines may fall, he will be none the worse for having some direct and intended preparation. By preparation I mean education—that substantial sub-structure on which all experience is more valuable for being founded. As Joe's mind has taken a mechanical turn, so should the preparatory education take a mechanical direction. I have been nosing around among the credentials, to wit, the out-put of our technical schools, and as a result have chosen one.

Joe is now in a condition to enter any of them, and the question with me is—whether to recommend him to pack up and enter this college, or to lay in a stock of overall stuff and go into the shop.

You will agree with me, that he must do both of these things at some time. Which had best be done first?

Suppose he puts on his good clothes and goes to college. From the very start he will assume upon the future great position he will take in the world. He will assume that he went to college because he was a superior sort of a Joe—none of your common stuff. He will develop the proper ambition and superiority, and will receive the encouraging smiles of his instructors; he will study hard, and, under the guidance of capable and wise instructors, will gradually absorb that very knowledge he went after.

Some fine day he will return and lay before me his sheepskin, and an admirable and really original and excellent thesis, and drawings most skillfully executed by his own hands, aided by facilities in the way of ruling machines which he may never hope to see again. I will feel the warmest pride in this boy of mine, and in answer to his inquiries I will probably say, "Go out and try the world, Joe."

* * * In about three weeks a young man of the name of Chordal will call on me and eloquently express himself on the unappreciativeness of a bigoted world, that don't know what is good for it.

* * * Joe will tell me of his conference with Mr. Simpson, who acknowledges that his business is falling off, on account of a lack of engineering ability in superintending the erection of their work. Oh, yes; Joe feels capable, and fearlessly goes off fifty miles to superintend fifteen men putting bowels into a big brewery. Men say to Joe: "What do you want done first?" Joe says he don't know. Men say: "This big pulley came from the shop without being balanced, the shaft runs thirty revolutions; shall we let it go?" Joe says he don't know. Men want to know which of the two kinds of babbitt this box is to be poured with. Joe don't know. Leading man of the gang writes to Simpson that young Chordal is a nice fellow and smart as blazes, but don't know anything. Simpson recalls his executive officer, and in a fatherly manner advises him to go into a shop and learn the trade, and tells him he will make his mark. Joe, the superior Joe, made of superior stuff, born to lead in his chosen line, trimmed to fit in the best technical schools, author of a thesis on centrifugal governors having valves unalterably related to the centrifugal elements—this Joe was not born to learn a trade.

* * * I make no suggestions to Joe, and bid him good bye, as he starts on another Quixotic expedition. Two brief weeks, and again I take his hand. This hand seems to have grown smaller and not quite so self-important in its grip. I ask after his conquests. He grimly and grittily smiles and proceeds. Says he went down to Philadelphia, and went to William Sellers & Co., whom he had been corresponding with ever since he went to college. They build machine tools, and at college their machine tools were held up to him as exponents of perfection, as test channels for design. He is nicely received and encouragingly talked to. He is asked if he is willing to spend a few years in the shop. He answers that he is not born for a machinist, but for an engineer. If Wm. Sellers & Co. can put him on a low round of the engineering ladder in some place, he will be very much obliged; then he will see some other parties he wots of. They appreciate the situation, and with real regard for the young man they own to such a ladder being on the premises; nay more, they acknowledge that some of the lower rounds still remain. Joe is invited to ascend, without any engagement which might result in mortifying termination. He reports next morning with a few classical books and a kit of drawing instruments of the most marvelous character. Each individual instrument and piece of instrument fits in a velvet bed, and each time he wants to use something he must take the pieces out and erect the instrument, and when he wants to put something back in the case he must dismember the whole thing and screw in all adjusting screws. His eight-inch compasses fit in the case when both triangular points are in, a condition in which no man on earth ever uses them.

He looks around among the draughtsmen and thinks that his eight-inch compasses cost more than all their instruments put together. He wonders how they can do any refined engineering with such tools, and the other draughtsmen look at his kit and wonder if that young man expects to do any quantity of practical work with such tools in such a case, and they wonder how long it will be before he will have them loose in a cigar box.

He is given a figured pencil sketch of a device, and is told to follow the figured sizes and form, but to detail it for shop use. Do no scheming whatever, but draw only. He does so. The draughtsmen admire the skillful execution, and the powers that be do the same. The lines are clean cut, nicely joined, and have extra thickness on the shadow side. His drawing is taken away for an hour and returned by his sponsor. It has been down in the shop, and Joe expresses his horror at the sacrilege. The sheet is dirty and greasy, and only his fancy shadow lines can be seen. Joe scorns to ask a question, and suggests that he make the drawing over with heavier lines. He does so; sees a striking resemblance between it and the shop drawings around him, which he saw little in to admire before. His sponsor calls again and asks if it will be safe to send that drawing to Savannah for pattern makers and machinists to work from. Joe asks who is going to take it, and is told the mail. Joe says he will write the proper explanations, and does so. Twenty-two pages of legal cap to one sheet of *detail* drawing. Sponsor asks what the legal cap is for. Joe says it is to explain the drawing. Sponsor asks what the drawing is for, and Joe says it is an aid to the legal cap, and, in return, is told that drawings are sent away daily without a word of explanation. It is the duty of detail drawings to explain themselves fully. Joe sees he has much to learn about drawings. He has mastered the art and that is all. He is now instructed to make a drawing of a two-foot pulley, six-inch face, proportions to be functionally correct. He goes at it. Refers to Rankine and Weisbach and Willis and Fairbairn, but never to Joe. He is too wise for that. He gets his pulley drawn, and is told to go down in the shop and compare it with a similarly sized pulley. He does so and doubts his eyes. The arms of the pulley are about eight times as heavy as the arms of his drawing, and he used five as a factor of safety—and the old pulley has two broken arms. He goes back and figures the whole thing over. He takes the data of strains to his sponsor and asks him to run over them. Same results; showing calculation to be right. Sponsor asks him where he got his strain data from. Joe says from the beltage. Sponsor asks him what broke the old pulley. Joe goes in search of knowledge and finds it broke in casting, and he makes his first memorandum of experience, namely: "Belt strains are not the heaviest strains a pulley arm may be subjected to." His sponsor tells him if he would spend a few years in the shop he would learn several things of value.

* * * * I see Joe again. He tells me confidentially that he is astonished at the number of things he don't know, which he must know before anybody will pay him ten dollars a year for his services. He has spent a year coming to a conclusion, and tells me he will go into the shop. Asks me if he can go into my shop. I tell him no; most decidedly not. He must go a hundred miles from me or any one else he can lean on. He can't get any self-reliance out of my place.

* * * * Joe apprentices himself in a shop, and wisely chooses a bad shop. No reamers, no fancy boring bars, no twist drills, no tools big enough for the work, no surface plates, no scraped angle plates, no system, no nothing. When Joe graduates from this place he will be full of experience indeed, and it is hardly likely that he will be the less appreciative of real facilities when he does get at them. His constant letters will bear constant evidence that he knows the necessity of the step, but feels it a let-down. He can't get into full sympathy with his necessities. He feels out of place, and knows he is in place. It is mortifying, disagreeable, hard, up-hill work. He holds a college degree, but his soft hands have got hard and callous, and big cracks have opened in them, and brass dust, and iron dust, and oil and dirt have got into the cracks, and he always has a rag on some finger. Joe will feel as though he had started wrong in some way. * * * At a late educational gathering, Prof. Henkle, of Salem, Ohio, wisely stated that "education is power rather than readiness." Joe will appreciate this, and will wish the readiness had come first.

Joe's post-collegiate shop life will be a hard one. Now, suppose I don't say college to him, suppose I let him go into some miserable shop which he will be glad to leave for higher fields; will not the seeds carefully sown by college professors fall in ground thirsty for it—ground which the old and poor and half-satisfying crops of the shop experience only stirred up into sturdy, ambitious receptiveness? Only he who has been athirst upon the barren plains can appreciatively absorb knowledge of certain water-getting processes. Will it not be better to clean up the dirty hands than to dirty up the clean ones?

* * * Do you know of any young man who went from shop to college, and wishes he had reversed the order of things? Do you know of any young man who went from college to shop, and wishes he had reversed the order of things?

* * * What books should machinists read? This question is asked of some one supposed to know about a thousand times a year. Mechanics, as a general thing, are pretty well advanced in years when they want these books. They can't comprehend anything fine or deep, or analytical, and cannot spend time to attain the necessary elementary book knowledge. They despise a book which treats them as children. Walker is a carpenter, and is patronizingly urged to go to the library and read up on his trade,

and rise in the world. He knows nothing of books, and takes the first one with carpentry on the back of it; say, "Constructive Carpentry Practically Considered." He could not define the title to save his neck, but proceeds to look into it. He finds many demonstrations and geometrical diagrams, but he can't get into sympathy with the thing; says the author's a fool who couldn't shove a saw, and he puts the book away. He takes another, the "Complete Carpenter." On the first page he sees a villainous cut of a saw, and he reads, "This is a hand-saw, used by carpenters to cut off boards. It has teeth upon one edge. These teeth are about one-eighth of an inch apart, and are bent alternately, slightly to the right and left. This bending is termed 'set,'" etc., etc. He puts this book away in disgust, and says the author thinks *he* is a fool who can't file a saw.

Walker won't read one book and can't read the other. The book for him must be tailor-made, and must fit him exactly, or he can't get any good out of it.

The thing is a problem, but there is one good thing about it. If a man has to ask what to read, it don't make much difference what he does read. A thirst for knowledge will find its own means of satisfaction, and this thirst will never come upon a man in middle life. There is no boy so circumstanced in this whole land, that a thirst for technical knowledge will not, in a way, develop and gratify itself before he is twenty. If there is anything in him, he will have formed an acquaintanceship with books in general, and need ask no questions relating to general direction of study. If such an acquaintanceship has not been formed, friends need hardly regret being unable to suggest a proper path of study. Of course, such reading is mostly done and mostly appreciated by the young chappies who are priming for the future. If owners of shops will keep one eye open for such tendencies they will find it an excellent index to character, and a pointer towards an excellent plan of encouragement which will repay ten fold.

* * * * I was in the office of a certain engineer, the other day, and a mutton-headed boy, about nineteen came in. He was a machinist. His father owned a shop, and he had served his time in it. He wanted to learn to "draft," he said. Said his father wanted him to learn; he wanted to learn himself, and his father would pay all reasonable bills. Torsion, the engineer, began to catechize him. What have you ever drawn? Nothing. What have you ever made rude sketches of? Nothing. What have you ever wanted to draw? Don't know as I ever wanted to draw anything, and could not make a "draft" if I wanted to, because I never learned how. That's all right, said Torsion. You will never draft anything, and will never be wanted to. I'll see your father this week. Torsion turned to me and said he had a dozen such fellows to deal with every month, and treated them all the same. But, said he, when some greasy boy slips in here, and pulls out some horribly original drawing, and asks me why the ink lines run when he puts color on, or how a fellow's to judge good India ink, or how this thing is to be drawn so another can understand it, then I quit work, and stay by that fellow, and place my time and library and office at his disposal.

* * * The Nicholson File Co., of Providence, sent me a copy of their treatise on files lately. Now this splendid little book would find more appreciation in the shop than would a new translation of the Iliad among the blues. Why, under heaven, didn't these folks get up this book when I was ruining files for a living! If I could take this book with me, and go back over the ground of my shop life and become owner of what I could save, or make, by the instruction imparted by it, I would feel able to and justified in putting a copy of this book into the hands of ten thousand file-users who never buy files.

CHAPTER XIX.

THE TRAVELED MACHINIST.—FAIR PLAY FOR APPRENTICES.—BRIGHT AND BLACK FINISH.

* * * * A machinist who has traveled and worked in a variety of shops, is always a more valuable and desirable man than one who has not done so. If a man comes to you for a job, and you find he has worked in twenty different shops, you feel satisfied that one, at least, of these shops was something like your own, and that, consequently, the man may fit. How long does it take a new man to get the swing of a new shop? If he is a little shy, he must pass the ordeal of fellow criticism. When he grabs a chipping hammer, he knows a dozen men are looking to see if he knows where to grab the handle. He don't know whom to trust, or to talk to, or to ask questions of. He don't know how your work is done, or whether you look to time or quality, or whether you sympathize with or blame one who errs. He don't know where to find things, he don't know what things there are to find, and it takes things a long time to get smoothed up. When they do smooth up, this man's value begins to count. If you and he had had years of shop association, would he not be worth more to you than he would to any other shop? If he is good for anything, you would know what he is good for. If he is good for nothing, what did you associate with him so many years for?

* * * * If Tubal owns a machine shop, and graduates an apprentice at the end of four years, and then offers that apprentice, say, a dollar and a quarter a day, and that apprentice goes to the very next town, and gets, say, a dollar and seventy-five, what would you think? Would you say the policy was short-

sighted on the part of Tubal? Would you say Tubal wanted the world to know, as if by a brand, that a workman of Tubal's manufacture was not worth much; or would you believe that Tubal was sordid enough to try to take an advantage of the semi-parental position he had occupied?

* * * * There are many shops in which it seems impossible for an apprentice to get justice after his time is out. The justice I refer to I gauge by the measurement of outside shops. I throw up my hat every time a young chap, who has served a faithful term of aprenticeship, skips from under a shop which wants to own him too cheaply.

I am glad, because it gets the boys whatever pay the world will give them, and it makes them travel, and travel makes them wiser.

* * * * Some machinists judge of a workman's skill by the general elegance and nice appearance of the work done. I never could look at machine work this way. Skill is an element of the process, not of the result. Many a rough thing may be skillfully done, and many a fine thing unskillfully done. The workman in a watch factory may be perfect, but that is no more reason that he is more skillful than the perfect man in a reaper shop.

There are many kinds of nice work. You turn a sewing machine upside down and find many qualities of work all equally well done. A neatly-shaped, well-surfaced, untouched drop-forging, strikes your eye and stands criticism. Flat parts have a flat finish—a hard, high polish, and pure surface generally, and you pronounce them well done. Small parts generally have a certainty and decisiveness about their shape and surface, and meet your approval.

Screws, without regard to their proportion of size or adaptation to purposes, if they have that instant appearance of an intention well carried out, we call tip-top.

But look at another machine, with the screws and other parts of such a shape as to indicate at once that such was not the exact intention; with polished surfaces, having a soft, wavy, or washed appearance; forgings, so far from the proper thing as to show tool work on corrected parts; castings with clearances filed in them; and certain surfaces which seem to have changed their intention when half done; these things, you say, are unskillfully done.

There is no doubt about one of these things being skillfully done, and the other not, but the very same workmen may have done them. The management was unskillful, at any rate, in one case.

A thing don't have to be elegant to be well done. The bad machine was undoubtedly intended to be well done without being nice. As such it was an abortion, and it will generally be found more difficult to do good work without refinement than to do it finely.

* * * * If you want good work, you tell a skilled man, provided with proper facilities, to do his best, and he does it, and you get your work. But tell him to make it as well as can be made, but to pay no attention to niceness, and your skillful man is mixed. He fails entirely to comprehend the situation, and thinking you mean general cheapness of work, he slouches everything, and probably loses his old skill in course of time.

* * * * Some of the work done on mowing machines to-day is as good as was ever done on locomotives, or machine tools, or sewing machines, or watches. The men are as skillful, and the intentions are as well executed. The men could not change places. The skillful man does bad work when he puts his work in the wrong place, as he does when he puts it on one piece of a reaper when the whole work should have been put on six reapers. Try to get good reaper work out of a bad machinist, or a machine tool man, or a sewing machine man. You soon find he don't know how. Try the reaper man on link work, or a lathe carriage, or a needle bar. You soon find he don't know how. The work in both cases will show unmistakable evidence of having been badly and unskillfully done, and still the men are known to be skillful. To put skilled labor at the right work is the duty of skilled management. Lead lapping a reaper journal would be an unskillful process. It is the fault of the manager, not of the man. Finishing an engine crank-pin with a file would be an unskillful process, the fault of the manager, not of the man.

* * * * A lack of uniformity in one piece is what often gives a workman away. He planes a flat piece, and half way across the job, the character changes. It attracts and repels you, for you see at once that whatever the intention was about the surface, that intention was not carried out. You can't say that the surface is any the worse for the variety, but there is a lingering suspicion that the workman is liable to give down on almost anything. You think the same, when you see a piece of shafting which changes color three or four times in its length. A clean, pure, continuous roughing cut always looks finer than a finishing cut that seems doubtful about how to look, and presents a variety of surfaces in a short stretch.

* * * * If a good, fine job don't look fine enough, you can go ahead and make it look fine enough. You simply stopped too soon, but if you want a good job with the hifalutin' left off, and you find it begins to look "ratty," you can only remedy the matter by going back on the original intention and doing it finely.

* * * * One of the most difficult things known is to get a tip-top job done with the finish omitted.

There are certain engine builders who build two kinds of engines, which they denominate "bright" and "black." "Both exactly the same, as far as real merit is concerned," you know. The bright kind has a miscellaneous lot of finish on the details, the shaft and wheel-rim and bed-top are finished, a polished governor is ordered, nuts and bolt heads polished, brass work of the nicest kind, blued set screws, &c.

Now it's all fine enough to stuff a customer with the idea that one engine is as good as the other, but it is false all the same. You get an order for a bright engine. You cast the cylinder. There's a blow in the flange. Do you use it? No. Do you break it up? No. You put it in the casting shed. What for? Why to use on some engine not "bright," you know. Another is cast and bored and a scab or two develops. You put it in the casting shed with the other. It will come into play all right. Some lunk-head drills a cylinder head wrong. You lay it away. It can be plugged and used on another engine. The pillow block gets poured with "that good babbitt." A stuffing stud gets a thread or two torn out, or it fits the nut too loose. "Make another, Harry, but save that one." Two or three cylinder studs are fitted too loose in the flange. Are they crowded in hard on the shoulder so as to pass muster? No. But they will be crowded into another engine in a month or so, but not a "bright" engine. The connecting-rod brasses don't seem to work just right under a tool. Save them. "Do you want iron set screws in here, sir?"

"No, siree, young man. Put in good, nicely fitted, tempered steel screws." The nuts on hand won't do for this engine. They are not good enough. Tom is told to spread himself on the piston packing. The fly wheel and eccentric keys are driven out to see if they were fitted well. The valve receives extra care. The crank-pin, for a wonder, is made round, and so are the main journals. Stub ends are made perfect. Hexnuts are hexagon and uniform. No lumps are allowed on the main shaft. The guides are straight and flat, and the cross-head is brought fair all round, no matter how much work it makes. The eccentric don't "cam" sideways, and the strap fits it when the job is done; and maybe a cut will be taken over the bottom of the bed, and the question as to whether the old foundation washer pattern was just the thing comes up; the finish on the connecting rod shows it to be good iron. If necessary, the president's desk will be wrecked to get well seasoned walnut to jacket the cylinder with, the spade handle on the valve-stem joint is the second one made for the job, spanners are made to *fit* stuffers, solid wrenches ditto, oil cups are selected with a view to lubrication, the cylinder oiler is studied on before selection, the cylinder cocks have drain pipes attached, and so on through everything.

Now, when you took this order for a bright engine, it was a hurried order, and you were busy on good paying work. You had a new "black" engine unsold upon the floor, made from the same patterns you proposed to make the bright ones from—just exactly the same, you know, "except in looks and price." Now, why in the world didn't you take that black engine apart, put a red-hot finish on the parts, put the extra finish on extra parts, order a bright governor, deliver the engine, get your money, and call the transaction complete? Why didn't you do this simple thing? Simply because you knew very well that the black engine was not good enough to make a bright engine of.

* * * * The idea that by omitting useless finish, and keeping the essential parts the same, the work will be cheapened, has led more than one fine mechanic into years of trouble. One of these superior mechanics says to himself: "I intend building machinists' tools; I see that those in the market are excellent and highly finished. This finish costs money; I will leave it off and save that much cost, and by doing the real work in a perfect manner, I will, in course of years, win for myself a name as a manufacturer of tools of superior excellence at low prices; I will thus be doing real good." Our enthusiast will go at it, and his first fruits will look rough to himself and his customers, and he will be astounded at the cost. He improves the character of the essential workmanship and strives to reach perfection. The work gets better, but the cost increases largely. To cut down the cost, he fills the air with system, and brings into play the keenest of manufacturing wit. This will run on for years, and he will finally be compelled to say to himself that it is impossible for him to compete with builders who do lots of unnecessary work on their product. There is no earthly hope of ever being able to get unfinished work as cheap as finished work. The cheaper design costs the most money. The amount of functional service, and the character of contacts, and the nature of material, is not a whit better, but still the cheapest machine costs the most money. The machine designer, who leaves that little thing called human nature out of the design, who thinks his own broad ideas will meet with a response in the minds of his workmen, makes a grand mistake. He must make a virtue of his demerit, and must invent arguments to prove that finish is a damage and that merit associates with paint only.

CHAPTER XX

SACKETT'S THEORIES OF WAGES AND FINANCE.—SYSTEM OF GAUGES.—NEWTON'S CASTING ROOM.—WHO SHALL CLEAN CASTINGS?—COUNTRY MOULDERS.

* * * * While I was in Sackett's office the other day, McMiller came in and asked for money between pay days. Sackett heard him and rated him soundly for being in need of money, and so careless of the future as to have to draw pay for the present necessities. Found he had not been sick, nor had any of his folks, nor had he taken a trip to the sea shore, nor bought bonds or real estate—bought nothing. Worked hard every day at good pay and wanted ten dollars advanced! Sackett began to look sick and disgusted. Went and fished old pay-rolls, and showed McMiller that he had received and spent more money in the last twelve years than any small store-keeper in the whole town could possibly have made. Mack couldn't say anything, but it made him feel rich to see what money had gone through his fingers, and awfully poor to see how little had stuck to them. Sackett got mad as he thought of the thing, and finally told Mack he could not draw any pay, but he would lend him ten dollars for a week; "but mind you," added he, "I am going to make an example of you. There is some excuse for a lazy drunkard with a slouchy wife, or for a smart young chap who dresses and lives proudly, but there is none for you. I never saw you with nice clothes on, and never saw you and your family out enjoying an evening at a theatre, or any other place, and I will bet a quarter you buy heavy sugar at higher price than sawed block, and pay more for coal oil than I do, and pay more for your clothes. You get good pay—a blamed sight better than I do, and I am bound some

Sackett got mad as he thought of the thing. * * * "Mind you," added he, "I am going to make an example of you."—Page 160.

one around this place shall make some money. If you and your wife, after studying common sense for the next year, can't show me a certificate of deposit for three hundred dollars, you shall earn your butterless bread in somebody else's shop." Mack said nothing, and went into the shop again, but Sackett didn't stop. "Half of them are idiots," said he, "just like Mack. He will go and buy a miserable coat of the Jews for eight dollars. The coat don't fit him, and would take the pride out of any man who ever lived, and I will wager he has bought six of them since I paid twenty-five dollars for the one I have on. I expect the same judicious plan is followed in all the family expenses. I can see why a drunkard don't save money, but why McMiller and his wife can't save money on three dollars per day, I don't understand. If I should raise his pay to six dollars, he would not live any better or save any more money. Chordal, I tell you some of the men in the shops make me sick. I hammered three thousand dollars out of the trade as a jour before I set up shop myself, and I never got three dollars a day in my life; but I didn't save my money by wearing Jew coats or washing myself with soft soap; and I went fishing once in a while without fear of starving Mary and the girls. The working-men's millennium will come when some man will drop among them and teach them common sense about money matters." As soon as this benediction or malediction, or whatever you may call it, was over, I left Sackett's place without disposition to argue against known facts.

* * * * I see that the telegraphic engineers are discussing the subject of a new wire gauge, but just what the grievances are, or what the proposed remedies are, I have been unable to gather.

My own personal objection to the wire gauge is its existence. The object of gauging anything is to ascertain some dimension. The dimension wanted is invariably expressible instantly in standard units of dimension, but the awkwardness of trade has buried the sweet simplicity of gauging under a cloud of technical "numbers" which don't express anything at all. To say that a piece of wire is number seven, don't give any direct idea of size, which is the only thing we want to know. The only information such an expression gives us is that the wire fits in some notch somewhere, and that said notch is yclept No. 7. To find out how big the wire is, you have simply to measure the notch. If the notch is hard to measure, or there is doubt about the notch fitting just right, the approximate size of the notch may be arrived at by measuring the wire—all very simple.

* * * * The whole plan of giving numbers to things, whose dimensions might as well be given right out in meeting, is a humbug. A number seven wire isn't the same size as a number seven boot, and there is no way of finding the size sought for, without being able to figure on what the notch, the wire, or the boot is said to fit. Why not say a number six barrel, or a number four dose of medicine, or a number nine mule, or a number fourteen locomotive, or a number thirteen and a half greenback, meaning thereby ten dollars, or a number twelve diamond, or a number eight journey, or a number seven postage stamp, or a number three cheese, or number ten pile of coal!

Imagine a brakesman yelling out at Cairo, "Number eleven, for refreshments!" All of this system of numbering could be easily carried out, and be a great deal handier than the present system of wire gauges.

The practical difficulties in the way of such systems would make them a nuisance, just as the wire gauge is now. When you write to a man to know how big a certain wire is, it is presumed that you want to know just what you ask; that is, how big the wire is. In reply you are generally told that it will fit tolerably nice, or "scant," or "full," in a certain hole marked No. 14.

If you don't care much, this may satisfy you. If you care a little about the matter, you had better send for the identical hole referred to. If you care very much you will send for a sample of the wire.

* * * * From the looks of things, one would suppose that in the year one, some man made the first piece of wire, and filed a notch to fit it. After being some time in business, he had made several sizes of wire, and had filed several notches. Then these notches were numbered and became the happy standard of an intelligent people. Nobody knew the dimension of these wires or these notches, and probably there was then no particular reason for caring. After a while, somebody wanted wire which wouldn't fit any of these notches. Here was trouble in the camp. What business had any man to want anything which would not fit any of the old holes? The wire drawer forgot, the day before he numbered the notches, the day when there were but three notches, maybe. In obedience to the law of progress, the wire gauge was overhauled, and new notches, to fit new wire which had been made, were added, and all were re-numbered. The new gauge, we will suppose, was "adopted." Now, it is very much easier to universally adopt a new thing, than to universally throw away an old thing, and, as a consequence, there were two wire gauges in use very early in the game. Then troublesome customers got more odd sizes, and new gauges were adopted, and even to-day there are in use in wire and sheet mills gauges bearing the following distinctive names, viz: Birmingham, Stubs', Washburn & Moen, American, Brown and Sharpe, Trenton Iron

Co., Standard, Music Wire, Steel Wire, G. W. Prentiss and English. Some of these gauges are just alike, and simply have two names, but it's well for a man to know what he's doing when he orders by numbers. Why not abolish all those long names and give the different gauges, designating numbers? It would be so handy, you know.

* * * * Somebody took a notion to measure wire gauges one day, and then we came into possession of memorandums of the sizes. But these sizes were all in fractions, and not in units. They could not be pronounced hardly, and didn't sound like a size at all. For instance, No. 32 brass English gauge is .01125 of an inch thick, if you know how thick that is, and No. 16, instead of being half as thick as No. 32, is .065 of an inch, or no relation at all.

* * * * Brown and Sharpe, in devising their system, found that in existing gauges the sizes jumped irregularly. There was a big difference between two neighboring small sizes, and a trifling difference between two neighboring large sizes—sometimes there was and sometimes there wasn't; it was all haphazard. If our coinage was on the same plan, we would have a five-cent piece, then a seven-cent piece, then a twenty-cent piece, then a sixty-cent piece, then a dollar piece, then a two-dollar piece, then a two-dollar and fifteen-cent piece, then a two-dollar and eighteen-cent piece, and so on, skipping around at random; so we would have to use big money to make small change.

* * * * The fault with every plan of fine measurement is that it gives us results in awkward fractions. The inch being the unit, everything small must be some unpronounceable fraction of an inch. What we want is a unit so fine that the minute measurements of modern practise may deal in whole numbers.

* * * * The much-abused metrical system,

whether we ever fall in with it or not, possesses one great virtue. Its divisions become units. While the name of millimeter implies a division or fraction of a meter, it nevertheless is a unit and stands on its own bottom, which a vulgar or decimal fraction can't do. If a millimeter was small enough we could give minute sizes in them, without division. But it is not fine enough for the coarsest work of to-day. It is about four one-hundredths of an inch, when we want our fine unit to be at most a quarter of a thousandth. If we carry the metrical division two steps further, we have some kind of a meter which will be about the third of a thousandth, or about the difference between the two finest numbers on the American wire gauge. This extraction has a name, but I don't know what it is.

The metrical system has been carried upward and downward from the meter, and the results have been named, I presume, but the every-day books don't give anything finer than millimeters. Somebody who knows more about French than I do, can probably tell you what the name of this fine unit really is, or what it might properly be.

* * * * This nameless little meter could be read on a pocket vernier gauge, and would give a simple expression to any fine, practical dimension dealt with in the work of the artisan. With such a tool, it might be possible that some day a paper maker would know something about the thickness of paper. I never saw a paper maker yet who had any earthly conception of the difference in thickness between two pieces of paper. One is heavy, the other is light. If these paper men were bright they would devise some system of numbers for the thickness of paper.

* * * * Newton has had a splendid shop running for about six years. He built it after deliberate planning, and he seems to have almost every modern convenience. But with all his conveniences finely schemed and finely executed, Newton finds he has been guilty of a grand oversight, and he sometimes expresses a wish that the whole shop would tumble down so he could build it over again.

* * * * It is really a fact that Newton has no place to keep castings. His foundry can make them, and his shop can work them up, but in the interim between operations there is not a place where these castings may rightfully lay their heads. There is no place for them in the foundry, the cleaning room is fully occupied by castings being cleaned, and there is no yard-room which is not legitimately and fully occupied. Every manager knows that, while there is no necessity for harboring old, useless, out-of-fashion, or cracked castings, many tons of standard work must be kept on hand untouched for many weeks.

Poor Newton now finds that there is only one place to put these castings in, and that is in the machine shop. As a consequence, he now sees piles and piles of castings wherever he may look. Alongside lathes and planers and drills and slotters and boring mills, and under and on top of lathes, planers, drills, slotters, and boring mills, are these things piled. They hurt the eyeballs of the manager, they annoy the men, they prevent cleaning up the shop, they demoralize things generally.

The place originally planned for a setting-up floor, is now a trifling space, bounded on all sides by a craggy shore of untouched castings. In the disorder of these castings, there is no keeping track of them, and it is almost always easier to get new castings from the foundry than to unearth old ones from these piles. Newton swears he won't put up with it any longer, and is now planning a general confiscation of the pattern store room as a casting store. He will put another story on the pattern shop to give him a pattern room. He purposes to divide his new casting room, *nee* pattern warehouse, by low fences into small spaces devoted to each separate product he builds, so that castings may be found instanter, and the whole stock kept free and in subjection.

* * * * This reminds me that in some little country shops there is forever and eternally a wrangle over the question of whose business it is to clean up castings. Sometimes the foundry will clean up castings nicely, more to see what the castings look like, than to perform a duty, and sometimes they won't. Sometimes the foundry wants core rods, or anchors, or spiders, or some big core to saw up into little ones, in which case they may clean the casting before they get done with it. Sometimes the cupola tender has time to clean castings, and sometimes he doesn't. Sometimes there will be a gawk of a man employed for the purpose, and the foundry will want this gawk for a shoveler as soon as the castings are shaken out.

* * * * Some lathesman has had orders for a week, to snatch a certain gear as soon as it is cast and "bore her out two and seven-sixteenths full." This morning he is told that the boys managed to get a good one cast last night, so he goes into the foundry and, among a lot of other stuff, he sees a lump of sand, which he recognizes as being pregnant with the thing sought for. He kicks the thing around a little, curses it a good deal, jabs some of the sand loose with an old core rod, and puts some finishing touches on it with an old file stub, and then trundles it into the shop, leaving a track of burnt sand wherever he goes. When he gets to his lathe he concludes to take a little more loose sand off. He rattles it off with a hammer. Then he chucks the job, and in knocking it into trueness he gets some more sand off. The lathe catches all the sand removed by this process. Then he bores her out two and seven-sixteenths full, and throws it on the floor. Some viseman cuts a key seat in it, and it is ready for shipping. Not a grain of sand has been purposely removed, which did not in some way interfere with the handling or working of the job. No one has pretended to clean this casting. If this machinist had gone to the foundry-men and said anything about cleaning, he would have been told that nobody had time just now. If he had gone to the head boss of the shop, he would have been sent to the foundry-men. If he had stood around that pile of castings till somebody did have time to clean his job, the aforesaid head boss would have happened in and told him to "clean her up and get her done." Our machinist knows all about this, so he don't say boo to anybody. He takes as little sand off as possible, and gets the job off his hands.

* * * * The worst moulders in this wide world are the moulders who work in these little country shops. Unlike the country machinists, they don't know how to do good work with poor facilities; and, unlike city moulders, they don't know what facilities to ask for. Not one in five of them knows anything about moulding. Not one in a dozen can cast a ten pound sash weight without a two pound shrink in it. Not one in a dozen can cast a straight-armed pulley at all.

The foreman of such foundries is generally the loudest mouthed braggart that ever rammed sand. He will brag of the fine shops he has had charge of; he will brag of the difficult castings he has made, when others have failed; he will brag of his superior knowledge of irons, and of sand, and of facings. And still he will turn out castings, day after day, which are not near so good looking as the pig iron he melts up.

They will be warped, and strained, and crooked, and hard beyond all belief; he will use parting sand for facing, and will complacently deliver castings with the sand fused into the outer surface; he can make cores which hot iron will melt, and the hub hole in one of his pulleys will be a vitreous cavity, which no machinist, city born, might ever hope to bore out; he will leave cores out where needed, and put cores in original places; he will put anchors just where they ought not to be, and he will fix core rods and spiders so that they will get welded to the casting; he don't seem to care if a casting runs a pound or ten pounds short, and if it is so bad a case that he can't get it off his hands, he will splice it with hot iron the next heat, instead of making a new one; he will lose one piece out of twenty, and when he gets his ugly castings done, he won't clean them up.

* * * * When I was in Cincinnati, I was told of an old shop, and a big one, in that city, which followed the plan, when they made a new pattern, of making one casting, just to see if the pattern was right. And a Cincinnati pattern maker told me that an inventor came to him once and wanted a pattern made. He asked for a drawing; the inventor said he didn't have any. He asked him to make one, and the inventor said he didn't have the least idea how to make a drawing; he asked him to explain what kind of a pattern he wanted, but the inventor didn't know how to explain anything; he told him to make a model, but the inventor was no mechanic, and couldn't. Then he told him he could do nothing for him, and the inventor went away and came back next day with a piece of an apple whittled into the shape he wanted his pattern made.

CHAPTER XXI.

JOURNALS AND BEARINGS.—THE YOUNGER SACKETT IN WYCOFF'S SHOP.

* * * * I almost come to the conclusion, sometimes, that a good journal running in a good bearing, both of ample area, good material, and proper condition, will run forever without wearing out. And sometimes I come to the conclusion that it will wear out. Any conclusions which I may happen to come to will have no effect on the general durability of journals, but when I consider that almost everything a machinist makes turns around, I think that it don't do any harm to talk about journals. If a truth is told, it's all right, and if an untruth is told, it's all right, too, if the untruth is big enough, because thought will be directed, and a truth will develop after all.

* * * * What is an ample area for a journal? What rule should govern the sizes? Probably half my readers would answer: "The smaller the better." "The smaller the bearing, the less the friction," etc. A person posted in the general laws of friction will simply tell these men that their belief is false, and will often propound the simple laws of friction, and say that any experience leading to any conclusion adverse to these laws is a false experience, based on false observation. This is about all the average practical man can ever get out of the average theoretical man.

Such things as this lead the practical man to have little faith in the theoretical man. He knows very well, that if he prick punches the centers in the end of a shaft, he can turn it very easily with his fingers when the shaft is put in the lathe. If he prick punches deeper, the shaft turns harder. If he drills and countersinks deeply, the shaft turns very hard. If he rests it in full-sized bearings, maybe he can't turn it at all. He knows that an eccentric may turn very easily on a shaft before it is keyed, but that the strap moves hard on the eccentric.

He often spins a twelve-inch pulley around on an inch-and-a-half shaft, but when he gets a twelve-inch pulley, fitting no tighter, on a six-inch engine shaft, it won't spin worth a cent. These things stick in the practical man's craw, and the assertion that a large journal has no more friction than a smaller one, won't go down with him. He is certainly right, and so is the theorist who denies it without meaning to.

* * * * The "contaction" of a bearing acts precisely like, and is, in fact, a friction brake applied to the surface of the journal.

The radius of the journal becomes the lever on which a resistance acts. The greater the diameter, the greater the leverage. If power be applied at a lever, the longer the lever the greater will be the resistance which can be overcome, and if friction be applied at a lever, the longer this lever the greater the power required to overcome the friction. The resistance of a journal is in direct proportion to the diameter of the journal. A six-inch journal will resist motion just twice as much as a three-inch journal. Journals should be no larger in diameter than strength demands, if low frictional resistance is sought for. The strains on a shaft, and the strength of the material, with proper allowance for safety, give us the least diameter of a journal.

* * * * When the theorist, whom the practical man don't seem to like, says that the size of a bearing don't increase the friction, he is talking in a general way of the extent of plain surfaces, and is correct, but he will generally mislead the practical man, and thereby lose his respect. Friction does not increase with the extent of surface, but an alteration of leverage is another thing.

The practical man thinks he is entirely right when he is not. He thinks a long journal offers more resistance than a short one, when it does not. He thinks a board will slide easier on its edge than on its flat side, when it will not. Some one has illustrated this by a brick. It takes the same amount of power to slide a brick on the floor, whether you lay the brick on its side, or its edge, or on its end. It is simply a question of weight and power required per pound of weight. Lay a second brick on top of the first and the friction is doubled, because the weight is doubled. The friction would be precisely the same if both bricks were laid side by side on the floor and moved at once, notwithstanding the fact that in the latter case the extent of surface is doubled. The extent of surface or the length of journal has no effect on friction. If there are ten bearings on a line shaft there is a certain friction. Put ten more bearings on the same shaft and the friction is not increased. There will be just half as much on each journal as there was before, and just as much taken altogether. Increasing the number of bearings reduces the friction on each. If there is a weight of a ton on a bearing a foot long, there will be the same weight on the bearing, if lengthened to two feet, but the pressure will be reduced in the long bearing to half a ton per foot in length.

* * * * It won't do to have too much pressure per square inch on a bearing.

Take the brick case again. I think a brick is four-by-eight, or thirty-two inches area. For an even number, say that it weighs thirty-two ounces, or one ounce per inch of area. This brick slides on the floor easily, and don't wear out the floor or the brick much. But pile fifteen bricks on top, and the pressure becomes one pound per inch. The thing works hard, and, furthermore, it wears out the lower brick and the floor. If we substitute a brick eight inches wide for the bottom one, we double the wearing surface and reduce the pressure to half a pound per inch. We can keep enlarging the lower brick until we get the pressure down to an ounce per inch, just where it was with the light load, and we noticed that the apparatus didn't seem to wear out any at that pressure. But it takes sixteen times as much power to move the sixteen bricks as it did one brick, because there is sixteen times the weight.

Increasing the size of the lower brick is increasing the area of our bearing. This will save wear, but it won't save power. We must try another plan. We put buckshot under the lower brick, and, lo and behold, it don't take any more power to move the sixteen bricks than it did to move the single brick before. We have converted sliding friction into rolling friction. We keep the thing going, and after awhile it begins to work hard. We investigate, and find that the buckshot have become flattened somewhat. Our rolling friction is gone. We put in new buckshot, and continue to do so as fast as they give out.

* * * * After this buckshot operation goes on some time, we would find out something. We would find that if we move the brick fast enough, the buckshot never flatten. They revolve with immense velocity, and centrifugal force keeps them round.

Then we would remember that liquids are composed of minute globules, just like buckshot, and we would find that some liquids were composed of fine, strong, large, durable globules, while others were weak and flimsy.

This would soon lead us into squirting liquid under the brick instead of replacing buckshot, and we find

that our old buckshot was simply a lubricant after all.'
* * * * The liquid we use may be oil, and we can learn much by watching it closely. We find that it wears out just like the buckshot; that it gets flattened and useless, and that if we run it fast its globules hold their shape well; and if we stop, they flatten right down, and let the brick touch the floor. We find that if the brick touches the floor while in motion, heat is developed, and when our globules get hot, they seem to melt and run together and give down entirely, and let the brick right down on the floor. Now, when we first found out how very easily the load moved, with the buckshot, we naturally piled on a ton of bricks and took the full benefit of the lubrication, and now we find that when this very heavy load comes down and bears right on the floor, we can't move it at all.

It gouges into the floor, or the bearing gets to cutting. We did find a way to prevent wearing, and we did find a way to avoid friction, but we find that by some unskillful proportioning of things we are apt to undo all the good which is done.

We investigate and experiment, and finally determine on an oil which has a good firm solid globule, which is least affected by heat, and least liable to wear out or get smashed. Next we find a pressure per square inch, which, if we look to a proper supply of fresh oil, will not smash the oil or force it out from under the brick. Next we try and find something better than brick and wood to run together.

We find that two different materials will run nicer than a single material, and, maybe, wind up by putting a fancy brass arrangement under the bottom brick and fixing a plain, hard steel plate for it to slide on. Then we are careful not to run the thing so fast as to develop so much heat that it affects the oil before it can pass off into the atmosphere.

Now we find that we have a nice cool bearing which wastes but little power in friction. But some day we will forget the oil, and the brass will touch the steel, and great heat will result, and what little oil there is will become useless, and the thing will work hard and begin to cut, and finally stick and stop. Then we will tear it down and find our fancy brass arrangement ruined, and some brass stuff brazed to the steel plate. As the brass concern is ruined, we make a new one.

* * * * After this thing happens two or three times a bright idea will strike us. We will see that we have made half a dozen fancy and expensive brass devices, while the simple and cheaply made flat plate has only been smoothed off once in a while.

We turn things around and make the fancy thing of hard steel and make the simple plate of brass.

Then we say: Wear out if you want to, you ain't much trouble to make new anyhow. We remember this experience, however, and ever afterwards when we scheme out journal work we are guided by this golden rule : " Always make the cheaper surface of the softer metal." We follow this rule in constructing crank pins and their bearings, main axles and their bearings, car axles and boxes, and every thing else.

We get the softer metal to wear as well as possible, but are always careful that it shall not be so good a stuff to wear as the other metal. We can jack up a freight car and put a new brass in for very little money. A brass made out of hard steel would last ten times as long, but the wear would fall on the axle where we don't want it.

Before you get through with this letter, you, like myself, will conclude that there are many things Chordal don't know.

I know for certain that all journals should be as small in diameter as proper strength will permit ; that the diameter of a journal has no earthly connection with its length; that plenty of bearing area will insure durability; that a certain pressure per square inch of bearing area will allow durability; that a certain greater pressure will insure immediate destruction; and that somewhere between these certain wide limits there is a pressure which is practically reasonable.

But I don't know what that pressure is, and I cannot approximate it.

* * * * I can give you some few every-day figures, and let you do your own averaging. A freight car on the Pennsylvania railroad, running out of this city, gives, when loaded, a pressure of two hundred pounds per square inch on the effective bearing of the axles.

A pillow-block on a stationary engine up town gives one hundred and twenty-five pounds.

The driving axles of a certain Mogul locomotive bear two hundred pounds per square inch, and the crank pin and cross-head pin of this same engine bear twelve hundred pounds per square inch.

My neighbors next door build a little eight-horse threshing engine, having a crank-pin push of sixteen hundred pounds per square inch of bearing surface.

There's precious little satisfaction in such figures as these.

* * * * If the crank-pin area of a locomotive was increased till the pressure got down to two hundred pounds per inch of bearing, an increase in the width of the right of way would have to be secured to let them pass, and the telegraph poles would have to be moved; and if the pressure on the driving axles was increased to sixteen hundred pounds, I don't believe the engine would run a week.

Now, what's the reason a driving axle or car axle won't stand the pressure that a crank pin will? They are both lubricated with the same stuff—to-wit: miscellaneous oils mixed with grit sucked up from the road bed.

* * * * Let us return to our experimental brick pile for further information. Assume our sliding surface at the bottom of the pile to be so small as to give some trouble. We can work it right along, but it needs care. Heavy, continuous work causes it to heat, bind, and stick. If our sliding motion, instead of being steady and continuous, is a bouncing, jerky one, we can get along better. We investigate and find that though we dose the thing with lots of oil, only a trifling quantity stays to do business. This quantity is just sufficient to form a film of globules between the surfaces, just like a single layer of our buckshot.

If the pressure is continuous, the surplus oil, forced out, can't get in again, and when the little that was in gets smashed up and useless, the whole thing gets dry and heated and cuts.

There's plenty of the surplus oil lying around anxious to do some good, but the pressure don't let up long enough for this oil to get in between the surfaces. If our whole load is lifted every second or two, fresh oil is sucked in between the surfaces, and every thing works better. There's a sort of a slap to a crank-pin bearing, and this very thing is to the benefit of the bearing. The crank pin of a passenger engine is practically worn on one side only. But this same side is constantly shifting from one side of the brass to the other; not with a rubbing motion only, but with a total let up and shifting of the pressure on the brasses. A car axle won't do this. It's just a solid demnition grind, on a shifting surface, it is true, but with no let up on the pressure.

* * * * There is still more in the brick pile. We can see how theory, as some folks call it, and practice should go together. Let us suppose that you were the party who did the experimenting with the bearing under the pile of bricks; that you spent six months' time, five hundred dollars in money, and used up lots of good judgment and patience; that all this happened one hundred years ago; and that you wrote down in your little book: "A hard steel plate, sliding on a hard brass plate, lubricated with good lard oil, works well under a load of brick giving a pressure of five hundred pounds per square inch of bearing area, if the surfaces are in good shape." Let your name be Morin, and assume that in course of years your little book gets printed and accepted as an authority on such subjects.

Now then, please to imagine Mr. Wycoff getting up a machine having a horizontal sliding surface operating under great weight. Young Tom Sackett, who calls himself an engineer, watches Wycoff on this job. Wycoff's heavy load is, by a coincidence, a pile of bricks, and his good judgment tells him that a brick surface won't wear worth a cent, so he proposes to put brass and iron surfaces where the wear comes. He makes the surfaces the size of something else at the bottom of the pile. He don't "theorize" over the matter, for he is a practical man, you know.

Tom asks Wycoff how big these surfaces are, and W. says: "They look all right." Tom says if he was building that thing, he would figure on it a while and try and get it right the first time. Wycoff says: "I don't believe any in your theories. It is simply stuff out of books. I have been thirty years at this business, and I guess I ought to know how big a bearing to put under a pile of bricks." This thirty-year business is the old millwright's gag and Tom hears it often. He retorts by saying: "I know men who have been at the business sixty years, and they don't know half as much as you do, Mr. Wycoff. I may have learned something yesterday that you never dreamed of. Your thirty years' experience printed in a book and proven by others might save many a man a peck of trouble and anxiety some fine day." This whole discussion goes on pleasantly, and Tom has touched Wycoff in a tender spot—the thirty-year place. He begins to wonder if, after all, this thing he has misnamed "theory" is simply a knowledge of the successful experience of other men.

Tom follows him up and says: "Now, Mr. Wycoff, you may have those plates plenty big enough, but it's all luck if you have. Other men have done just such jobs, and they have worked with them till they were right, and there are ways of getting at the facts. You make your plates, and I will hunt up the documents and figure on the thing."

* * * * Enter Tom on Wycoff's premises the next day with a scrap of paper. He says to Wycoff: "I find by consulting standard authorities, that a hundred years ago a Frenchman named Morin, experimented with sliding piles of brick, at great cost of time and money, and he gives the results of his labors. I have figured on your pile of brick, and find that, according to Morin, you will have to make your plates twelve times as large as you intend, or you will have lots of trouble and a total failure."

Wycoff winces some and finally gets around the matter by telling Tom that a person so much interested in a thing had better undertake the superintendence of the job. It's a bargain and Tom takes hold.

* * * The plates are done under Tom's directions, and after the machine starts up he watches it. It runs ten minutes, gets hot and stops. Tom wonders and figures the thing all over, and says to himself: "If these big plates heat, what in the world would

Wycoff's little plates have done?" Wycoff says: "I don't know anything about the Frenchman, Morin, and I don't know what 'coefficient' means, but I see what's the matter. These plates are so big, and make so much friction, that the thing can't work."

In sheer exasperation Tom ejaculates the whole of Morin's laws of friction into Wycoff's ear and explains them, and makes Wycoff understand. Then Wycoff wants to know what *is* the matter.

They set a Johnny to taking the machine down, and he soon comes around and says: "See 'ere, lad, there's 'igh spots hon this 'ere plate, shall hi take em down a bit?"

Tom looks at the plates. All of the parts which really touched and made bearing would not cover a deuce of spades. He calls Wycoff and shows him; and then triumphantly adds: "and Morin says the surfaces must be in good shape." And then the practical Wycoff turns on this young student and says with malicious glee: "When you have worked thirty years at the machine trade, may be you will know when two sliding plates are in good shape. I left this thing to you, and here are the plates.

They consider this matter a "saw off," and determine that theory and practice, if kept from fighting, will, when united, do anything within the power of mortal man, and they make a strong associate point by acknowledging their individual weakness.

* * * * I never expected to see the names of Wycoff and Sackett associated so closely. Wycoff and the elder Sackett have always been friends. They were cubs and jours and tramps together, and now that they are in some degree competitors, they are neither cordial nor at loggerheads.

But young Tom Sackett considers himself a bright and shining light, and, being a gentleman of elegant leisure who likes to work, he can generally be found in the darkest and most benighted places. He naturally gravitates towards the premises of Wycoff. Tom has good sense and is of benefit to all concerned.

* * * * I ought, perhaps, to tell you that the elder Sackett is not what Wycoff would call a "theorist:" He is simply a skilled mechanic with tip-top business sense. There is no science in him, but he knows the value of science. He bases his whole practice, so far as originality is concerned, on the accuracy of mathematics, and he don't know a logarithm from a twinge of the lumbago. Sackett keeps men skilled in these arts and he uses them. He never puts his foot down without knowing before hand what happened to other men who have stepped on the same spot. He is no genius and can't contrive anything, but he keeps a genius and works him hard. If the sliding-plate job had been done in Sackett's shop, its dimensions would have been arranged with reference to how big it *ought* to be. Sackett is too wise to guess at a thing which can be determined with some degree of certainty, and too wise to use figures he don't understand. He calls himself the business manager of his concern.

* * * * Again do we return to the sliding plates. The plates were made large to increase the rubbing surface, and the chap who planed the plates sprung them so badly that they only touched in spots. The big plates thus became little plates, so far as bearing was concerned, and Tom Sackett, that bright youth, supposed that a planed plate was a plane plate.

Tom will some day learn that if a bearing don't bear well, it isn't much of a bearing. He will learn that a round bearing six inches long, if some botchy lathesman turns it badly, is often only a two-inch bearing.

He will learn that a six inch belt may do a certain

work, if it contacts nicely with a pulley, but that if some botchy lathesman scrapes a pulley up with the end of a file and leaves rings on it, his six inch belt may become a three inch belt.

* * * * A round journal touches in its box, on about one-third of its circumference, the balance being free. One third of the circumference is pretty near the diameter, and it is safe, when finding the rubbing area of a journal, to multiply the diameter by the length, which gives the practical bearing surface.

* * * * If a journal is not round, the first thing it does is to commence the work of grinding itself round. In course of time the journal will get round, but it has also got smaller and looser, and the metal ground off stays around to do mischief and do cutting. A journal made perfectly round in the lathe don't have to go through this grinding operation, therefore a round journal will run nice from the start; it don't get loose, and it don't lubricate itself with iron filings.

* * * * This applies to flat rubbing surfaces also. If you don't take the lumps off, it will try to do so itself, and, in doing so, will groove badly and sprinkle itself with iron dust. The bearing will be in very bad shape just at the time it would be in very nice shape if the work was well done.

* * * * A badly turned journal, while it is rounding itself up, will cut rings in itself, the same as sliding surfaces cut grooves while wearing the lumps down. Badly turned journals and badly fitted flat surfaces never doctor themselves.

* * * * If two plates which rub together are found to be nice and flat, and bear practically all over, they will not work well, if the file marks or any other marks run in the direction of the motion. Such marks are, in fact, little grooves which interfere with the side flow of oil, and particles of cuttings get into these grooves and act like "pins" in a file. They scratch. Surfaces having finish marks in the direction of motion are cut already when new. The same may be said of journals when round. The finish should not leave any kind of marks around a journal.

* * * * Never draw-file a piston rod or pump plunger. Finish them in the lathe with well-defined encircling finish, and three days wear will give a dead polish which will stay. Never draw-file engine guides or such things. Bring them to a true surface by any process and then cross-file them lightly, even with emery paper, so as to show that there are no marks running endwise. Such guides will come to a dead, true, hard polish in a few days, and they will stay, if the surfaces are of proper size. With wrought iron, steel, or cold-rolled slides this is particularly important, as there is a vicious end grain anyhow, and cross-finish will neutralize it.

* * * * Scraped surfaces, aside from their being presumably flat, wear nicely as the endwise scratches are bound to be lacking.

* * * * A steam cylinder finished endwise would make trouble from the word go. The tool marks around a cylinder are beneficial, as indicating the absence of marks the other way.

* * * * A journal nicely rounded up, and finished by lead-lapping, has little or no marking around it. A final lead lap finish given *endwise* insures the absence of other scratches, and the journal will be ready to commence its life work, not its death work.

* * * * If bad workmanship fails to take the lumps off bearings, a substitute may be sought in a material which fills the hollows up to the level of the lumps. Metalline and sundry plumbago lubricants do this. The fine particles of this stuff flush up the surfaces and give perfect contact of self-lubricating surfaces. A bearing so outrageously fitted, that no amount of oil will keep it cool, will often behave itself, if fitted with metalline, and no oil applied. Surfaces must be large enough for the work, but metalline corrects, in some degree, bad workmanship, and it carries its buckshot with it.

CHAPTER XXII.

MR. HUBER'S NEW BUTTON SET.—POOR DAN TAKES THE FLOOR.

* * * * Mr. Huber is one of those lucky men who own boiler shops. He works about twenty or twenty-five boiler makers.

Mr. Huber got some button sets made, and one day last week went into the said boiler shop to introduce the aforesaid button sets. When Mr. Huber went into the boiler shop to introduce the button sets, the boiler makers all went out of the boiler shop on a strike against the introduction of the button sets. I wish these men would put their cause of action into writing. It might be shown that the button set was a bad tool calculated to injure the reputation of a boiler maker who used it. In such case the boiler makers ought to hear more about it. Probably the button set is a really bad tool, and that a conscientious boiler maker would scorn to use one for the same reason that he would any other bad tool. If Mr. Huber should take a drift pin into his boiler shop and say: "Here now, you boys, when holes don't match by the width of a county, you just drive this here pin in and make them match." I suppose, of course, the men would get on a strike at once—only they wouldn't.

The fact is, that the introduction of a bad tool into a boiler shop is not a certain method of starting a strike. Maybe the button set is a good tool. I can imagine some idiotic workman striking because some new tool worked better than the tools he was used to. In my own State, and in several other States, a certain class of men are kicking against oleomargarine, or artificial butter. They want the business stopped by legislation; they want the product destroyed and the producers sent to the penitentiary. Not because the stuff isn't good, mind you. If it was bad, they wouldn't say a word. It's entirely too good, and that's what's the matter; and that's why they want legislatures to enact laws which will hang any man who attempts to extract butter from the other end of the cow.

* * * * Maybe Mr. Huber's boiler makers think the button set is too quick a tool, and will allow Mr. Huber to reduce his price list ten per cent. This would give Mr. Huber lots of business, and he would have to enlarge his boiler shop and get more boiler makers. This is dreadful to think about!

* * * * I know two chaps who tied up about four dollars' worth of boiler tools in some old overalls, and went out into a distant country and started a boiler shop. They did repair work. They put on cold patches, put on new sheets, put in new rivets, put in new flues and tubes, put in new fire boxes, etc. They did their bending over wooden logs, and kept three boiler makers at work constantly. They got big prices and saved some money.

* * * * After building two or three new boilers in this crude way, they took it into their heads that they would get some kind of a rig to punch holes for rivets. They had been drilling by ratchet entirely. The man who had been "running" the ratchet drill saw trouble ahead, no work, a starving family, etc.

He was quieted, just on the eve of a "strike," by assurances that his job was steady, and that he might run the new punch when it came. Still, he felt uneasy, for he foresaw that the punch would do a day's ratcheting in half an hour. Where he was to get his other nine and a half hours' work was a mystery. Things looked still blacker when he remembered that there was not work enough to even keep the ratchet drill going.

* * * * This artist of the ratchet knew lots of

things, but one thing he didn't know. He did't know how hard the bosses had to work to get a job at the prices they were compelled to ask, and he didn't know how little margin of profit there was in it after the job was gotten. He didn't know that his own low wages, as operator of the ratchet drill, made the cost of boilers so high that six contemplated saw mills were never built—just on that account. He got a dollar a day, and saw suffering and idleness ahead. In the bitterness of his woe he would have smashed all the punching machines in existence, if he could have done so.

* * * * The new punch came all the same, and poor Dan was placed in charge. With saddened heart he saw the vicious tool punch holes ten hours a day. He wondered where the new demand for holes came from, and he wondered how the bosses had been able to raise his wages half a dollar a day, and how they managed to find work for three more boilermakers than they had before.

* * * * Three years' time saw poor Dan as boss of three punching machines. He tried to wonder what the fifty men were doing who might be ratcheting these holes, and then he remembered that when the ratchet was depended on, only one man was employed in making holes while now there were four, and besides that there were thirty boiler makers at work in the shop. Instead of sheets being bent over a log, labor-saving rolls were used. There had been a kick against these rolls. A steam riveter stood in the middle of the shop and worked steadily; and a business-like tool cut half a dozen tube holes at once, and orders for boilers came in, and boilers went out, and saw mills were built, and lumber got down to a price, and wages got up to a figure where a boiler maker could live in a house that was a house. Poor Dan!

* * * * One fine day one of the bosses brought

into the shop a gauging rig for one of the punches. This thing was some sort of a self-feeding frame, which spaced the holes and punched them on big circles so as to bring the rows straight when the sheet was rolled up into a tapering ring.

* * * * This gauge made trouble; and Mr. Mulligan, as spokesman of a meeting of boiler makers, explained that the devilish gauge was well calculated to take the bread out of boiler makers' mouths. He went on to explain in eloquent terms that all these labor-saving traps were throwing men out of work and leaving their families suffering; that the bosses were, by their means, enabled to do the same work with less men, and could put that much more money in their own pockets; that he had nothing against the bosses, but the working men must guard their interests or prepare to suffer. Then he showed by figures, which never lie, that this gauge would do the work of three men laying out work and do it better; that the steam riveter was doing work that six more men ought to be hired to do; that the bending rolls were doing work that three more men ought to do; and that the punching machines were doing work that ten men ought to be doing. He said he liked the bosses, and didn't favor destruction, but he really felt that if all these things were back in the form of pig iron, there would be a hundred men working in the shop instead of twenty-five or thirty. He was in favor of expressing to the bosses the general good will of the men, but of insisting on the new gauge being abandoned. They would work hard and do their duty, but it was not asking too much of the bosses to ask that the new gauge and similar traps be kept out of the shop in the future.

* * * * Then poor Dan took the floor, and, with permission of the chairman, asked Mr. Mulligan a few

Then poor Dan took the floor, and, with permission of the chairman, asked Mr. Mulligan a few questions.—Page 190.

questions. Mr. Mulligan was a free and generous soul, and went into the catechism class cheerfully.

First question by Dan.—Mr. Mulligan, did you ever work in a boiler shop when some great labor-saving device was put into use and kept in use? If so, state the circumstances.

Answer by Mr. Mulligan—I worked for McLean when they got a flanging machine intended to revolutionize the trade. The thing was a fraud, and was laid aside in a month. It was an experiment and a failure.

Second question by Dan.—That's not to the point. I want cases where the devices staid and did just what was intended. Do you know of any such?

Answer.—Well, when I was at Crofts' they got a big punching machine, which punched six holes at once, and did the work of about four common machines. It worked well and is working yet, for all I know.

Third question by Dan.—How many men were discharged at Crofts' when the gang punch went to work?

Answer.—Discharged! Why, none.

Fourth question.—Please name over such things as you would consider labor-saving arrangements; things which you have seen introduced into boiler shops where you have worked. Give us a fair count.

Answer.—Well, here goes. In the matter of hole work, I would mention cold chisels, which will chip three holes without breaking twice, ratchet drills which drill more holes than a man can chip, a frame to hold the ratchet drill up while you use it. This saves lots of work. A crank drill. This saves. A power drill. This saves lots of work. A punching machine. This saves lots over a drill. A gang punch saves still more. Getting better steel for punches saves lots of labor. Clean marking saves labor. The use of French chalk instead of white chalk saves labor. In cutting out work, good chisels compared with bad chisels will let one man do two men's work. A man with a healthy scientific muscle will do the work of two brute force men or two weak men. Oiling a chisel makes it cut faster. A power shear saves lots of work. In handling work, crowbars save men, and cranes save still more. In riveting, one gang of two men will do much more than two gangs of one man. This parceling of parties reduces the amount of labor required to do a certain amount of work. Steam and hydraulic riveting will save lots of work.

Fifth question by Dan.—Mr. Mulligan, are you opposed to labor-saving tools in the boiler shop, and if so, why?

Answer.—Yes, I am. It takes the bread out of a man's mouth, and as the iron machine don't want the money it earns, the boss takes it.

Sixth question by Dan.—In what shops have you been best paid; in shops with every labor-saving device, or in shops where muscle did everything?

Answer.—Well, I never got what I call good pay, but I got the poorest pay in the poorest shops.

Seventh question by Dan.—Did you ever know of a boiler maker being discharged, because a new man was hired who had a big muscle and could do a big day's work?

Answer.—No; never heard of such a thing.

Eighth question by Dan.—Mr. Mulligan, did you ever see, or did you ever hear of a case where the introduction of a labor-saving rig of any kind whatever in a boiler shop resulted in the discharge of a man because the machine did his work?

Answer.—Well, I can't exactly say I ever did, but I have been around some, and I ought to have seen some such case.

Ninth question by Dan.—Mr. Mulligan, what has become of all the boiler makers who have been thrown out of work by sharp chisels, by punching and shearing machines, by bending rolls which will run a sheet right through, by riveting machines, by muscle in the arms of other men, &c., &c.?

Answer.—Well————. I don't know, I guess they work at something.

Tenth question by Dan.—Don't you guess they work at the boiler maker's trade, and don't you guess there are twenty times as many boiler makers working to-day as there were before riveting machines were invented?

Answer.—I don't know anything about the figures, but I do remember when boiler makers were few and far between. When I was a cub, I believe a year's work of all the boiler makers in the world would not keep the boiler makers of to-day busy three hours. It beats the deuce where all the boilers go. It seems as though everybody wants boilers now, and they are so cheap everybody gets them. Trade slackens once in a while, but it used to slacken then ten times worse.

Dan.—Thank you, Mr. Mulligan. You're a square chap and a bully boiler maker. Now, Mr. Chairman, all I've got to say is this, I worked in this shop years ago, and I drilled with a ratchet drill every rivet hole, made in the place, and three men worked in the shop and there were not holes enough wanted to keep me busy. The shop now has steady work and pays good wages, and sells boilers so the people can afford to buy. You take the labor-saving tools out of the shop, and every mother's son of you will tramp, except two men, and I will go back to the ratchet, and I bet I can drill more holes than there will be to drill. Labor-saving tools have been a friend to me, and have got you your jobs, and I, for one, will welcome anything of the kind I see coming along. I move that we tell the bosses to get all the gauge rigs they can use.

CHAPTER XXIII.

TURNING SHAFTING ON THE HOTCHKISS PLAN.—
A SIMON PURE MACHINE SHOP.

* * * * I really believe that a machinist who likes to see things, can find more solid enjoyment in some of the rough-and-tumble jobbing shops located in the woods, than he can in some high-toned manufacturing establishments, gotten up without regard to cost. The workmen turned out by such concerns are invariably of more value than those raised in nice shops.

* * * * A new man comes along and says he worked ten years in Hotchkiss' shop. Now, Hotchkiss has the reputation of selling the nicest shafting known to the market. You want a man to turn shafting, and, of course, you ask this new comer if he worked any on shafting in Hotchkiss' shop. He answers truly that he never did much else. You consider yourself lucky, and set the man to work. You soon find that he turns the worst shafting in the world, and gets out about twelve feet a day. You go for the gentleman, and ask him why he can't do some decent work and some reasonable quantity of it. He explains, in a very condescending manner, that if you want good work you must furnish good facilities. He explains that, when at Hotchkiss', he used a special lathe with a wonderful carriage arrangement, carrying numerous tools, and with a centering and straightening attachment, and a burring rest for finishing to size. With this rig he turned a hundred and fifty feet of nice shafting in ten hours, and says he can do it every day in the week if you will bring him the apparatus. Now, you know all about this kind of thing. You have been in Hotchkiss' shop, and you know this man speaks truly. But you ain't in the shafting business, and don't propose to go into the business. You have shafting jobs now and then, and want to do the work fair in quality and reasonable in price. You don't expect to do it as cheap as Hotchkiss does, who makes a specialty of it. You see at once that this man, who was all right in Hotchkiss' shop, don't know anything about turning shafting at all. You hunt up a boy in the other end of the shop—a long-legged, long-headed youth, who has spent two years with you learning the *machinist's* trade. He knows how to turn shafting, and you know it. You put him on the long lathe, and he gives you forty feet of shafting in ten hours, and it's forty times as good as the machinist from Hotchkiss' shop could turn. If your long-legged boy ever gets a job in Hotchkiss' shop, Hotchkiss will have a rough diamond capable of high polish.

* * * * You give the new man another lathe and set him to boring pulleys. He bores about three miserable holes in a day. He finds no pulley-boring machine, no good chuck drills, no reamers, no nothing. He ridicules the idea of doing work without tools. He never looks at his own deficiencies, but looks at the deficiencies of the shop. He is a nice fellow, but is not smart enough to admire the men all around him, who, every hour in the day, are doing things he can't do at all.

* * * * You tell the new man he is a failure on a lathe. You set him to key-seating some big pulleys. They must be chipped and filed. Does he go and get good, solid side chisels dressed, and does he lay a wide, straight edge in the hole and draw one mark to chip his key-seat to ; and does he sit down on a block and send three heavy, nice, clean, straight, flat cuts through the pulley ; and does he file five minutes and show you a nice, clean key-seat, out of wind and free from chisel marks, all done in forty minutes? No; he don't. He never cut a key-seat, and never saw one cut in this way. He was brought up alongside a slotting machine, and he is now five hundred miles from the nearest slotting machine. He knows he can't do this job, and is smart enough to tell you so. This man is no machinist at all. He served a five years' apprenticeship, and worked eight years in one of the best shops in the United States, but he is actually of less value than your youngest cub. You put the case to him fairly; tell him you need men and like his looks, and that if he can point out any work in the shop which he can do properly, you will be glad to keep him. He feels badly; and after looking around, decides that he can't do what the poorest men in the shop are doing. He will do one of two things: If he's a coward, without any coarse grit in him, he will abandon the "machinist" trade and tramp back to Hotchkiss and beg for a job on that shafting lathe. If he has the right stuff in him, he will start in and learn the trade. He has sense and experience and don't need to commence just like a boy. He can start anywhere he chooses, at such wages as his work shows he earns, and increase his wages as he increases his value.

* * * * You go into one of these rough-and-tumble shops and watch a man at a lathe. He whistles and sings and skylarks and smokes, maybe, and does a hundred other things which the high and mighty think ought to send a man to the penitentiary. But don't that chap do the work, though! Don't he earn and get good wages, and don't the proprietor make more out of him every day than the high and mighty do out of three men who were brought up to use every modern facility, and who are stumped if one of the aforesaid facilities happens to get broken. Watch this *outre* machinist as he works. He runs an eighteen-inch lathe, perhaps, and the work brought to him might well be, and, in a better fixed shop would be, distributed among big lathes, little lathes, Fox lathes, planers, slotters, milling machines, cutting machines, drilling machines, screw machines, bolt cutters, gear cutters, etc. But this chap does everything which is laid by his lathe. Some he does tip-top, some he leaves slouchy, but all of it is done as well as is required. He does this all the time. He lives on it. Every job he does is something he, or anybody else, never did before, but he does it all the same. This man is no mere machine wound up and set to running a shafting-turning machine. This shop isn't a manufacturing concern with a system adapted to a special product.

This is one of my Simon Pure machine shops, doing job work, new and old, and this fellow we see is a lordly lathesman, a real machinist. You may set him down in any shop in the world where there's a lathe, and a job to do, and he can do it. He will jump at new and better ways, but is not helpless in the meantime. He's no baby. He's a machinist, and he is worth money every day. Oh, ye puny chaps that claim to be lathesmen! You only know one way of doing things, and that's the way you were *taught* to do it. You only know how to do one job, and that's the job you worked on while you were being taught, and you can't do that job when you get in another shop away from home. Aren't you ashamed to ridicule a poor, one-horse machine shop when every man in it is immeasurably your superior? Aren't you ashamed to claim fellowship and equal wages with these sharp fellows, full of mechanical wit, who do work every day which you don't even dare to undertake? You say they can't do it well. You can't do it at all. You don't know how to tackle it. * * * *

* * * * Look at the job this lathesman gets. He is sitting on a casting and handling a connecting rod strap. It's a rough forging for a strap to hold square boxes. You can't see a bit of lathe-work about it anywhere, or a chance for any. Pretty soon he gets his present job done. Now he puts a miserable looking angle-plate against his face-plate, and sets this strap in some shape. He fishes a dirty piece of paper out of his tool box. This paper contains a memorandum of sizes which he took down verbatim as the foreman gave them. He goes to work, and in two hours, lays two hours of planing on the floor. He has surfaced that strap nicely and squarely all over the outside. There's one job of "lathework" done. There is but one planer in the shop, and that is too much crowded to be doing anything that can be done in any other machine. That same planer will stand still six months in the year, so it would be folly to get another, and thus be ready for a rush which never comes when you are ready.

* * * * Here goes for the next job. Twelve stubs about two feet long, one and three-quarters diameter, to have thread cut eight inches on one end. No turning, simply a thread to be cut. They belong to a bridge bolt job, and the bolt cutter has no dies for this size. Soon this job is done. It isn't nice lathe work. Nothing to be proud of, but it is o. k. in every way. What next? He puts on a chuck and proceeds to chase out twelve hot-pressed nuts for these bridge bolts. Ough! how your teeth grit to see a lathesman having to do such a job. It's a nasty job, but there's no tap that size, and soon it's done and off this chap's mind.

* * * * Next comes some nice lathe work; a couple of valve stems and two or three small wrists. They are finished to the sizes given and nicely polished.

He gets them done, and feels proud of them. Bless him, any lathesman can do such work.

* * * * Here's a brass casting for a two-inch stop-cock, and by it lies the old one. It's a repair job. The old one is bursted wide open. The plug is swelled, but not broken. Does a foreman come around and instruct this man how to do this job? No, sir. His orders were to "rig up that cock." He takes the casting, chucks it, and in half an hour has a two-inch pipe thread chased in each end. Now he chucks crosswise, and you suddenly notice that this cock must be bored tapering. How is this fellow going to bore this hole? Will he go and get a nice taper reamer? I guess not in this shop. Will he fit up some kind of a reamer? Not he. He is fitting up an old water-cock, not making new reamers. He'll set the head of the lathe over, won't he? No, he won't. The head of the lathe can't be swiveled. Will he set the Slate taper attachment over? Guess not, as he never heard of Slate; and don't know what a taper attachment is. Will he use the compound rest? He may some day, when such a thing gets into the shop. Will he stick a wedge under the back wing of the carriage? No. He never heard of it, and is not so deep an inventor as to think of it just when he wants it. Will he wrap a cord around his cross-feed screw-handle and tie it to his tail-stock, and thus get the taper? No, he has no time to invent this ingenious plan. Will he find a fancy little sliding-head boring-bar somewhere? Not a bar. Has he a mandrel which he can screw his chuck on, and thus do the job in the steady rest? No, sir. He won't do any of these smart things, and he won't tell you that the shop ought to have a Fox lathe for such work, and he won't tell you how the Metropolitan Cock Company bore them out, for he don't know, and, I am sorry to add, he don't care. All he cares about is to lay that cock down on the floor and call it done, and as well done as is needed.

He whistles a very peculiar air in a very soft manner and turns his cross crank slowly to keep time. The result is a hole which is tapering, if it's nothing else. It would have taken him just about as long to bore it straight. He takes the job out. Puts on a face-plate, and puts the old cock plug in the lathe. He chalks it and hammers the swells out, or in, rather. Then he sets his lathe over and takes a light cut over it. Then he marks a close fit in the cock, but keeps the plug large. Now he goes to a vise and *files the hole.* It was tapering all right, but the sides were not straight. He files carefully but boldly, watching the tool marks in the hole, and trying the plug. Soon he is done with the filing, and, returning to his lathe, completes the fit of the plug. Now he grinds it in, and soon there isn't a file mark or a tool mark in the hole or on the plug. It is simply a first-class, water-tight taper job, quickly done in a third-class manner. He screws the thing together, and bounces the next job. Time on old cock, three hours and a quarter. You or I could not do it as well or as quick with all the cock-making appliances in existence. This man never fitted up a water-cock before. He is a machinist, and will hustle out any job you will bring him, and will do it as well as you want it done, and no better. * * *

CHAPTER XXIV.

GEOGRAPHY IN MACHINE BUILDING. — GETTING READY FOR BUSINESS. — TWO CASES IN POINT.

* * * * Many manufacturers jump at the conclusion, if they have something to sell which it is to a party's real interest to buy, that the party will buy if he has the money. This won't do at all; economical devices cannot be sold on their merits. Geography enters largely into the question: people in one locality are frugal, thrifty, and rich; they spend a dollar to save two, and by that means gain their riches. In another locality the people will positively decline to spend a dollar to save ten. They are not frugal, they are not prudent; they are thrifty and they are rich. A Texas farmer would starve to death in Connecticut; he would not work hard enough to get a living out of the soil; the soil is different, and he comes from a different class of people.

* * * * The steam engine is essentially an element of modern economy; the steam engine is not the same the world over by a great deal. In our Southern States many long-stroke, slow-speed engines use their steam at nearly full stroke. In the Middle States proportions are changed; the lap of the valve is increased, a variable cut-off added, and, once in a great while, an automatic cut-off is found. In the older New England States we find the finest types of automatic cut-off engines predominant, and, in many cases, a condenser added. In the old countries of Europe every pool of water is found steaming hot with the discharge of numberless condensers.

* * * * If a hundred horse-power engine, using steam full stroke, is kept in fuel for fifteen dollars a day, it is doing well. If the valve of this engine be altered and the throw increased, ten dollars will buy the coal required each day. If it cost ten thousand dollars to lengthen this valve, the investment would be a capital one. Such a change costs, in fact, about fifty dollars. If a good automatic valve gear be put on the engine, six dollars and a half will pay for the coal required. The three dollars and a half a day thus saved would be good interest on ten thousand dollars. The change can generally be made for five hundred dollars. If water is handy, and a good condenser be added, five dollars a day will pay for the coal required. The dollar and a half a day thus saved will be good interest on ten thousand dollars. The change can generally be made for a thousand dollars. If a man has a hundred horse-power engine, using its steam full stroke, and will, at one bold stroke, make it properly automatic and condensing, he will save ten dollars a day, or ten per cent. on thirty thousand dollars.

* * * * You would think, if you were the proud builder of a tip-top condensing engine with automatic cut-off, if you held this hundred horse-power engine for three thousand, or four thousand, or five thousand dollars, if you offered it for sale in localities where wasteful engines were used, that there would be such an overwhelming rush of orders that you would go crazy. But such would not be the case; there would be no rush of orders from such a locality, and if you went daft it would be from disappointment. The place to sell such engines is right where people use such engines. I don't build such engines myself, and have had no experience in the matter, but I leave it to any high class engine builder in the country who has ever tried to introduce his engines in localities where the greatest economical changes could be wrought.

* * * * It is the miser who seeks new ways of

saving money. It is the prodigal who welcomes new suggestions as to spending money. If we get along with something mean, we don't care if it gets a little meaner. If we appreciate that which is good, we will seek for that which is better. Bad leads to worse, and good leads to better.

* * * * Speaking of investment, leads me to think that there is a great geographical difference in our capitalists. I made a short stay in the Middle States lately, and noticed that as a general thing there was but little capital invested in what in the East would be considered as well-equipped factories. I refer here to metal industries exclusively. Eastern manufacturers are cautious about picking up a thing, but when they do it they have a good grip on it. It is no unusual thing to find a new building in New England, out of which, for two years, come an army of workmen, all drawing good pay. This is to be a factory some day. Thousands and thousands of dollars are being spent in equipping the concern with the most efficient machinery. Not a pound of goods going out—not a dollar coming in.

Every little expense which promises to return itself a hundred fold when things start up, is borne with patience. This thing would work in the West for about three weeks, and then capitalists would begin to ask when this paying-out process was going to stop. There are exceptional cases, of course, but as a general thing Western capitalists have been very slow about investing in manufacturing business. It don't seem enough like trade. In trade you pay money for an article which you sell instantly at an advance. As soon as you part with your money you have its equivalent. But in the factory things are different. The big money goes, perhaps, into special machinery, which is not for sale or salable. The main money is invested in a process. In New England the intention seems to be to fix for making money, no matter what it costs. You will see little of this kind of business done in metal in the West.

The New England factory evidently purposes commencing when it commences. In the West " business " commences as soon as money commences to go out, and Western men are not up to paying out long at a time without looking around for a return.

The Westerners will take up with a good thing, get it into crude shape; manufacture in a sort of a way, go into the market, and fail on account of the general prematureness of the thing, and they will do it all before the New Englander decides to put money into it. But when the thing is pronounced all right, the New Englander does take hold of it sure enough.

If the article is a new invention, whose raw principle is full of certain promise, special skill is employed to get it into a superior practical form. This is often omitted in the West. After being reduced to a practical, useful form, special skill is employed to get it into a shape adapted to systematic manufacture—to machine construction—to cheap excellence. This is almost always omitted in the West. The sample being done, special skill is employed to contrive and construct special machinery for its production. This is almost always omitted in the West. These things cost a fearful sight of money, and the Western folks have not learned to stand the strain.

In New England, after the crude principle is approved, after the most useful form is given at great expense, after the form has been adapted to manufacture, after a world of special machines have been contrived and built, after two or three years' time, and say two hundred thousand dollars have been expended —then, and not till then, are the factory doors thrown open, and the world informed that this is a screwdriver factory, or some such thing. Then the product is offered, and then the public buy. The article they buy is as good as money and skill can produce it, and sales will continue till such an article is no longer needed. All this may happen after the same article, in a general way, has failed on the market, owing to a premature delivery. You know I am no Yankee, so I am not blowing. I may possibly have a better motive.

* * * As an example of New England operations, let me cite one case : A steam engine of entire new type was devised. It was taken to a celebrated concern. It was approved, and taken in hand. An engineer skilled in the science of steam and mechanics re-designed it. An engineer skilled in manufacturing joined hands and heads with the steam man, and the result was a machine which looked all right to the steam man, and which the factory man said he could make well, and cheap, and profitably. Then a few were made as any single article would be made.

In the West these few engines would have been sold and some money brought in. But not so in this case. These engines were put to work, surrounded by skilled tests. They confirmed the judgment of the parties who were "looking into it." Did they go to work and sell them then ? No, sir. They then began the tests for *durability.* Hour after hour and month after month —every hour that there was steam in the factory boilers, did these engines whirl away at their heaviest loads, under every possible change in work and handling, and under the closest of scrutiny. They are running yet, and will be running next Christmas. When this test is over, will these factory people commence to make this engine for sale? I doubt it. I do not think they will ever "make" these engines. When the tests are over, the system of manufacture, already in view, will be elaborated, and then a fortune will be expended in appliances; and then, and not till then, will the public be asked to buy. The engines will be *manufactured*, not "made," and that "manufacture" means a well studied and economical production which is to the benefit of all concerned. All this, of course, in case this engine proves "durable." It may be disappointing, in which case the whole thing will go into the scrap pile; and the cost will be charged to expense, and will be a small loss to a concern which has accumulated millions of dollars by a continued demand for articles treated in the same careful, cautious, painstaking manner.

These heavy investments, based on a hope of future return, are not an inventor's worship of his idol. This engine came from afar. These are capitalists looking up investments.

I honestly think that, if this same engine had been sprouted in the West, it would have been in the market years ago, and more than likely it would have been "dead, buried and resurrected, and its body strung on wires."

* * * * Another case: A Western firm "made" a certain machine. Cut prices began to bring the blood. There was competition from New England. Both parties made the machine quite well. The Western firm resolved that something must be done to cheapen the machine. It could not be made any lighter, for it only had panic thickness anyhow. Wages could not be cut, for there was no substance to cut at.

The question came down to a simple question of reducing the amount of work on the thing. The common Western plan of cheapening a product is to leave something off. They did this thing: they reduced everything, and cut and slashed as long as they thought the machine would pass muster. Then they cut prices twenty per cent. Now, the Yankee manufacturers of this machine had never been well fixed, as they called it, for manufacturing; the last wind from the West began to hurt; something must be done with that machine. Did they think of reducing the value and cost of the thing by leaving some of the work off? They did nothing of the kind. The Yankee never takes that view of matters. They let the product alone and hopped upon the process and revolutionized it. They invested thirty thousand dollars in special machinery and commenced on a new lot of machines. The special machinery had been designed to do the work as well as possible, and when the lot was complete it was found that there was more profit in the work at the last cut price than there had ever been at any previous price.

They had kept about ten men on the work heretofore. The Western concern had about the same number. The East now cut the price ten per cent. more, intending at one swoop to kill their competitors, and enhance the demand for the machine.

They did so with this result: The Western men dropped the thing, saying they had done everything that good mechanics could do in the matter, that the Yankees were working at a loss against which no good business house could compete, and that it was entirely too sick a cat to get well. The new machines were so much nicer than the old ones that they were hardly recognized, and now over sixty men work on these machines.

* * * * Here is a case where cut prices forced the use of the much-abused labor-saving machinery, and where the much-abused labor-saving machinery led to the permanent employment of forty men in a new industry. I could write you down ten thousand instances of similar cases in this last particular.

CHAPTER XXV.

WORKING FOR NOTHING.—HOW CHORDAL GOT UGLY.—SIXTEEN GLASSES OF BEER.—MONEY SAVED ON MANDRELS.

* * * * What do you think of a man who will work for nothing? Of a man who will get up in the night and tramp off to a machine shop with a tin bucket on his arm; who will put on overalls at seven o'clock in the morning and keep them on till six o'clock in the evening; who will stand at somebody else's lathe, or planer, or slotter, or vise, and hammer on somebody else's pieces of iron all day long, and keep it up day after day, and week after week, and month after month, and year after year, from the time he goes at the trade at fourteen years of age till he dies; and all for nothing? I don't mean the kind of men who find delight in seeing crude material develop and grow into useful, finished products, but the kind of men who have no earthly interest in development and growth, and don't care a cent about useful, finished products. Do you know any such men, working through their whole lives, and bringing the sweat at every blow—and doing it all for nothing? I know them, lots of them. There are a hundred thousand men working in machine shops to-day who cannot show twenty-five cents for the last twenty years' work. They have worked every day and have drawn their pay. But where is it? They have had no grave calamities, no bad debts, no heavy losses on indorsements, no forfeited bond for a friend in office—nothing which impoverishes men, but everything which makes men independent, to wit: income, sure and steady, and to be depended on every time. Of these hundred thousand men I speak of, over fifty thousand haven't got ten cents in their pockets at this minute, and won't have till next pay-day. They will work day after day, and draw pay after pay. But when they leave one job and travel, do they take any of this good money with them? Not much. They borrow to pay for the trip. These same hundred thousand will raise a row to get ten cents a day more, which is right in principle; but I want to know what becomes of this ten cents. They used to get thirty and fifty cents more, but they can't show that the old figure produced any tangible results.

* * * * It won't do to say broadly that men spend their earnings in drink, etc. It won't do, for two reasons: first and foremost, it isn't true, and second and hindermost, that's a good way to spend money if the sole object is to get rid of it as soon as possible, and that in reality seems to be the main object with the hundred thousand.

* * * * I tell you, and I can prove it by every "dead-broke" machinist in the land, that the reason the hundred thousand are always "strapped" is not because they drink, or smoke, or gamble, or wear diamonds, or keep fast horses, or nice places in the country, but simply because they don't know what to do with their pay. Let one of these fellows draw a month's pay. He goes and pays bills he owes, invests something in the worst clothes he can find, and keeps the rest in his pocket. It begins to fester right away. A workingman, with a few extra dollars in his pocket, often has really painful desires to find something to spend a little something on. He can't think of anything he wants, and feels the existence of a void. In a few days the stuff is gone, and then some necessities arise. Credit is drawn on. Small quantities of second-class necessities, on credit at a high price, is what uses up the cream of the next pay. I have known a well-paid machinist to get eight pounds of heavy brown

sugar on pay-night, when he had thirty dollars in his pocket which he had no idea under heaven what he was going to do with. The idea of getting fifty pounds of good sugar never occurred to him. Before the next pay-day he would be getting horrible sugar on credit, by the half-dollar's worth, at outrageous prices.

* * * * These very men, who do no good with their money, who can't show any little fund laid up; who can't show a decent wardrobe; who never gave a friend a present costing ten dollars; who never spend two dollars on pleasure travel; who can't show five dollars' worth of books; who have no wife or children made comfortable by wise expenditures; who have no balance in the office; who haven't got a hardened steel square in their tool-kit, because it costs a day's pay; who never buy good cigars, and who will buy bad whisky when tip-top whisky is the same price—these very men are the men to kick the hardest for higher pay. They will say: "I can't stay here long, wages are too low." They play hob if they find some other fellow getting five cents a day more than they do themselves.

* * * * As you use discretion in selecting extracts from my letters, I don't mind standing for an awful example. Years ago I worked for the Hall Steam Engine Company. That is to say, I put in time on their premises and got their money. I ran a planer. The aforesaid company was composed of Tom and Charlie Hall. They were not mechanics, but hailed from the salt sea. Tom had been master, and Charlie had been master's mate, on some sort of a sea craft at some time, and the shop was their quarter-deck, and is now, for aught I know. They were both good men, and showed more than common sense in some of the details of their business.

In the same town were located the immense railroad

shops of the Under Pavonia Railroad. These shops worked sometimes fifteen hundred men, and it generally happened that the men in Hall's shop were simply putting in time while waiting for some promised job in the U. P. shop. To do business with such men, you will readily see, required skill and management. Well, as before said, I worked on a planer at Hall's, and I wasn't waiting for a U. P. job, either. As near as I remember, my wages were three and a half a day. I worked on a while, and finally learned that a German near me, by the name of Szcheinfule, or Swivel, or some such name, was getting three seventy-five a day. Now, you know, this wouldn't do. It didn't make any difference in my finances how much money I got for my work. I had worked for three dollars and for six dollars, and it was all the same. At that time I didn't have any wife and babies, and I didn't have anything else, and no amount of wages would give me anything else. I kept grinding over the matter of this fellow getting more money than myself. I sat on that planer table and brooded and talked to myself, and got ugly. Now, whether you know it or not, machinists generally have no sense on the question of wages or business. They can't talk reasonably, and generally they put off talking till they get mad, and then they blurt out like fools. That was my case, anyhow. I kept getting madder, and finally bolted into the office. The president, Mr. Thomas Hall, who, by the way, was a member of the Legislature was there; so was the master's mate. I talked loud, and asked them what they took me for, and if they supposed I was going to work alongside of Swivel for a quarter less per day; told them I knew my rights, and I wanted my pay raised or Swivel's cut down. The seafaring men waited till I exhausted my drivel, and then Tom Hall said: "Chordal, when we had our hands full of work and men were scarce, the U. P. shop came here and took all our men, by offering them temporary jobs at four and five dollars per day. Every man left us but Swivel, and he didn't come in and bulldoze us for a raise, either. He stayed. This thing happened, not only once, but a dozen times. Swivel is not a first-class man. If we would discharge him, to-morrow we could hire him back for two dollars a day; but he has acted square with us, and men like you may come and go as much as they please, but this man Swivel will stay at the same wages he gets now. We are paying this man for what he has done for us. If you ever prove yourself worthy of such a compliment, we would be pleased to have you let us know it. We advise you to go and sit on that planer another day, and to-morrow, if you think it wise to be silly, you can do so."

* * * * My better judgment prevailed, and ever since then I have always had a great deal of respect for a machinist who, without any nonsensical self-abasement, could assure himself of the respect of his employers.

* * * * While I think of the Hall Steam Engine Company, let me tell you of another case: A young fellow came to their foreman, Rogers, and asked for a job. Rogers said he was sorry, but he could not possibly scare up a job. The fellow said he had been to the U. P. shop, and there wasn't the ghost of a show there. He went off. The next night Rogers and myself were drinking beer at the Tivoli Garden, and who should come with our beer but this same chap who had asked for a job!

There he was with a white apron, and about sixteen glasses of beer. Now, while a machinist is queer about his pride, he always has lots of it, such as it is.

This thing touched the three of us. Rogers, on inquiry, found that the fellow was "dead broke," and

Who should come with our beer but this same chap who had asked for a job! There he was, with a white apron, and about sixteen glasses of beer.—Page 214.

that this was the only thing that had opened up. He was getting a dollar a day of sixteen hours. Rogers told him to take off that apron and square up with the house; told him to come to the shop in the morning and he would find him a job as a laborer, and as soon as there was a chance he could have a good job. The fellow came, and was set to work unloading coal-car lumber.

On pay night, this same fellow raised Cain, and quit incontinently because he only got two dollars a day when men in the shop were getting three and a half. He knew his rights, you know.

* * * * It is true, that the balance on hand is a real source of annoyance to the hundred thousand machinists I have referred to. Some will read this, and I defy any one of that number to deny it. A man with a big family accumulates money and property at a dollar and a half a day, and a man right alongside of him, at three dollars and no care, never has a dollar to his name, and never has a dollar's worth of goods to show, and he don't drink unreasonably and he don't gamble. Between you and me, I think this is just as important a question to many of your readers as the question of how to make a fluted reamer which won't chatter. What does a man need to care about the chatters, if the reamer don't bring in any returns? The object of life is to make a reamer which won't chatter, and to be able to show some of the comforts and pleasures of life as the result of having made a good reamer years ago.

* * * * If the owner of a genuine, simon-pure machine shop, and by that I mean not a systematized manufacturing establishment, wants his eyes opened, let him take a note-book into the shop and keep an account of the *money spent* in turning up mandrels for one month. There are some nice machinists in the country, who don't know what I am talking about when I refer to turning up mandrels, and if they would go into one of these common shops they would not recognize a mandrel if they saw it. In ninety-nine shops out of a hundred, each man fits his mandrels as he goes along. He keeps them lying on the floor under the foot of his lathe, always. All the mandrels in the shop are, of course, common property.

If Walker wants to turn up a job, he takes the piece with him and goes down among his lot of mandrels and tries to find one which will fit the hole he has bored. He don't find one big enough, so he goes to Dix's lathe, and don't find one that isn't too large. He makes the grand rounds, and then drops into the blacksmith shop, and picks out of the scrap pile a piece of two-inch round iron, maybe eight inches long, and maybe eighteen. He goes back in the shop and centers it, and starts as though he thought of drilling the centers, but he concludes he only wants to use the thing half an hour, so there's no use in drilling. Then he gets it in the lathe, and when he gets one end squared up, he concludes that it is too much trouble to turn the thing around and square the other end, so he proceeds to make his fit. First a heavy cut, then a light one, then two more light ones, then he files it, and then he tries it, and then his chin goes up and his eyebrows come down, for his mandrel fits like a mouse's tail in a flour barrel, as he expresses it between oaths. Now it luckily happens that he has only turned up about three inches in length, so all he has to do is to turn another three inches and get a good fit, you know. He is bound to have it big enough this time. Soon it is done, and he proceeds to drive it in. The thing he drives through is *always* an old gear brought in from the scrap pile years ago. The hole in the aforesaid gear is so big that it would let his job right through, so he hunts up something smaller to lay on it. He finds it necessary to use two or three of these underlays, so as to reduce size properly. He has built up a cob house about two feet high, and, ten chances to one, one of the "cobs" is a nicely-bored piece of finished work. No matter; he puts his job on top of the pile and sticks the mandrel in. Then he hunts up a nut *always*. He don't find any loose one, unless he takes the one he uses for a candlestick and keeps stored on the inside of his lathe. He finally takes one off one of his bolts, and carefully balances it on the craggy, rough end of his mandrel. Then he calls Dix to hold the mandrel. Dix does so, and Walker goes for the sledge and comes down on the thing three times. Too tight. He lets Dix go, and, turning the thing end for end, sets the nut on the mandrel, and comes down heavy to drive the mandrel out. Mind you, he is getting mad all this time, for he is having bad luck. He strikes a crooked lick and knocks the whole cob house down, and the hot-pressed nut splits, one half just missing Lambert's ear on its way to the foundry, the other half goes out the front door into the street. He erects the structure again, and fishes out his candlestick. After knocking the greasy nut off two or three times, he gets his mandrel out and files it smaller. He is getting a little bit madder. Now he takes it out, takes the dog off, goes and hunts up the nut under a vise bench, and starts the mandrel. It drops in clear up to the shoulder. He was too mad when he filed it last. He is entirely too much out of patience now to turn up a new place, so he goes to a vise, and, screwing his mandrel in it, he proceeds to raise a burr all over it with a prick-punch.

Everything is lovely now. He cools down and finishes his job, but in the meantime his job slips once or twice, and he is compelled to prick-punch some more.

When he gets done he throws the mandrel under his lathe. The next time he uses that mandrel he will want it a quarter of an inch smaller, and will make it so, and he may or may not have luck in making his fit. But still the necessity of drilling the centers, or of squaring that other end, does not force itself upon him. In a month or so this mandrel has been made to do for some size by every lathesman in the shop. It is one and seven-eighths at one end, and three-quarters at the other, for it has been used for everything it could be made to answer for. In course of time Walker is looking for a mandrel about an inch and a half. He has his job with him and is searching under Moore's lathe, and finds this identical mandrel, and, as good luck will have it, there is a place on it which exactly fits his job. He is smart enough to put it in the lathe to see how much the small and limber end of it has got bent during late drivings. He finds that no part is true, and that no two parts are true with each other, which shows that it got a new bend each time it was used. The part he wants is almost true. He can see it wink but thinks it will do. He uses it. Here are five botches at once: first, a mandrel which is not true; second, an inch and a half mandrel which must use a two-inch dog, and which is made very limber by having part of its length three-quarters of an inch in diameter; third, a mandrel without drilled centers, etc.; fourth, a mandrel with such a rough surface-fit that it must be driven with a sledge; fifth, a machinist who will play unnecessary parts in the business; and, sixth, a shop owner so reckless of money as to pay each year for mandrel turning, an amount which would three times over buy a good set of hardened and ground steel arbors. Take your note-book into the shops. If you have a good set of mandrels they will save big money, and will make your sizes uniform, because the boys will get into the habit of making a two-inch hole two inches. Such mandrels are ground after hardening, and the surface fit is such that a lead or copper hand hammer will drive a three-inch mandrel for twenty-four inch work. When Walker wants a mandrel he would know just what to get, and when he would go after a dog he would get the right one, instead of lugging his job all round the shop to find a mandrel, and then lugging the mandrel around to find a dog to fit the big end.

Don't dream of making nice mandrels. Go and buy them the same as you would buy wood screws, from some one fixed for making them. * * * *

CHAPTER XXVI.

FINDING ONE'S VOCATION.—HOW BOB DID IT.—PATTERN MAKING IN COUNTRY SHOPS.—DEVICES BORN TOO SOON.

* * * * Men, and especially mechanics, are always wiser and better after making some big mistake. They are in some degree insured against the mistake in the future. The best machinists it has ever been my good luck to fall in with, have been men who have gone at the trade after a long experience at something else. A man don't find out what is in him till he has wrestled with circumstances for a short lifetime.

* * * * One of the cant expressions of a narrow-headed mechanic is, "Every man to his trade." Such men are very jealous of the success of any one who slips into their craft edgewise.

A short-sighted father grabs his fourteen-year-old boy, who has never shown any loud preferences for the vocation, and shoves him by force into some trade. The boy goes at it passively, and without becoming in any degree a smart mechanic. He learns the use of tools and regular methods of procedure in regular cases. In irregular cases he is a mere cipher, and don't count. After a term of three or four years, he asumes the dignities of a journeyman. He knows what he has learned, and nothing else. He gets the lowest pay which a boss dares pay to a full-fledged workman, and that is, maybe, a trifle more than he is worth. He works on for years, but is nothing but a skilled machine which must be adjusted for every new condition. This man grumbles at the poor pay a good mechanic has to work for. Some one suggests that perhaps he is not a good mechanic, and points to real mechanics around him who, by some hocus pocus, get a great deal better pay than he does. Then this stock mechanic looks around, and indignantly protests against Smith, who has only worked half as long at the trade as he has, getting more pay than himself; and he points derisively to Jones as a man who never did serve a time at the trade; and to Robinson, who was an apprentice a month ago.

These three men get better pay than he does, and these three men are infinitely better mechanics than he will ever be. The probabilities are that he has struck the wrong trade, and will never be one of the best, or even ordinary, elements of it. Such men are to be pitied.

* * * * The only hope for them is, that they will discover some vocation which they can excel in, and will go at it. A man of middle age, who has had a long, even if unpleasant, experience in hard work in certain branches, can go at a new trade and be excellent in a month, perhaps. The manipulation of tools, the knowledge of materials, and the general routine of mechanics' work, is similar in many respects.

A good marble cutter will make a better vise hand in a machine shop in one month than a printer will in two years. No mechanic ought to blush to use his own judgment in such matters, and, even after years of hard tugging, cut loose from a bondage inflicted by a short-sighted guardian, and go at something which the mature judgment of manhood tells will be successful. This mutual switching around of good men who have got into the wrong holes, will finally get each man into the right place. Whenever one mechanic, good or bad, sees a man coming into his trade from some other trade, he can feel justified in giving him a welcome, instead of muttering "Every man to his trade."

* * * * Once in a while you hear some despondent workman say, "There's the trade I ought to have gone at," and once in a while I say to such a man, "Go at the trade now." Forty years is none too old to go at the thing a man feels he is cut out for. Every man is entitled to a little ordinary every-day success before he dies.

* * * * Because a man, after fifteen years' hard work, has failed to make a tip-top blacksmith of himself, it don't follow that he won't make a good surgeon, or dentist, or executive officer, in almost any business; and there's many a good blacksmith, if he only knew it, who is trying to accomplish something as a preacher, or lawyer, or what not. I say that "Every man to his trade" is a good motive, and I say that it is every man's privilege at any time in life to find out what his trade is.

* * * * This whole thing is brought to my mind by acquaintance with pattern-makers, and I expect every one who has had anything to do with pattern-makers has had my experience. There is not a shop in the country employing half a dozen pattern-makers which don't get into a pinch once in a while, and have to put a carpenter, or a cabinet-maker on pattern work to tide over a rush. After a while one of these wood butchers will come around and say he would like a steady job under instructions. He wants to quit his present trade and go at one he believes he will excel in.

He's my man every time. If you want a good pattern-maker, this is the kind of stuff they are made of, and it is generally a hundred per cent. better than ten-year-old stock that don't know what it was made for, and won't know for thirty years more.

* * * * There's always a foolish kick in the pattern-shop when this man goes to work. The pattern makers want to know why this man don't stay at his trade. The answer is simple: It's because he don't want to.

This man comes with years of experience in working wood with wood tools, and with a mature mechanical judgment in the perception of things. That he has good sense is proven by his choosing his vocation before he dies.

* * * * I know these pattern makers like a book. There's Bob, for instance, is an old pattern-maker, and the best one I ever had anything to do with. You take your drawings to Bob and he makes the patterns. And the patterns are right, too. You don't have to measure to see if there's shrinkage here, and rappage there. You don't have to find out if this core will cut through where you don't want it to, or if that core is in such form that it can't be set. You need have no anxiety about sizes, or about bosses coming in the right place, or about sharp work where you want fillets. You need not bother yourself about the matter at all.

If your drawing was right the patterns will be right, and you can order them into the foundry without any anxiety, or fussing, or wondering. It's Bob's business to make patterns which will make castings like the drawings, and he understands his business, and attends to it. He don't stand around with sharp tools and wait for instructions how to make this, how to part that, how to dowel this, where to glue that, and when to put these rapping plates on, and where to put cores, and where to draw in green sand, and all such. That's his business. Bob's a pattern-maker, and a good one, and I defy any pattern-maker to prove Bob off in any points of his trade. Did Bob's father kick him into the pattern-makers' trade? Not a bit of it. Bob was a steamboat carpenter, and went to pattern-making when past forty, I guess, because he saw he was the man for the trade.

* * * Bob is one of these men who don't like

to see any man come to work in a pattern shop, who is not a "regular pattern-maker."

* * * * I never will let up on my admiration for the rare pattern-maker who can make good, nice, everlasting patterns when required to, but who also knows how to nail a thing together in ten minutes, if you only want one casting off the pattern.

In the small jobbing shops in scattered western towns, the proprietor is generally a machinist, and the pattern-maker is a man with responsibilities. If the pattern-maker is a good man, the concern may succeed, but if he is a poor stick the institution is bound to fail.

There are no draughtsmen around these shops, no lordly engineers with square roots, and cube roots, and logarithms, and torsion equations, and density tables, and all such.

The pattern-maker is generally the man called on to furnish the high art for the establishment.

The foundries connected with these shops take off a heat of about eighteen hundred pounds once or twice a week, and about nine-tenths of the work is cast from patterns made for that heat, so you will see that this pattern-maker—he almost always works alone—has his hands full. Thursday is the casting day, and five o'clock is the hour set for the fan to be put on. Tuesday night the pattern-maker will say he is ready, and you will find him working on some pulley pattern he has been trying to add to the set for a year.

Wednesday morning the proprietor begins to think of things which must be made this heat, and repair jobs will come in a rush, and by noon on Wednesday our pattern-maker will have laid that everlasting pulley pattern away, and will have mapped out a lot of patterns for the heat to-morrow, which would keep a common, high toned shop, full of pattern-makers, busy for a week. It don't seem to make any difference what comes, or how much of it, bevel gears, spur gears, odd boxes, thimble skeins, sash weights, a face-plate, a cross head, a stop valve, a lamp post, a stove grate, a dumb bell, reaper cranks, concaves, step-plates, couplings, and what not. He don't get any dinner or supper, maybe, and the fan belt don't get on till six o'clock; but Friday morning he will get down that eternal pulley pattern again. He has probably put in six weeks' solid time on that pulley pattern and it isn't done yet, but he has done some "odd jobbing" in the meantime.

* * * * We are not very conservative in this country, but still there is such a thing as a device being born too soon. The people won't have it, and a wise manufacturer sometimes lets it alone. The brilliant and radical inventor will sometimes find his offspring entirely too perfect for the time. Its very perfection of adaptation implies, probably, a radical departure from well-understood plans, and, too often, as a consequence, the very perfection of adaptation to function involves a perfect inadaptation to common surroundings.

* * * * If there was ever a short cut made all of a sudden, it was when the direct-acting steam pump was invented. As far as my knowledge goes, Mr. Worthington is the real inventor of this radical contrivance.

He found steam moving a piston in a straight line; he found pistons moving water in a straight line. The cause was as he found it; the result was as he desired it. But what a world of complicated, intermediate machinery he found between these simple terminal elements! He straightened the matter out, discarded the entire intervention, and produced a machine which consisted of a single transmitting piece of metal, moving in the simple and identical lines of inevitable force and required work.

* * * * All this was many years ago—in 1840. During the intervening years the steam pump has, without any real material change in structure, found its true place in the busy world and in the appreciation of users, but every day since its birth has been an uphill struggle for recognition, owing to the simple fact that the new pump was not enough like the old pumps.

* * * * The present value of the steam pump as distinguished from ancient donkey pumps is too great to calculate, but it required fourteen new generations of steam users to provide it with any reasonable welcome. Mr. Worthington might have saved himself a world of trouble and mental anguish by not inventing a direct-acting steam pump at all.

In later years, after the struggling infant has forced its way into popular use, hundreds of wise men see a good business in steam pumps.

I will venture the opinion that if Mr. Worthington had it all to do over again, he would commence at the other end.

CHAPTER XXVII.

COARSE-GRAINED FOREMEN.—THE CHRONIC MISTAKER.—THE BLUNDERER.—THE ANXIOUS MAN.—THE MAN WHO KNOWS.—THE MULLET-HEAD.—CLIQUES IN THE SHOP.—BENCHES FOR THE NORTH SHOP.

* * * * I really think it a good plan for workmen to make shops too hot to hold coarse-grained foremen. No proprietor in the land ever changed from a pirate to a gentleman without finding his costs reduced.

Tubal had a foreman who could not possibly disapprove without insulting. He ought to have known better, because every man should know that friends are desirable, and enemies not. Still, this fellow could not help it. There was not a man in the shop in sympathy with him. Every man looked upon him as a man to be shunned and thwarted. He knew nothing of what was going on, and could do no real execution. The men muttered and drew their pay and worked as little as possible. Tubal found himself almost driven from the market by the high cost of his work, so he kept dinging at the foreman, who told him the men were bad. Tubal let him go, and got Jimmy in his place. Jimmy went into the shop, and, without discharging a man, cut down the costs twenty per cent., by simply increasing the good feeling of the men.

* * * * It certainly does not pay to work men who have to be eternally and forever cursed into their work, and it is certainly as true, that it don't pay to follow such a course with men who don't need it. The dollar-and-cent view will take the big, big D, out of the shop.

* * * * If a good man does a bad job or breaks something, he is ashamed of himself and will remember. A foreman should be smart enough to appreciate this side of human nature and act accordingly. Let him assume that the man don't care, and begin to blast him, and the man will never care again as long as he works for that foreman.

* * * * There is a certain species of machinist who makes mistakes—always and continuously. His ten feet four inches and a quarter is an eighth short or long. His inch and a half is in the neighborhood only of an inch and a half. He forgets the washer on this job, and don't cut the thread up far enough on that one. He drills this hole too far from the edge of a flange, and drills that tap hole the size of the outside of the tap, and he never gets a hole the right size for a tap, and he never chucks a job true enough, and he sets a lathe over, so as to turn a crowning pulley very much more tapering on one side than on the other; he won't make a key bear on the sides, and no wrench will fit all round on the bolt head he files up; he taps holes crooked and runs pipe taps in too deep; he cuts shoulders up a sixteenth too far, and makes the driving fit on the wrong part of the job. He is a good workman, for all these things are nicely done. He simply forgets or neglects, or something or other, and is a nuisance, for you never can depend on him. When he lays a job down, you never can have the assurance that it is right until you measure every thing about it. The work that such a man does costs lots of money, because you must provide a special supervision over every thing he does. Such a man will turn a foreman's hair gray if he lets him keep on. He never will get any better as long as he works in the same position. To cure this man, reduce his pay and put him at the very foot of the ladder, telling him to raise his own pay by learning to be "sure." No men continually liable to small mistakes around me, if you please.

* * * * Another species works decisively and surely. When he goes for a size, he gets it as close as the case calls for. He don't slouch dimensions. You never think of running over his sizes. You know they are what you ordered, but—once in six months this man will make some grand blunder. He will turn something to eleven and a half inches which should be twelve and a half inches, but that eleven and a half inches will be a good and accurate size. He will get an engine four inches out of line, but he will never get it a sixteenth out of line. He will try to raise a smokestack under one of his guy ropes, but his rope will not be a foot too short. He will get things right wrong, and fit up his steam pipe out of one-inch pipe, and make his feed pipe out of four-inch pipe. He will cut a wide rubber belt four feet too short, but never four inches.

He will get on his two-thread gears to cut fourteen to the inch, but he will never get the fifteen-thread gears on. He will bore the taper hole in a piston wrong end to, but it will be a good hole and the right size. He will leave a monkey wrench inside of a steam cylinder when he puts the head on, but he won't leave any small stuff in there. He will do one of these outrageous things two or three times a year, and one of these blunders never teaches him to guard against the next. Between blunders, the blunderer is invariably all right. You can depend upon him. His blunders are so obvious that they will not pass into misfits. The blunderer never makes little mistakes, and the chronic "mistaker" never reaches the dignity of the blunderer. Give me the blunderer every time.

* * * * Another man is awfully cautious, careful and sure. It is painful to watch him. He calipers a fit, turns his work nearly to size, hesitates, doubts, and goes through the whole calipering process again.

When done, he will ache for a chance to try his work to see how it will fit. He measures everything twice and then isn't sure about it. These anxious men are never sure of anything. The more pains they take to assure themselves, the less sure they are. They have no confidence in themselves. No decision, no boldness. The thing grows on them, and they grope their way through life. When this man locks up his tool box at night he must always go back and put the key in the lock to see whether he locked it or not.

* * * * Another kind of a chip is the man who never becomes so preoccupied with a thing that he doubts details. He is a man of bold and decided action. He has self confidence enhanced by self confidence. Watch him caliper a job. He knocks his inside calipers with a motion that means something. They move an inch blow. The last hard blow is lighter, but decisive. Then come the gentle strokes, soft and delicate, but effective. Finally, he gets the fit, and when he does he leaves instanter. He has got all he came after. He goes to his lathe and sets his inside calipers, and when he gets them right he stops trying to see if they are right; he knows they are. Then he tries the job in the lathe. Good deal to come off. He gives the crank a pronounced turn and takes a big cut over the job. Does he hold his calipers in his hand, and think about the fit in the mean time? Not a bit of it. He starts his new cut, tries his calipers, and sees that he has the right size; lays the calipers down, and let's her go. His mind is now free. He don't wonder if his job is the size of his outsides; he don't wonder if his outsides are the size of the insides; he don't wonder if the insides are the size of the hole; he don't wonder if the "feel" in the hole was just about right; he don't wonder about anything. He *knows* what he has done. He will follow up his job with his calipers, and keep the thing turning straight, and, when done, he will lay the job aside, and don't care a cent who the first man is to try his work together. He don't know what relief is, because he don't know what anxiety is. There is no luck, or ill-luck, in the universe for him. A man who makes caliper fits with confidence holds the universe in his hands, and shapes his future with effective strokes. When he raises a sledge hammer, he hits where he intends to. He don't wonder where that hammer is coming down.

* * * * Another machinist is the mullet head. You call him a machinist, and he calls himself one, because he has worked at the trade about fifteen years. He has no skill, no pride, no taste, no knowledge, no judgment, no nothing.

He is too obtuse to reason with. He will do what you want done, if you can hammer it into his head what you want. If you can't do that, you had better give him some other job. He has no pride to shame, so there is no use talking to him. Inert matter becomes sentient and independent in this man's hands. You may pick out a three-quarter drill for him, but, sure as fate, it will drill a thirteen-sixteenths hole. He is stupid and ignorant, and that is all there is of it. If you set him to turning a grindstone, you must fix a ratchet on it, or it will be as apt to turn one way as the other.

This is the fellow who makes a swearing man of your Sunday-school superintendent. Swearing at such a man is a waste of talent. It ruins the swearer, and has no effect on the swearee. The man is out of place, and has chosen the wrong trade. Find a job more suitable for his abilities, such as tightening up fish bolts on a railroad. You can do nothing with such labor round a shop. If you pay him money enough to just support him in his mean, unambitious way, he still cannot give you value received.

* * * * Of all the bad things in the shop, the worst is the "clique." Workmen, foremen, superintendents, managers and proprietors, feel its baleful influence. There is but one way to circumvent a "clique," and that is to stamp out every man composing it. If you are superintendent, you owe it to your employer to see that no lack of unity exists, so far as your position is concerned. Use your authority justly and firmly. Give shelter to no vipers, and don't handle thistles with a tender hand. If there is an influence or an atmosphere which fails to co-operate with you in your duty, which clogs every movement you make, or which submits sullenly to fate, purify the thing at once. You fail in your duty to your superiors, if you permit the thing for any reason whatsoever. Put the question fairly, and discharge every man who hangs a lip. If one of the members of the "clique" is your superior, state your case to him and draw your pay. Be king; be a good king, deserve loyalty, and remove all disloyal influences.

* * * * I am studying about what kind of benches to put into the new North shop. I am sick of the usual things; they are too convenient to throw things under, for one thing, and I have about made up my mind to have them wainscotted, or sealed up, letting the bottom of the "sealing" drop back, say eight inches. The benches gotten up by Brown & Sharpe are the neatest I have ever seen, and look as though they had been studied over. I am prejudiced against drawers in benches. Our men will pile files in them, and do the files more damage than their regular use. Then they will throw in chipping chisels and hammers and wrenches and squares and soap and scrap iron and scrap brass and odd pipe fittings and sausages and sheet rubber, and I don't know what all. I am studying on a wall cupboard to take the place of the drawers, and if I succeed in getting up anything to suit my ideas of the proper thing, you shall hear of it. While I was visiting the shop of Brown & Sharpe, I mentioned my objections to drawers, and Mr. Viall, the superintendent, got the keys from the men and we made the grand rounds. Yale locks to start on—think of that, you who use padlocks!—and drawers that you could actually draw right open without any hammering or fussing. And when those drawers were opened, they looked as nice and clean inside as any apprentice's tool box. Here a neat clean sliding tray for scales and calipers and small tools generally; here a division for chisels, and here another one for files. These drawers didn't remind me of anything I had ever seen in a machine shop before, nor the men at work in the shop didn't either.

If they would let Wycoff have those drawers about a week, they would not recognize them, and would not want them back again. Oh, if I were only an artist, wouldn't I like to send you an interior view of one of Wycoff's bench drawers, just to show some of the boys the difference between machinists and machinists! * * * *

CHAPTER XXVIII.

PROCRASTINATION IN SHOPS.—INGRAHAM'S OPENING DAY.—MAKING REPAIRS.—SYSTEM AND ORGANIZATION.—SICK LATHES, AND HOW TO CURE THEM.—SHORT-WINDED PLANERS.—A POINT IN SACKETT'S SYSTEM.

* * * * How often, as we are engaged in our daily work, we find things wrong and make up our minds to make this thing or that thing right the first idle day, or when times get dull. And how often do we correct things when an idle day does come? Not once! I never was one to believe in the moral utility of rules or texts in a machine shop, but I believe a shop would not be a bad place to hang up a worsted motto bearing the golden words, " Now is the accepted time."

* * * * The owner or manager of a shop daily finds some detail out of gear, some big thing or some little thing. He thinks it ought to be fixed, but not now—some other time; and, as a consequence, it never does get fixed unless it happens to be one of those things which comes to a stoppage some day and has to be fixed. Then, of course, it is in a hurry, and gets cobbled instead of being fixed sure enough. Every man around a shop, ordinate and subordinate, experiences the same thing. Johnny, a two years' boy at a lathe, thinks it about time to tear the apron of his lathe to pieces and oil it up; but not now, wait till his job is done, then he will do it before he gets another job. Not much, Johnny. You will never fix that apron till it sticks and can't be worked, and then you will have to do it just when you don't want to, and when your judgment tells you the time can least be spared.

The foreman thinks the drill sockets are getting in

bad shape. They ought to be overhauled, but not now. When? When work becomes extra rushed and these same sockets get on a strike all at once; then is the time you will do it, and then is the time you will be too much rushed to half do it.

The superintendent thinks he will put a new foreman in the foundry, for he has found that a slight rush of work throws his present man off his balance, and reduces his capacity just when it should be enhanced. He is a nice man, and a good foreman within his small and inelastic field, but we are liable to emergencies, and this man must go. Not now, of course, but—when? When the emergency comes, and the foundry is driven, and the old man won't do, *then* the new man *must* come and enter upon new duties under the most unfavorable circumstances.

The stockholders say, "We must absorb the Toggle Works; they want to sell and we must soon find something to take the place of Harding's orders which are to leave us." But not now. Oh, no! We must wait till Harding has been gone a month and things look thin, and the Toggle Works, with eyes as good as ours, know how essential it is that we buy their business at their price.

* * * * It has been my fortune to be a hand on the opening day in several little shops, and right here my mind goes back to Ingraham's, and I must tell a story. Ingraham started a little shop away off out of the world. The inhabitants had never seen melted iron, or much of anything else, and he had things arranged to make his first heat an occasion of importance in the town. Grand announcement—flourish of trumpets—circulars of invitation to the best folks in town—lemonade—brass band—ice cream—raised seats for the ladies, and all such. The day came, so did the people. The fire had been lighted and the cupola charged. Ingraham superintended, and explained, and smiled acknowledgments of many congratulations.

But the iron wouldn't come down, and never did come down till the bottom was knocked out. Ingraham was a bachelor and could be confused sometimes, which may account for the iron being under the fuel.

* * * * But, aside from music and ice cream, I remember that shops within my experience were always started with the intention of fixing things better after the thing got moving, and I never saw anything fixed till a radical change became imperative. A lathe is speeded too fast. The proper pulley had not come, and the main shaft was ready to go up, so a larger pulley was put on to drive the lathe. Was the right pulley put on when it did come? Not much. It went into stock, and in two years some lathesman insisted on having that pulley changed, if he was to run the lathe and do lots of work.

Thick stuff gives out, and two-and-a-half inch stuff is used for a couple of vise benches—temporarily, of course, but they danced tools and work off for years, till Dennis himself happened to use one of the vises, and found out what the boys had to put up with.

There must be a foundation under that planer, of course; anybody would know that, but we can start it up, you know, and fix the foundations when the masons are here again. Yes, I know. Masons come and masons go, but that planer goes on for ever.

* * * * The only time to do things is when the consciousness that they are necessary arrives. When we have nothing else to do, we don't want to do things. That's human nature set to music in the Arkansas Traveler, and brought to mind each day in the shop. An excellent rule is, to do things right, and stop when they are done right, and the rule is justified by the simple fact that it is almost always cheaper.

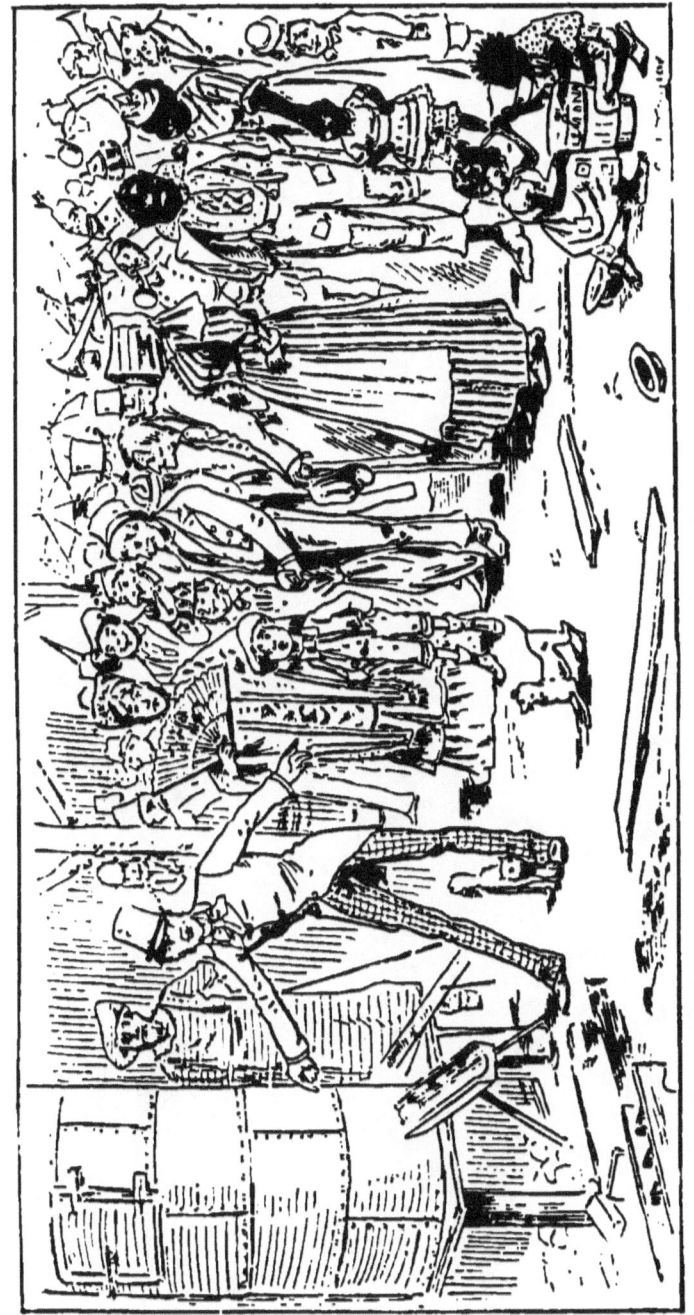

Ingraham superintended and explained, and smiled acknowledgments of many congratulations.—Page 238.

* * * * I have set up many engines, cutting and fitting every pipe, and I, at one time, was the worst slouch that ever did such work. My ambition seemed to be to get lines of pipe in position and get things started. If I had doubts of a pipe joint I would say to myself, "I guess that will do; if it won't, I will fix it." Soon every joint was made on the same plan. Of course, the doubt was only settled when steam was let on, and then the thing got "started" under a cloud of steam which would even prevent inspection. Then the whole thing had to be gone over. Common sense overtook me one day, and I changed my tactics, and settled all doubts about pipe joints when I made the joints. I saved time, money and good nature by the conversion.

* * * * If repairs are to be made, I think it cheaper to make them at once, even in a rush of business, than to await an idle day which we hope will never come. If a shop starts with loose joints, premature or temporary arrangements, or lack of system, it will run so till a new shop is built.

Few men have the foresight or money to provide for everything, but the omissions referred to are seldom dictated by economy or ignorance.

* * * * It is a notorious fact that a millwright will stay on one job as long as there are any inducements—social, political, financial, geographical, religious or otherwise—to do so. He only quits to go on a better job. This is a long and expensive way to reach good results, but we seldom find in a mill any temporary or shiftless executions of the original plan.

* * * * Tell a hap-hazard manager of system and organization, and you make him sick. He thinks you lay out more work for him than is involved in the regular business which your system is simply an adjunct of. The fact is, you tell him too many novel things at once, and he thinks all hands must quit real work and devote themselves to keeping your red tape chalk line straight.

Not so. System is not work, but is simply a law of action for reducing work. It does not require special executors, but permits few to accomplish much. It loads no man with labor, but lightens the labor of each by rigidly defining it. Hard work begins when system relaxes. System never, under any circumstances, interferes with variations in human action, but includes them. Elasticity is not a quality of system. Comprehensiveness is. System is the result of two rigid laws: a place for everything and everything in its place, and specific lines of duty for every man. The laws being written, understood and executed, lighten the responsibility of every man. In many shops half the things are everybody's business and never done; the others are nobody's business and half done.

Law without execution is no law, and in the shop we find empty law adds to illegal work.

Many shops let their system drop during the hard times, and when things are picking up they wonder why their capacity is so limited. I know one excellent shop which had a tip-top pattern system, in which there was a fixed responsibility for everything, and no dependence placed on the memory of any man. A stranger could enter the place and receive five minutes' instruction which would enable him to find any pattern of any piece of three hundred machines. Those instructions would be: "Each machine has a short symbol as shown on its drawings, and every piece has a number also shown. Each pattern or piece or scrap is stamped with the symbol and number. The pattern storeroom contains all patterns not in use or being repaired, and shelves are symbolized to correspond with their symbols. The pattern storeroom has a sign on the door."

With such instructions, a stranger could be given any drawing and asked for a piece shown thereon. He could bring it in ten minutes, even if totally unacquainted with the premises, providing the piece was at home. If he didn't find the pattern, he would find a slate telling him to call at foundry, or pattern shop, or at some malleable foundry a hundred miles away. A simple arrangement this, and it did not cost ten cents a year, and saved many dollars.

As simple and satisfactory plans pervaded foundry, machine shop, blacksmith shop, wood shop, boiler shop, storeroom, wareroom and office, and more work was done by less men with less hard work than one often sees.

* * * * But the man who organized this thing was wanted elsewhere, and went. He had been gone five years, and has organized another concern which has, within the last few weeks, had to buy a railroad to use up its earnings.

A few days ago I visited the first concern, and found that the organizer had carried away the statute books, and the system had gone to the bow-wows. There were patterns in the pattern room, in place and out of place, with marks and without marks. There were patterns stored in the pattern shop, in the drawing room, in the drawing vault, in the storeroom, and I don't know but elsewhere, and there were castings stored in the foundry, and casting room, and machine shop, and wareroom. There is no one man about the place who could find a piece of pattern or casting without a scientific search over the whole place, or an inquiry as to its whereabouts. The short cut, of course, would be to ask some one supposed to know, who would tell you, or send you to some one else who might know where the particular piece was. If some subordinate would get sick, the shop would kill him with business messages.

* * * * Few men can organize, and they do wrong if they fail to leave the law behind them. In the above case, the owners could say to a new executive officer, "Take this and maintain it." As it was, "this" had gone with its maker. I never heard of anything great being accomplished in productive, legal, military, naval or social art without organization, and I never knew organization to fail to result in economy. Of the detail of the law, and of examples of organization in shops in this country, I may write you hereafter.

* * * * Printed rules stuck up in a shop are objectionable and hurtful, because, instead of defining a man's duties, they dictate his conduct.

Monarchies exist on the ability of the educated few to dictate and enforce good conduct among the ignorant masses. Republics look to the self-dictated good conduct of the masses. Specific rules imply license beyond, and, as a consequence, monarchies don't dare to run a bell-rope through a railway train, or leave rules of conduct out of the shop.

If you want to elevate the morals of your shop and of republican citizens, cut the conduct clauses from your duty regulations, and kick every man out who has not sense enough to "conduct" himself. * * * *

If an unfortunate mortal finds his shop full of consumptive lathes, he immediately sets about remedying the matter, that is, if he has any competition in his business. Intelligent labor will double the product of a lathe, but such skill can work the same changes in a lathe having proper power, so something must be done with the machine itself. If the lathe is stiff enough to stand the racket, its power may be increased with very little trouble and with no expense. Inquiry will show that the fault is in the beltage of the cone. The proportion between belt velocity and cutting velocity is wrong. If the lathe is run slowly enough, there will appear to be power enough for the cut. This results from the increased velocity of the belt, but behold—the cut is too slow! It is known that the cutting tool will bear a velocity of twenty feet per minute, and here we have but, say, twelve, which means that forty per cent. of the lathesman's wages is wasted, and would be well invested in a better lathe. If, in this case, the speed of the countershaft be increased sixty per cent., the lathe will be found to have sufficient power at the proper speed, but it will also be found that the lathe will not do business at all satisfactorily upon its full swing or upon large diameters. This is bad, but is the best that can be done with such a lathe, for, owing to wrong design in the back gearing, the belt is incapable, under any circumstances, of doing the proper amount of work upon large diameters. The change in speed of countershaft costs only a change in line shaft pulleys, and makes what power the belt may have available for work, and within the new limits of swing, the lathe will yield an increase of product in a year, which will buy a new lathe and allow the old one to be strained through the cupola. As such cases are apt to occur in every shop, it might be well to give a mathematical rule here for changing the speed of the counter shaft, but experience tells me that formulas are terrifying in most shops—that is, the rank and file of the shops in the country. A trial based on a hint is better in many cases. It might be well to say, however, that the point of least power in all lathes, of whatever make, is when the belt is on the largest step of the lower cone. Lathes doing general shop work should be capable of work at the point of the tool, amounting to *not less* than thirty-five thousand foot pounds, and when the belt is on the large step below, it should be capable of transmitting somewhere near that amount of power.

The strain of a lathe belt will average forty-five pounds for each inch in width. The width of the belt in inches, multiplied by forty-five, gives its strain, and 35,000 divided by this strain gives the least velocity in feet per minute at which the belt should run, and also the surface velocity at which the small step of the upper cone should run. Its proper speed can then be found without trouble.

* * * * After the belt, the weak point in ill-constructed lathes is in the teeth upon the cone pinion, if this pinion is of cast iron, as is the case on cheap lathes, and in the teeth of the back gear wheel. The final or front gearing of lathes is rarely found too weak for their usual work. Once in a while a lathe can be found with a "lump" in its speeds, that is, it runs faster with the back gear in, than it did with the back gear out and the belt on the large step below. Many a man will run such a lathe a month before finding this fault, and will gravely change his belt to suit changes in size of work without noticing the effect. It's much like the man who wound his clock every night for fourteen years, before he found out that it was an eight day clock. In lathes of the triple-geared persuasion one may frequently find two of the aforesaid lumps in the speeds. Errors like these cost the shop owner money continually, and it is well for him that they are getting rare. Well-intending and well-established tool builders are not guilty of sending out such machines, the errors generally lying with those builders who copy other makers' tools and recklessly add some inspiration of their own, without re-calculating the whole thing; such, for instance, as adding a step to a properly designed cone, or changing the proportion in one pair of the back wheels. The speeds of a good lathe will increase in a geometrical ratio, giving the smallest variations for the largest work, and the power will be sufficient to tax a turning tool to its utmost.

* * * * Short windedness in a planer is as common as it is in small lathes. One seldom finds a large planer refusing its duty, but five out of ten small ones will positively refuse to carry a key seat tool three-eighths wide, with a thirty-second depth of cut. This chronic disability in planers is really more annoying than in the case of lathes, for there are generally fewer planers in the shop to appeal to in cases of emergency. If a small lathe will not hold a cut, we may put the job in a larger lathe, but in many shops there are no larger planers.

* * * * Talking about system, Sackett, one day, explained to me that he put work into a man's hands and got it done. His foreman never need concern himself about the matter. He himself, of course, had nothing to do with the man; the foreman was his boss; but the man had a duty which it was expected he would do without either prompting or officiousness.

* * * * When I commenced this letter I intended to tell you something of Sackett's plan, but I have wandered off. Some other day will do, and then I may tell you that when there is something to receive in Sackett's shop, there is a person to receive it, and when there is something to ship, it is somebody's easy duty to ship it, and when there is something to order, there is somebody to order it. A thing is not delayed on account of some factotum being harassed with a thousand duties, undefined but still accepted, and there is no vast army of loafers with a single duty.

Sackett's place is run with less men than any similar shop I ever saw, and each man has work enough to keep him employed without harassing him. No man complains of excessive burdens. One can work for Sackett in the daytime and sleep o' nights. If any man lays off to fish, or lies down to die, another man knows his work and no interruption ensues. I have known of patterns being made in a shop the second time, because some man who carried the whole shop in his head had gone into the army.

CHAPTER XXIX.

PAINT ON MACHINERY.—FUNCTIONAL MACHINES.—SHAFTING AND HANGERS.—A NEW WRINKLE IN SHAFTING.—A NEW TOOL WANTED.

* * * * I am studying up on the subject of paint, as it relates to machinery. We can all remember when all machinery had to be painted a grass green, and decorated, maybe, with stripes of more or less contrasting hues. The age of green paint was also the age of ornate curves and general elaborate design. Certain prominent machine builders commenced designing their machines on what I call the functional plan, that is: each element was treated as regarded its duty only; the form was such as was dictated by its functions only; lines of strength were placed in the lines of strain; and under no circumstances was a pleasing shape sought after, save such as resulted from an apparent adaptation of parts to their work, or what might be termed the harmony of utility. Utilitarianism in machine design ran so far, that simple machinery began to look complicated. Instead of soft blending lines, rigid protuberances became the order of the day, a thickness of metal having been determined upon, this thickness was maintained, and the exterior of a casting presented every little projection and complicated sinuosity which characterized the interior. Bosses were sharply developed, flanges stood out severely, and reinforcements were placed in plain view. The Whitworth machines are a fair sample of this class. American builders have followed, as far as they dared, but none would carry the idea out entirely. Philadelphia builders would design an engine lathe with every important part shaped to meet the essential requirements of function; they would abuse the privilege they had of making a thing ugly, but when they came to the legs of the lathe, they attempted to gather in the very sunlight of lighthearted beauty in design. A cultivated pedal taste is not to be violated even by a Philadelphian follower of Whitworth. Such designers left off all attempts at exterior neatness, because it was not essential to utility, and they left the striping off the green paint for the same reason.

Then came that happy thought, steel-colored paint, so called, because it had the color of raw steel. This color, on account of its light shade, developed shadows in all details, and brought every line into plain view. It unearthed errors in the surface of castings, and developed a higher grade of foundry skill, and, coincidently, brought to our notice the value of "filler."

* * * * Machines designed upon the functional plan meet the approval of all cultivated mechanics, men who have a discriminating judgment, and are capable of appreciating the rare beauties of purely functional adaptation. The machine builder who seeks his customers among such men will find peculiar satisfaction in his commercial success, and will receive the gratifying applause of his peers!

* * * * The thoughtless have been led to think that this severe and rigid construction is essentially cheap, because it looks cheap. The fact is that machinery designed on this plan is essentially expensive, and can never, under any conditions, compete in price with machines equally well constructed, but designed on the old composite plan.

The thoughtless adopt the functional plan, and design their machines accordingly; they leave off the painted stripes; they leave off the features they have been using solely for looks; they leave off the green paint, and attempt to get steel color, but find it has degenerated into a hideous, colorless blue; they send these machines among an uncultivated class of patrons and —lose their trade.

* * * * The average machine purchaser of the day is not a discriminating mechanic. He simply has need of a certain machine. He applies to Brown by letter, and places his order for a steam pump, perhaps. Brown used to finish his work nicely and well, and used to paint neatly and tastily. But he has got the fever, and gone into the function business without thinking who his customers are. He leaves off his nice finish, because he says it does not add to the utility of his steam pump. He leaves off his tasty painting, because it does not add to the utility of his steam pump. He leaves off the modulating lines, which, in having the same strength, involved a little more metal, because they did not add to the utility of his steam pump. I don't understand why he don't leave off the fraudulent, steel-colored paint, and let it go unpainted, for paint does not add a particle to the utility of his steam pump. The surfaces will rust and look bad, but the surfaces are not moving surfaces, and good looks will not add to the utility, etc. But one thing he soon finds out. Good looks add to the utility of the steam-pump *business*. Machine buyers are not foolish enough to "think the less of a jewel, because the casket which contains it is a beautiful one;" in fact, by the direction of their purchases, they show that they are foolish enough to prefer the beauty of appearance, even at some sacrifice of utility. Now Brown, as a builder of steam pumps, knows that it is a ticklish business. He knows that each steam-pump builder retains his customers by a very delicate tenure, and that they are prone to run after strange gods. He sends his ugly, functional steam pump to Smith, the purchaser. Smith is no cultivated mechanic, and knows nothing of pumps, steam or otherwise, but he knows a nice machine when he sees it, as every body does, you know; and when this pump reaches him he don't see one. He is not favorably impressed. The pump *may* do. That is the highest compliment he can pay it. Virtue in machinery, to be apparent to Smith, must be upon the outer surface. If this steam pump wins its way to Smith's favor it must be a good one, indeed, for it works against prejudice. If Smith had received an elegant machine, something made to *please* as well as to *do*, he would on its arrival unhesitatingly have taken the thing to his bosom, and have said to friends: This is a *good* machine. In that case, the pump must be a poor one, indeed, to fail, for it has a friend by its side, one who has committed himself in its favor, and who will not eat his words, if he can make them come true.

* * * * As a user, I would prefer machines designed on the functional plan. As a spectator, I would prefer to see them; as a builder, I would prefer to build them; as a seller, I would prefer to sell them. But as a builder of machines for others' use, I would prefer beauty enough to guard against neglect; as a seller whose business must leave out sentiment, I would have to sell machines, which would help to place themselves in the good graces of the average uncultivated buyer. Questions: Does a beauty of appearance, produced by what the world knows as paint, necessarily destroy or detract from the functional utility of a machine? Does the first impression which a purchaser forms of a machine add to or detract from the future opinion of the machine? Is the average machine buyer a cultivated mechanic, who can see merit, even through steel-colored paint, or is he a man who has the terms "nice" and "good" mixed in his mind? Because I paint my work with a view to please the average buyer, does it follow that the workmanship or the design of forms is less correct? If I turn out machines known by myself to be correct, how many long years of missionary labor must be expended in bringing my customers to that view of things? Won't a little exterior ornamentation help to place my really meritorious machines? Is not the paint cheaper than the missionary labor? If the real merit of design and workmanship goes with the paint, am I not doing as correct a thing as if I left the paint off? If I leave the paint off, and act as missionary, don't those who do paint, with or without merit under the paint, outsell me? And when my missionary labors are completed, don't my rivals step in and enjoy the fruits without the labor? Don't proper painting tend to cause the eye to wander all over a machine, and don't dead painting, steel color for instance, cause the eye to take in details separately? For that reason, don't I need to put a higher finish on details?. Does this higher finish on details add any more to the utility than paint on the general surface? Isn't this extra finish of details more expensive than the extra painting of the whole? What is the special virtue of steel-colored paint? Is steel-colored paint any longer steel-colored? Because one man has a well-established trade among cultivated mechanics, is it any reason why I, who sell to the aborigines, should build steel-colored, functional machines? My machinery being properly designed and constructed, and made for an uncultivated market—should I paint such machinery with a view to a pleasing effect in such market?

* * * * Some years ago—a good many, happily —if a man happened to have a line shaft, and found that his steam gauge must show twenty pounds before he could revolve the shaft, he thought little of it. When he put up the building, he put up the clumsy shaft with its common boxes bolted squarely up against posts. The shaft was put up in line, and if it staid so, well and good, and if it didn't stay so, well and good. But in course of time, people began to reduce the diameters of shafts and to increase their velocities, and in course of time it got so a man could revolve a long line shaft by hand, and finally the art improved to that state which requires a shaft in such nice shape that the merest trifle of force will turn it. Such a result is attained by making the shaft round, and straight, and small; by making pulleys light and in balance; and by making bearings in good style and in perfect line. It is immaterial what the form of the bearing is, so long as its wearing surface is in proper shape, and its bore in line with its neighbors. Experience with shafting developed the fact that it was easy to make a good box, but very difficult to get it into line, if of ordinary bolted box form, and that settling floors, etc., would soon disarrange all the fine adjustments. The first step towards a nice device was to arrange the boxes in a holder, so that the proper adjustment could be made by set screws. This rendered erection an easy matter, and allowed the boxes to be brought into general line, but it failed to provide for bringing every part of every box into collimation. That is, a true line might cut the axis of every box at some point of the box's length, but there was nothing to prevent the axis of each box assuming independent angles. The adjustment provided consisted of vertical and horizontal movements by screws, and the fault above referred to was obviated by designing the box in gimbal form, so that each box was universally self-adjusting, so far as its individual axis was concerned. Such boxes or hangers could be put up in a position of approximate accuracy, and then brought into line by means of the vertical and horizontal adjusting screws, great care being taken to deal with the axis of the box at the center of its length, or point of gimballing action. That being done, the balance of the box's length would attend to itself.

Such hangers have never been improved upon, and probably never will be. They contain erective and corrective adjustments and self-adjusting features, as far as attainable. But, along with the universal hanger, has come the idea that they are self-adjusting and may be put up recklessly. This is a grand mistake, for, while the universal movement will generally prevent corner or "cant" wear, it does not in the least reduce the general ill effects of general bad alignment, and there is no justification for putting such hangers up in bad shape, and no justification for omitting any of the facilities for adjustment. Some makers have adopted the ball-and-socket hanger on account of its peculiarly solid form, simplicity of structure and low cost, and it is often copied under the impression that it possesses all the virtues of the old gimbal hanger. When the ball-and-socket hanger is up and in line, it is the real equivalent of the gimbal hanger, but it lacks an important feature of convenience in erection and re-adjustment. The horizontal adjusting movement is omitted altogether, and a substitute found in sledge-hammer manipulations.

* * * * Speaking of line shafts, the Colt's Fire Arms Co., of Hartford, have something peculiar in the way of line shafts. There are many lines of many hundred feet, and all the shafts are twelve inches in diameter. The idea is to use no pulleys, but to run the belts directly upon the shaft. The speed of driven devices is arranged by using proper-sized receiving-pulleys. The shaft is of cast iron, very light, and is reduced to four inches at the bearings, which are about twelve feet apart. The shaft, or drum, is made in sections, each having an internal flange at each end. Each journal is in spool form—that is, it has a flange at each end, and these journal flanges are bolted to the drum flanges. There are no elastic features introduced, the whole being as rigid as possible. Where motion is transmitted from one line to another, pulleys are used, the hubs being bored to fit the drum, the same as if it was of the usual size. A pair of vertical engines drive the initial shaft, and the line shaft is caused to act as the crank shaft of the engines. Crank discs are placed on the ends of the line shaft, and receive motion directly from the engines. A line shaft, large enough to act as a driving pulley, will be a new idea to many, and will be apt at once to suggest criticism. It is evident that excellent intentions will sometimes fail, and that time will see many odd-sized pulleys strung upon this drum. Such pulleys might be called lagging. We, who are used to putting a belt on a dead pulley and then on the live one, will wonder how they get along without the privilege.

* * * * I wish to ask if an invention is not called for in the way of a good substantial, *adjustable* chuck-drill, if such qualities may possibly be combined. Chuck drills are generally made of flat steel or old files, and thus far nothing has been gotten up which will equal them in their peculiar capabilities.

Among agricultural implement makers it is the main tool. Their expert boring hands put these ugly looking drills through one-sided, rough-cored holes dead true, a hand reamer finishing the job.

* * * * I have noticed one queer thing about chuck drilling. In the agricultural shops, where the work is all rough, a green boy will be set to work at a chucking lathe, instructed a short time in this work, learns nothing else, and soon bores good, true holes without any appeal to luck. He never even finds out that his drills have a tendency to travel and run out. On the other hand, the fine lathesman, working on nice work, often uses these drills to follow cored holes or to cut from the solid, but he never, even by chance, succeeds in getting one to go through straight. He never seems to get the "swing" of the process. He never acknowledges this, however, and attempts to console himself by saying he only wanted to take the sand out and didn't care whether it ran true or not. It will always be found that such men set such a drill at work with good resolutions to have it go through truly, but the affair ends in good resolutions, and the drill soon goes on its winding way as usual.

CHAPTER XXX.

ELASTICITY OF WORKMEN.—HOW CHORDAL GOT BOUNCED. — A GLORIOUS MECHANICAL TRAMP. — RESURRECTING SHOPS.

* * * * Did you ever find that a lack of elasticity on the part of your workmen thwarted you in your good intentions? Have you not found out that even American workmen get into a certain habit and kick vigorously against any change? This kick always takes the form of contempt for the man suggesting the change. If you have ever received such kicks you have also given them. This stubborn grooviness, this lack of the exercise of reason, this conservatism of craft, is one thing present in some degree in all men, and its degree of absence represents the real degree of progress. A new foreman goes into a shop. He finds roughing cuts taken at a proper rate of feed, but he finds that the quick-finishing cut is unknown. No knowledge of tool surfacing by sliding cuts seems to exist. The wiry, rough tapering and changing surface of the fine feed is the standard for rough work, and these defects corrected by the file are the standard for nicer work. A smart foreman bounces this thing instanter, and he will have a hot time of it. He takes off his coat, grinds up broad-nosed tools and shoves clean, true cuts over work, but there is no smile of approval. No workman meets him half way. The results are new, and therefore unacceptable. This isn't always true, but I am speaking of the many cases where it is true. There are several reasons why the men don't rebound to the new suggestion. For one reason, they see a man claiming to show them something about their business. That hurts. For another reason, they are called on to see and acknowledge that another man's process produces better results than their own. That hurts. For another reason, it looks quicker. That hurts.

* * * * Our new foreman, having full power, may, if he chooses, override the prejudices of his conservative workmen, and force them to a good plan by the simple exercise of authority. But if our new foreman is smart, he will not do it that way, for he will be loosening the ground under him at the very start. He finds the men are good men, and he is a poor general indeed if he starts out by putting indignities upon them. He would humble their pride instead of enhancing it. If he takes the wrong tack, he can very easily increase the cost of the work, when the very opposite is his intention. If he gets one new man, an experienced broad-tool man, he can make these chappies ashamed of themselves, and effect the very object sought.

* * * * Such things come up every time a new foreman starts in. I have been on both sides of this business myself. I very well remember turning up a lot of circular saw arbors out of three-inch cold-rolled iron. They were about six feet long. Now, like every other country machinist, I had got it into my head that a saw arbor was a particularly nice job, and I also got it into my head that I could turn up a better one than the oldest man in America could.

To have a shaft so true that a sixty-inch saw, clamped between five inch collars, should run dead true, seemed to be an essential quality in saw arbors, just as though it was not as easy and proper to make a hundred other things just as true. Of course it would not do to turn this job end for end after trueing one journal. The thought that this would apply equally as well to all journaled jobs never occurred to me. These arbors had a five-eighth key seat cut between the journals. I had turned up lots of these arbors. It was my special prerogative. I guess I got them all right and nice and true. They were not turned in the body at all. The collar work was fitted up and the journals skimmed, that was all. No filing, all water cut. Four inches projection beyond the outer journal allowed this whole thing to be finished at one dogging. From my lathe these arbors went to a planer and had the key seats cut. Now anybody who knows much about cold-rolled iron can imagine what became of my fine true journals and collar faces. But I never imagined anything about it, and the foreman never did.

* * * * But one day a new foreman came. Eddy was his name. I don't know whether he ever saw a saw arbor before or not, but he was a thorough mechanic and knew more about saw arbors in a minute than I did in a week. I didn't look at it that way however just then. He brought around some of these arbor jobs, looked at them a minute or two, bit his lip a little, and then sent the jobs to the planer to have key seats cut in them before they went into the lathe.

I was in arms in a minute. This wasn't the way I had been doing the job. I claimed to have sense and reason and regard for people, but instead of co-operating with this man just when he needed it, and just when the co-operation of every man in the shop would be of real value to him, I grew morose, sullen, stubborn, defiant, and rebellious. I might state right here that Mr. Eddy showed a keen appreciation of these new and valuable qualities, and he proved it by giving the mutinous Chordal the grand and instantaneous "bounce." Eddy was a good mechanic, a good sort of a man, and all that, but he was a miserable general. He did not go and get one of my brag saw arbors in which the key seat had been planed after the lathe work was done. If he had, he might have shown me my elegant arbor sprung about a thirty-second. No lecture would have been needed; I think I could have seen the joke without a diagram. Eddy's good sense told him that saw arbors should be straight, that turning the job nicely would straighten it, that keyseating would spring it, and that it would be a wise plan to do the crooking part of the business before the straightening part was done. He comes and orders me to plane the keyseated piece as straight as possible, and then do the lathe work. He did'nt take the trouble to ease away my prejudices, so that I might be wiser and his path more smooth. He kicks one blockhead out and puts another blockhead in his place. It took me over two years to find out why Eddy changed the manner of making saw arbors, and during that two years I lived in ignorance, and he had my contempt. He failed in his obligations to his men when he omitted to educate me, in some roundabout and unsuspicious manner, up to the new standard. A foreman should be a general, but a machinist is not a soldier. He is, or ought to be, a skillful man. It should be: "know how to do," instead of "do this way." Eddy had no right to throw the burden of educating me in this special thing upon some other foreman. He had no right to let me pass through his fingers without my being wiser for having worked for him. He had no right to allow a mistaken contempt to rest in my mind. A workman has a claim on a foreman in the matter of the reason for certain operations of skill.

* * * * The cynic only knows no heroes. The dullest routine practice finds unknown somebodies who by bold originality have entitled themselves to that highest expression of praise, "better than I."

This constitutes fame. We who live in shops have our heroes too. Men who have done what we would die without having done. Men whom we can respect without envy. These are the men whose garments touch us daily. They are the heroes and examples of the shop.

One of the greatest of these, to me, was a certain quiet, dignified gentleman, called DeLow, whom I once mentioned to you. He was not the hero of an art, but was the hero of an artisan. He was simply a machine shop foreman, and was for twenty years before he died. His rarity entitles his name to mention, for few foremen so well understood the requirements or capabilities for good of their position. He was, in the "mechanical" sense of the term, a tramp. His life was not interwoven with any one shop. One day he said to me: "I know of no more pitiable subject than a foreman out of position after long years of narrow service in one shop. Gold in the shop he staid by so long, but the most inelastic lead in a new position. Nobody wants him. His usefulness is over, and if middle aged he calls his life a failure."

DeLow's usefulness was of the cosmopolitan order and instantly available.

He always worked for just eighteen hundred dollars a year, and would often refuse higher pay for positions as superintendent, manager, etc. He said: "I am a foreman machinist. My province is the machine shop, which I must *control*. I am responsible for the quality and cost of the work. Chapman with his little shop paid me $1800 when his own income as proprietor was less then $1200, but he showed his sense by employing me, odd as it may seem, for he never made five cents out of that shop before I went there. He offered me a half interest in the concern freely, but I declined, for proprietorship is not my profession."

* * * * I once became acquainted with the owners of a shop. They had a splendid field, a good plant, but wretched shop management. They were not mechanics and depended on some leading workman, having no executive ability whatever, for the running of the shop. They opened their hearts to me, and I suggested DeLow to them. They studied the thing over, multiplied his 1800 by all the digits, and finally sent for him. He came and conquered. Quietly but certainly revolutionized that concern, gave their work a reputation, increased their capacity two-fold without expense, made the thing *pay*.

But he only staid a year. He went to them and said he must be king in the shop. His position and prerogatives must be respected by both men and owners. They understood his motives and peculiarities, and concurred, but, on several occasions, had walked around "the dignity of his great office," so with the best of feeling all around he went elsewhere. He went to Wycoff's and staid a month; he went to Hunter's and didn't stay at all. He wanted more dignity than Hunter had to spare.

The peculiar fitness DeLow possessed for his profession, as he called it, would be hard to describe. All who employed him admired and respected him, and revere his memory to-day, for he was one of those men who, though our employes, make us feel that the world is better for their having lived in it. I have met machinists in twenty states who have worked for him, and all hold his memory in high regard, which is a rare thing to be said of a foreman who does his duty by his employers.

Many of these men say they are better workmen and manlier men after having worked for DeLow. I know that any man who worked a year for him is a more valuable and better paid machinist than before.

In the shop DeLow was firm and just, handled his men's self respect with the greatest and tenderest caution, if they had any. Building upon that quality he increased a man's usefulness. If the man lacked the quality of self-respect, he discharged him incontinently.

He gave man and apprentice the best work he could do, and paid him accordingly. If incompetent, he reduced the grade of work and pay. He kept a man in his proper place, leaving the choice of place to the man's capability.

He had wealth of resources for emergencies, but I never heard of his putting finger to work, never saw him touch a file or a hammer, and never saw him idle. He was the quiet and dignified physician of the machine shop's ills.

I knew him to resurrect two concerns, dead even to mortification.

* * * * Speaking of foremen; I hold my foreman responsible for every thing which passes him. I refer to moral responsibility of course. If a job is too poorly done or too well done— both are faults equally — I blame him. He cannot lay it to the workmen, for it is his business to see that his work is properly done by his men. He should work by inspection, not by faith.

Some men don't think work can be too well done. There is as much work done too well as too poorly.

There is work upon which refinement is wasted. I put up about two hundred sorghum mills one season. The requirements were well understood by my customers, by my foreman and myself, in spite of which, one lot was fitted up with the nicety of a Corliss valve gear. It made the mills cost more and made them not a whit better. My foreman laid it to the men, said they would work on a job long after it was done. I told him he could not shift the responsibility to the men. I ordered a certain thing of him, and, it being in his power to furnish it, he should do it. If he would work fine men on such work, he must stand the blame.

CHAPTER XXXI.

SUCCESSFUL THINGS THAT WON'T DO.—SCREWING-ON VERSUS CASTING-ON.—THE TEN-YEAR-OLD METHOD OF POLISHING.—MIGRATING WESTWARD.

* * * * When the lover of music allows his tastes to degenerate into a knowledge of art, he may bid farewell to the real pleasures of music. When he loses sight of music's high and only office, that of pleasing a natural sense, and sees in it only demonstrations of achievement, he leaves music and approaches art. He cares no longer for what is done. He asks how it is done and who did it. He looks for the signature of the producer, and has no ear for the sweetness of the product.

The painter and the critic bury their love of the beautiful under the distorting glass of a most terrible art. A souvenir of a master takes more value than a masterpiece without credentials. Authenticity in the signature becomes of more moment than merit in the work.

* * * * The blighting rigors of art and artists sometimes get into the shop. The name-plate on a machine will sometimes secure a respected tolerance and defence for the most pronounced failures, and often the meritorious offspring of some interloping nobody will quietly do the proper deed unhonored.

* * * * When we talk of educated mechanics, we mean men who know lots of things outside of their own experience. If they come from schools and colleges, they are well posted as to purity of design and propriety of movements. They know how things ought to be done, and they know how things ought not to be done. They know of applicable principles, and they know of things which won't do.

* * * * Sometimes these poor men, in their walks in the world, discover that the most successful things are those things which won't do, and they often find the proper thing a total failure. Such things make a man sick.

* * * * The most reprehensible bigotry is the bigotry of art, and next comes the bigotry of commerce. That good thing isn't good because *we* didn't make it, and this bad thing *is* good because *we* did make it.

* * * * If an artistic machine designer is of the bigoted kind, and the proprietors have a good share of commercial bigotry, their draughting-room is a nice place for a student.

* * * * A student under such circumstances, surrounded by smart but narrow men, will grow more ignorant every day. He absorbs home examples as types of the only correct form, and a departure from these home forms is the basis of his future criticisms.

The susceptible youth spends his young days in an atmosphere of self praise. His world is composed of "we," and the outside "they" are never studied. When this young man goes out into the world he don't meet "we" so often as he expected, and he finds the contemptible "they" all around him. He comes to the conclusion that the world is ignorant.

* * * * I was once wandering through a machine exhibition and had struck up an acquaintance with a party from Fitchburg. We stopped to examine a lathe made by the Niles Works. The exhibitor told us the tube was cast upon the tail stock, while all New England manufacturers screw them on. When together, the appearance is exactly the same, and there can be no difference in the value of the completed article. I have never been able to account for the Fitchburg man's wonder, and his expression, "I don't see why they don't screw them on."

* * * * We were admiring a Sellers' planer, and watching an Englishman who had evidently never seen one before. His mind evidently went back to the old screw planers, and traced the thing down to the present, for he finally said, "I see, now; they used to make them all screw; now they make them all nut."

* * * * The more cultured a mechanic becomes, and the more he travels, the more he sees of the sickening successes of bad things.

* * * * If we pick up a mechanical work of reference, we find complete detailed descriptions of machines which have a general air of correctness about them. They are placed in such books as types of advanced practice, and the experienced practical man will discover in many of these orthodox arrangements types of the most pronounced practical failures.

* * * * Maybe you don't know it, but I claim to be one of these critical mechanics myself. I know good work when I see it, and have tolerably fair ideas of forms. I like to see surfaces of good character and of proper proportion brought into good contact. I like to see things so shaped as to look right and proper, and I like to see good finish where finish is put. I don't like to see things look wrong all over, in design, workmanship, choice of material, and adaptation; and when I am forced to see them, whether I like it or not, I don't like to see them doing their intended work with a nicety and perfection which command the applause of every ignorant beholder. I see just such things every day.

* * * * Years ago there was gotten up, somewhere in this State, a portable engine for threshing purposes. It was simply known as the New York engine. From an intimate knowledge of this engine,

I feel justified in saying that from one end of the machine to the other there was not a detail which the cultured machinist would not criticise. The boiler wasn't calculated anyway at all; its bracing isn't what's called right; it seems to have none of the proportions the books tell of. The cylinder seems wrong for the boiler, and the ports seem wrong for the cylinder, and the valve seems wrong for the ports, and the eccentric seems wrong for the valve. The piston-rod is held in the cross head, and has been held in there for years by a plan which won't hold it, you know. The connecting rod is one of these things which won't do at all. The main brasses are bored castings dropped rough into the iron pedestals. This won't do, of course; no formula will fit the fly-wheel, so, of course, the fly-wheel is wrong, and all the formulas you can find will twist the main shaft off as soon as the engine starts.

I have seen much of portable engines, and I give it as my opinion that this same engine is the most excellent and successful engine in the market—an opinion which I feel corroborated by the hard solid fact, that the most successful portable engine-builders in the country to-day are those ten or fifteen men who have copied this engine outright, or with some slight variations in keeping with the general make-up of the engine. Among the sensible copyists, I know two or three who have no respect whatever for the engine they build, but whose success they are bound to respect.

* * * * Many a machine builder of high degree, finds that the real hard work of his life is to battle against the successful things which won't do.

* * * * The machine designer, when he gets cornered, always has a number of plans on hand which are not acceptable. He will say, I can do it this way, but this is no way to do it. I can do it that way, but

I once saw a ten-year-old Nigger boy finishing flat-irons on an emery wheel.—Page 272.

that's wrong. I can do it this way, but it would be absurd. I can do it that way, but I don't want to. Such cases produce dyspepsia and baldness.

* * * Sometimes the same man is disposed to make use of some simple contrivance, which, by some reckless springing of parts or imperfection of movement, will do the very thing he wants. The Yankees, I believe, call this manslaughter, and understand its value in a pinch.

* * * There are devices which will not stand critical analysis at all, but experience shows them to be of the utmost utility. Of this character is the link motion of a locomotive. We can never hope to find such another perfect success of such an imperfect principle.

Another case is found in the running-gear of a buggy or other vehicle. Not a torsion joint about the perfect thing, and flexibility is essential.

* * * Returning again to the trammels of art, did you ever notice what queer notions some machinists have about finish? They don't seem to care so much about the thing when it's done, as they do about the plan of doing it. In railroad shops some one man is always harping on file finish. I have worked in more than one of these shops, and I have never yet seen one of these men who could put a finish on a job with a file. The most he can do is to file a job in good shape to be finished.

This thing of getting the scratches tolerably shallow and very parallel, and then calling the surface a finished one, won't do in these days when we see good finish every day.

A finished job is a polished job. If it's a polish without proper surface under it, it don't look well; and if it has good surface without proper polish on it, it don't look well. A highly finished surface always has a high polish, and machinists condemn it because they can't do it. I like to see a well finished and highly polished surface, and it's nothing to me whether it was done with a rasp, or a file, or a grindstone, or a belt, or grit wheel, or what not.

I have never seen any good polishing which was not done by a wheel or some such rig. I have heard lots of blowing about hand finishing, but I never saw any of the finish worth blowing about.

I once saw a ten year old nigger boy finishing flat irons on an emery wheel, and he was doing work a thousand per cent. nicer and better than anything I ever saw done at a vise.

* * * * For the benefit of Eastern workmen, who may seek work in the West, I will give a point or two which I have picked up since I have been out here. If you come with a pocket-full of testimonials and recommendations, you can't get a job. If you set yourself up for a genius, you can't get a job. If you sneer at the Western style, you can't hold a job. If you go to bragging, you can't stay in a shop. Bosses don't want to hear what you did in Jericho, but want you to dry up and show what you can do in Rome. Simply coming from the East won't make you a lieutenant general in the West. The most useless machinists that have ever got into some of these Western shops are crack men from the East. If they were good men, they too often get disgusted, then dispirited, and finally sink to the level of the worst around them. If they were bad, they get worse. Good hard-headed manliness, combined with good horse sense and tip-top skill, will win every time among these shops. Don't brag what you can do, but show what you can do. Don't assume that you are a better man than another, but try and prove it to *yourself*. Don't let on that you miss the facilities you were brought up on, but gradually learn the new way, without ever forgetting the old way. You may be the happy means of improving the shop you work in, but you can't do it by bluster. You must do it by nice management. If you are a skilled man, you ought to learn how to manage your skill before going into strange countries. If you don't, you will bring discredit on your native place. Bear in mind, that in going West, you go among the smartest and crudest workmen in the world. The minute you set foot in their land, you will find them doing a thousand things you don't know how to do, and would be ashamed to do if you did know how; but you have got to do it, nevertheless, and the men who employ you will be glad when you improve your surroundings. If you could not do well East, you will starve West, and if you did well East, you can do better West; above all things, let your superiority assert itself <u>without the aid of "blowing"</u> from you.

CHAPTER XXXII.

SETTLING MECHANICAL DISPUTES.—ADVANTAGES OF HAVING NO FOUNDRY.—MECHANICAL QUIXOTISM.—FORGES AND SHELVES FOR THE NORTH SHOP.—THE STEAM ENGINE INDICATOR.

* * * * Our craft must often prove a law unto itself, for every few days some little thing turns up in business which would puzzle the highest kind of a joint commission. Machinists are, of course, governed by law, just like common folks, but a man who tries to do business with the statutes as his sole guide would soon find he had no business to do. Business men can't afford to quarrel, leastwise among themselves.

The metropolitan boards of trade settle more real differences than the metropolitan courts do, and it has often occurred to me that such a board would be a handy thing around machine shops.

* * * * I am not what the world calls a "kicker," but it seems to me I am called on too often to pay unjust bills. I have no foundry, and get my castings from foundries best prepared to do the work. I thus avoid the necessity of getting blast furnace and such heavy work out of a brass foundry, or its equivalent, as I should do if I tried to combine the whole art of founding under my own shop-roof. This plan of having no foundry is immensely satisfactory in many ways. I can get common castings on short notice any day of the week. I can get heavy castings and light castings, hard castings, or soft ones, gray iron, or cold blast, or brass from shops better fixed for each particular kind of work than I would be the day before I was ready to die.

* * * * If I had my own foundry, I could charge to ill luck, or bad management, many of the little and big things which now come up between my contractors and myself.

* * * * For instance, some time ago I was building a lot of nail machines. You never saw better patterns than were made for this job. The patterns were black, as usual, and every core-print, or stopping-piece was yellow, to show that a part required attention in some way. Every pattern was numbered, and every core-box was numbered to correspond.

One piece of these nail machines weighs about eighty pounds, and has a large, square slot cored through it. Twenty of these machines were under way, and these pieces had progressed but little, when it was discovered that the slot-core had been left out, and the prints cast on. I sent the castings back to Brown's foundry, charged him with these castings which he had been credited with, and also sent him a bill for the work I had put on the castings before I discovered the blunder. Brown came over with the bill, hopping mad. First, he said the castings were all right; then he said the patterns, were wrong, and it was my fault; then he said it was his mistake, and that he would make new castings, and pay for the cigars besides, and charge the cigars against the moulder's wages; but he would be eternally every thing under heavened, if he would pay my bill for work done on the castings. He said that I had accepted the castings, and that he was entirely too liberal in taking them back at all; that I was a smart machinist to allow my men to weigh up castings, and then do forty dollars worth of work on them before seeing that they wouldn't do; said he would pay for his mistake, but not for mine. I toned him down somewhat by saying, that all castings coming from him were weighed up to his credit, on his reputation. They might send castings of the core-boxes for all I knew or cared, or they might send somebody else's castings.

Then Brown took the ground that if I had a foundry myself, these mistakes would occur just the same, and I would have to stand the expense of new castings, and now I wanted to shove the thing off on him. I suggested that I didn't keep a foundry for that very reason. His was the foundry, and his the gain by good luck, and his the loss by bad luck. Then we both decided that this was getting off the track. The question was not one of replacing bad castings, but of paying for work misplaced through what I had to acknowledge was my own oversight, if not my real fault. I don't know what will become of my bill.

* * * * Another case: I wanted three big shells cast; they were made by Walker, swept up in loam, he furnishing sweeps and working to dimensions given in the order. The order read "three shells, eight feet long, forty-nine inches outside diameter, and as thin as can be cast. Thickness not to exceed three-quarters of an inch." My estimate had been based on a thickness of three quarters, and Walker's price was five cents per pound. When the shells came, the weight ran away above my estimate, and inspection showed them to be an inch thick at the thinnest part. One of the shells proved unsound, and another was ordered and came—*five-eighths thick.* I figured up and docked Walker's bill fifty-five dollars. I suppose there will be a row over this matter, too. I don't think Walker would have been justified in sending me castings two inches thick. Why? Because I wanted thin castings, and ordered thin castings, and his sending me one shell five-eighths thick, showed that my order could be filled.

* * * * The cause for growling is as often on the side of the foundryman. I know a case in point and a very plain one, too.

Bennett was building a hydrostatic press for compresing coal slack. The pressure applied was six thousand pounds per square inch. He used a pump cast from ordinary iron in his own foundry. The pump burst as soon as the ram felt full pressure. Then Bennett strengthened the pattern where the pump broke, and cast another from common iron. Burst instanter on reaching full pressure. Then one was cast from cold blast iron. Burst instanter. Then he boxed up the pattern and sent it to Luke & Matthews' brass foundry. Back came a nice brass casting weighing about forty pounds. It was fitted up and put on, and it burst as the others had done. They sent the casting back, and then overhauled the whole construction of the pump, and found a defect in design. Bennett cast a new pump of common iron, and everything was lovely. It would stand ten thousand pounds per square inch, probably, without bursting. Pretty soon, Luke & Matthews sent bill for the brass casting, twelve dollars and sixty cents, less the value of the metal in this identical casting when it was returned. Did Bennett pay this bill? Not any to speak of. He indorsed it "casting good for nothing," and sent it back. Then Luke went over, and very justly got on his ear. He had furnished exactly what was ordered, to wit, a perfect casting from the pattern furnished. The faulty design of the thing was no fault of his. Bennett said the pump wasn't good for anything, and he would't pay for it, not even for the metal turned off it. Luke said he wasn't talking about any pump; he wanted pay for a good brass casting furnished as per order. I don't think Luke & Matthews ever got their money. Any jury would of course have allowed the bill, but it don't pay business men to appeal to juries. In business, mutual good will is often worth more than legal rights, and principle almost always has to give way to policy.

* * * * How far the machine shop proprietor is to use discretion is another vexed question.

If a man orders a certain thing of me, which thing my own sense tells me won't do what he expects to do, am I to tell him so, and suggest more economical equivalents, or am I to deny all relationship with my brothers and execute his order, knowing that in the end it will have to be done over again, whereby I make more money and my workmen get more work? If you have a friend who appears thirsty for reputation, and don't seem to care what turn the reputation takes, just tell him to go into any business, and be square, honest and open with customers. His reputation as a fool will surely come. If he by a miracle succeeds in business, he will be held up as an example to young men.

* * * * There are in this world a class of machine men possessing high views, noble ambitions, and an unbounded pride in their art. Their mechanical ambition takes form in construction, executed on honor. They take no sordid view of craft; a balance sheet is simply a vulgar, incidental necessity. Everything they do represents progress. They set the copy for the world. They dive deep into research and greenbacks and bring up data, which add to the perfection of their product, and to their reputation as leaders in their trade. This data, or knowledge, or whatever else you may call it, is their contribution to an admiring public. The admiring public buy their product, only so long as they will compete in price with others using the same data, free of cost of getting, and no longer. Give such a shop an order for a job based on certain requirements. They estimate the price on a plan of execution which their ready invention has already contrived. The contract is closed and the work commenced. A new plan opens up and is executed at double the proposed cost. You pay the same as contracted for. The thing delivered has, say, ten times the capacity of the thing proposed. The constructors, in their noble pride, have far exceeded themselves, and have had no thought of the contemptible contract price.

* * * * This thing can only go on a certain number of years before the fact develops itself, that the candle burns away at one end and don't grow at the other.

The remedy is to put a partition across the shop; do high and mighty and lofty and admirable execution on one side, the wick side of the partition; and do ordinary machine work on the other side. Leave sordidness behind when you go on one side, and leave pride and high aims behind when you go on the other side. The candle won't grow any shorter, and it won't grow any longer, either.

* * * * To increase the length of the candle, extinguish the lighted end, and live and die in darkness.

* * * * The chief end of some lives is to accumulate gross tallow, to accomplish which they will begrudge the little grease imperatively required to lubricate the wheels of life. There are other lives absorbed in watching, and bettering the process of dry distillation which illumines the paths along which the whole world moves in safety and pleasure.

* * * * I never go into heroics. You and I have hundreds of friends engaged in changing dull and heavy material into moving mechanism, a process akin to the creation of life, in which it differs vastly from ordinary trade and commerce. The two tendencies I speak of are obtrusively present, or ought to be, in the experience of every shop owner in the world.

In many cases the tending forces counter each other, and the results are *nil*. This is the worst that can possibly happen.

* * * * I am figuring on the forges for the north shop, and am debating whether to put in good iron forges with hoods and stacks, leaving a clear floor, or to build up with brick, as usual. My experience is, that it takes more iron work to tie a brick forge together properly, than it does to build a good iron forge entire.

* * * * Question: Is it possible for a blacksmith to do good blacksmithing, if the inevitable little brick shelves, caused by the narrowing of the chimney walls, are absent? Where on earth would he lay his chalk, and his matches, and dressed and undressed tools, and his miserable little lead-pencil, and his better-looking slate-pencil, and his rule, and his soap, and the numerous odd little scraps of steel he saves for some unknown and unknowable purpose, and the hardy which he knows can't be mended, but which he hates to throw away?

* * * * I have some very unorthodox views of the steam-engine indicator. It has two functions: one in the hands of the engine tender to allow him to keep his valve motion at its best practical point, spite of adjustment and wear; and the second in the hands of the expert to allow him to study on the action of steam. Its first function it performs in a perfectly satisfactory manner, and in the second also, perhaps, though that question is now being pretty well overhauled. Experts decry the use of the indicator in the hands of engine men—think the art will become degraded, etc. Not a bit of danger. An engineer, with skill enough to give a fifty-horse engine proper attention, can use indicators for the purpose specified as well as any expert living, after he has learned the simple trade (for it's nothing but a trade) of taking diagrams, and these diagrams will tell him just what he wants to know. But there he stops. The scale, the logarithms, the hyperbolic lines, and isothermal lines, and adiabatic lines, and doubtful tables of density—these belong exclusively to the expert, who, if he doubts the accuracy of the cards taken by the engine man, may make others for himself with more delicate instruments. If the engine man happens to be an expert himself, so much the better. I believe indicators should be permanently attached to every engine of considerable size, and that the tender should be skilled in their use. This might be bad for experts, but would exalt their calling, which seems to be what they want.

I saw a couple of cards taken from a high class engine in New York or Boston, I forget which, by Mr. Bacon. The first was fearful, and must have suggested to Mr. Bacon danger of a coal famine. The second was after the valves had been set where they belonged, and was a beauty. I don't know how much figuring was done on these cards, but a good engine tender would have looked upon them simply as an indication that his valve motion was off. The makers of first-class engines adjust them by indicator to the best practical conditions, and the engineer could, with a model card in his hat, keep it so forever, if he had indicators.

The common plan is to let bankruptcy approach, and then send for a scientific expert to do purely mechanical labor on the engine—labor which should have been done a week after the engine started, instead of two years after. * * * *

CHAPTER XXXIII.

OLD CASTINGS IN THE SHOP.—HOW NEW TOOLS ARE SUGGESTED.—HOW THEY OUGHT TO BE.—COMBINATION MACHINES.

* * * * If great care is not constantly exercised, castings will accumulate around a shop. There are odd castings cast too often, castings acting as monuments of error, or of folly, and stock castings made from "old style" patterns, and therefore useless. Inventory after inventory sees these castings weighed up at standard price when, in fact, they are only worth the market price of scrap. They will get the best of any shop, if not systematically kept down to zero. Not weeded, mind you, but destroyed root and branch.

It looks hard, and will cause pangs, but I unhesitatingly declare it to be the most economical plan to melt up every pound of casting not standard to-day. If the design of a machine is changed to-day, melt up those castings which ceased to-day to be standard. Odd castings always block the entry port against economical and labor-saving system. If a customer wants a casting, he will pay for pattern and casting, but if you succeed in finding something approximate, he will pay you for the casting, but never a cent for the valuable time consumed in hunting it up.

* * * * The practice of littering the shop up with useless scrap is not confined to rough-and-tumble shops in the country. The finest tool and locomotive shops sometimes take the disease, and if it is not checked it will invariably prove fatal. Parts of machines which are found defective will always be useless, and are not worth a day's shop-room. Tons of such stuff can be found in many fine shops. Damaged tools are steel scrap and nothing else. They have no proper place as items in an account of stock.

* * * * Another tip-top thing to melt up is an old lathe, or planer, or drill press. It is not a good plan to save such tools in remembrance of the good they have done.

Many a shop starts up with good, fresh tools adapted to do the work of the age. Time runs on; lots of good work is done; lots of money is made; and the tools are wearing out.

New and enterprising builders succeed in changing the character of popular demand, and the old shops often find that, in spite of a splendid past record, their products won't suit the buyers of to-day. They condemn this new generation of buyers, and finally, in self-defence, are compelled to change the style of their products to suit the unreasonable demand, and then they find that their ancient tools, while well adapted to the ancient product, are totally inadequate to the new requirements.

* * * * I say they find such to be the case, but I doubt the general correctness of the statement. They only find that the trade seems to have absorbed new tricks which they fail to get hold of. They are proud of their old skill, and look upon a lathe as a lathe, and a planer as a planer, and having lots of them they don't see through things. The competitive price list bothers them, and they gradually fall into the belief that the new race of machine men conduct business on a reckless and unjustifiable basis.

* * * * A lathe is a standard staple machine, always designed for the same general range of work, but at the same time the ancient lathe is a much different tool from a modern one. A modern lathe too much played out cannot do the work of a lathe in good shape. Old tools tend to make old workmen out of new men, not in skill but in habit.

* * * * When a boy starts at the trade, he buys a four-inch scale or rule and carries it in his pocket. In five years' time he gets much good out of this nice little tool, but gradually and surely it is playing out. The corners get rounded off, it gets red rust on it and he wipes it off; it gets black rust on it and he polishes it off. This trick soon gets away with the lines and figures. He still sticks to this old scale, and his other little tools will be treated in the same manner. If a scale be used up, it is not as good as a good one. If the end of a scale be squared off on a grindstone to bring the corners up square, it is not as good as a good one. If a scale be used for blocking in the tool post, or under planer jobs, it will not long stay as good as a good one.

* * * * Now the honest fact is, and few workmen seem to find it out, that a four-inch scale and all such tools are articles of consumption. They should be replaced with new ones as soon as their decay becomes well set in. A four-inch scale should not be kept out of use to make it last longer, and it should not be kept in use after its time is out. Such a tool should be thrown away every six months and a new one got in its place. The expense of such renewals is the merest trifle, and it is well justified by the fact that it lets one use good tools and use them plentifully.

* * * * This principle holds good with lathes as well as with scales. Other things being equal, the new shop with new tools will generally scoop the old shop with old tools; and other things being equal, the old shop which is prompt in getting new tools, will generally scoop the old shop which thinks it can get along with tools whose good record belongs to past ages.

There is time to invest good dollars in good machine tools, and there is a proper time to throw these same tools into the scrap pile and make good castings of them. It don't pay to belt them up in some corner and use them for special work. It don't pay to make bolt cutters, or horizontal drilling machines, or polishing machines, out of them. They should be got out of the shop entirely. Their very existence on the premises exerts a bad influence, which is simply one element in a concomitant system.

* * * * At one time in my life, I formed the habit of sorting things out of the pile of scrap iron, laying aside such as I thought would work in some job some day. The "sorted" pile became the largest, and when some job would come along, which seemed to call for some of my pet cullings, I would tell Gus to wait a minute till I went out and got just the thing we wanted. Then commenced a search. "Am sure it's there. Saw it not over a year ago. Here, Bill and Mike, tear open that scrap pile." Soon I find it. "Told you so; it don't look as big as I thought, but I guess we can make it do." I figure on the thing, and finally take it to Gus with his orders. When the job is done it is a patched job, and weighs six pounds. Castings at five cents make thirty cents as the value of the piece finished from the scrap pile. Let's see what it cost. Gus loafed an hour, and the men worked an hour on the pile, and Gus worked two extra hours trying to adapt the unlucky "find," and I staid by the job two hours extra. That makes a dollar and seventy cents as the cost of that chunk, for which I can only charge forty cents in the rough, for our shop is a jobbing shop, and the bill is made for the rough casting and for Gus' time only. Chunks of iron culled from the scrap pile generally require an amount of superintendence, which raises their cost to quadruple the cost of new castings from the foundry. Experience has converted me often, and now I refuse to abide on the premises while a "select" scrap exists.

* * * * Is there a machinist living who cannot picture to himself the foreman hunting for a casting —the occupied shamble over the interfering pile, the peculiar expression of conscious memory, combined with a half-despairing look of puzzled disappointment, and, above all, the inevitable, loose-jointed, dirty two foot rule? * * *

* * * * Every once in a while we see something made of wood, which has a shape entirely different from anything we have ever seen before. It won't be long after this peculiar shape reaches public view, before some manufacturer of wood-working machinery is offering a machine to produce that new shape in wood.

This manufacturer does not build the machine to order, nor does he design it at the earnest solicitation of half a dozen men who have noticed the pressing need. He gets no orders, no inquiries, no hints, till the machine is in the market. If machine manufacturers waited till there was a demand for a new form of machine, they would do little in the way of advance.

* * * * As a general thing, the machine buyer is a man who don't know what he wants. He goes into the market to find out what he needs, or he acts on the suggestion of some seller, who looks into his place and guesses his wants. The country grocer may go to town to buy a heavy butcher knife to cut plug tobacco with, and may come back with a regular tobacco-cutting machine, made for the purpose, though he may never have dreamed there was such a machine. If his demand for it had determined when it should be put in the market, he would never have seen it.

* * * * Of course, almost any observant machine builder can see something every day, which he knows he can build a machine to produce, but judgment steps in and tells him it won't pay to build the machine. Men get picked up on too hasty action in just such things as these. The idea of a machine strikes them, and forthwith they scheme the plan, and build the machine, and put it in the market; and then they often find the market don't want the machine. It is a question of good judgment entirely, for there is no guide whatever. There is no such thing as an ante-production test. Many machines gotten up in a routine sort of a manner have proved happy and profitable hits, and many other machines, deliberately planned to fill an obvious vacancy have fallen flat. One of the fine points, in machine-making management, is to know when to get up a new machine and when not to.

* * * * Woodworking machine builders are a hundred times more progressive than builders of machine tools. With all possible respect for our many advanced tool builders, whose names I might mention, I feel justified in saying that it is very seldom that one of them brings out a new tool. There are two causes which lead to the new tool being brought out: one is, that they need just such a thing in their own shop, and the other is that some customer ordered them to get it up. When it comes to looking around to see what is needed, the machine-tool builder does precious little of it.

* * * I don't believe that the idea of getting up a lathe on purpose to turn car axles ever originated in the brain of a machine-tool builder. Some railroad men were probably looking around for a tip-top lathe for the work, and that suggested the whole thing. I can't imagine a machine-tool builder watching a common lathe turn axles, and then drawing the conclusion that a properly devised axle lathe would be a good thing to put in the market.

The average machine-tool builder will travel all over the country and watch every kind of metal industry, and never take a single hint. He will watch the agricultural implement industry. He sees work done in the most impossible manner, and hears a continuous prayer for better methods. He watches the portable engine business, and sees cylinders bored in a lathe, and sees connecting-rod bodies and straps worked on planers and shapers, and sees cylinders drilled as usual and tapped by hand. Then in the steam-pump shops he sees cylinders bored in lathes, and sees the same old drilling and tapping. He sees that this work is extensively carried on, that it is regular manufacturing on a large scale, but he never draws a conclusion. He would be most happy indeed to build anything these folks are kind enough to come and order; but building and offering some new machine, which they can't afford to do without, never seems to occur to him.

* * * * Steam-pump men and portable-engine men would break their necks reaching for a good machine to drill and tap their cylinders. If they want such a thing they must invent it, design it, and go to a machine-tool shop and have the thing criticised as a machine not properly gotten up.

The machine-tool shops don't do any cylinder tapping, and, as a consequence, will never originate a machine for the work. A machine-tool builder don't have much taper keyseating to do if he understands his business, and, as a consequence, he will never bring out the little machine needed for that work in nearly every shop in the country.

* * * * One of the modern frauds in machine construction is the combination machine—a machine combining within itself the capacity for doing the work of two classes of machines. Such combinations are apt to involve opposing features of sufficient and insufficient strength. Some years ago, some party put a combined lathe and milling machine on the market. It was a common lathe with a milling machine built on the left hand end. The combination consisted in using the lathe arbor for the milling-machine spindle, and vice versa. When you did lathe work the milling machine was idle; and when you did milling, the lathe was idle. When you used one machine, you were working on an investment nearly large enough to get two full-blooded machines instead of one mongrel. Such a combination is bound to make a very poor average of speeds, strengths and movements, and you have to get a combined sort of workman to run it.

* * * * Some combined or universal machines are made comprehensive enough to turn clothes pins in the winter, and do brick work in the summer.

The changes in capacity and nature are often made by adding separate fixtures, which are laid away when not in use. Aside from the main fault, this involves several bad things. The machine is not ready for business just when it is wanted. On miscellaneous work this is a grave fault. You only want a certain operation carried on for a few minutes, maybe, and if you can't get it when you want it, you don't want it at all. How often we see some man take some trifling job to a machine, and, finding the belt broken, or things gummed up generally, finally finish it by hand, or by some other foreign process!

* * * * In some universal machines, the time required to rig up some converting part of it is more than would be required to do the job without the machine.

It is in the nature of a workman to hate to fuss with something extra, when he would rather be doing something on the job in hand. How often we see a lathesman working on a job bolted to a face plate in an insecure and shaky manner. If he takes a big cut, the whole thing will tumble down, and he knows it. He could stop and rechuck his job, and go into it for all it is worth, but he don't want to. He prefers to take tender, nibbling cuts on the uncertain thing, because he is *cutting iron all the time.*

* * * * Odd fixtures and attachments lying around the shop are never in condition to use. They get dirty, and jammed, and broken, and in many cases they are remodeled to use for something else. Every machinist knows what sort of a thing an odd compound lathe rest is, and he knows what becomes of the two-jaw chuck, which is only wanted once a year. When the year comes around, and you take a look at the chuck, you conclude that you don't want it at all. The common steady rest is a fair sample of neglect from inconstant use. Planer centers in the country shop furnish another sample.

A combined slotter and drilling machine makes a happy family. If both are efficient tools, the combination is too expensive for a tool which can only do the day work of one machine. The most likely thing in such a combination is, that the slotter will become weak and the drill clumsy.

* * * * Some inventor filed an application in the patent office for a patent on a combined washing machine and churn. The thing made the rounds of the rooms, and each examiner indorsed his opinion on the document. One examiner wrote as follows: "You may clean out and scald this churn if you will, but the smell of the linen will hang round it still."

* * * * The greatest and main objection to universal machines is the idle investment and great cost of short jobs on them. In a machine with, say, twelve capacities, you invest the price of about six machines, and really get the ten hour use of but one.

In household implements, not running at a continual expense, and in which you change the function by grabbing the other end, a universal combination seems proper. It saves search after many separate utensils, saves room, and saves expense; but as soon as an implement gets into continuous motion, under the charge of a paid attendant, the combination feature seems to be a mistaken virtue.

CHAPTER XXXIV.

ARRANGING MACHINE SHOP FLOORS.—METHODS OF FINISHING WORK.—OUR ARTIST SKETCHES A COMMON BOILER FRONT.

What do you know about machine shop floors? When the good manager builds his shop, he shows on a plan the proposed position of every machine. Maybe he don't intend to get these machines right away, but he makes his calculations for them, and when they do come, he can put them in a place reserved for them.

But one thing he cannot do, and that is to put in all his foundations before his floors are laid. No man living can predicate a foundation for a lathe, or a planer, or any other machine tool. Some tool makers even cannot furnish a foundation plan till they have the machine built.

Then again the good manager never gets the tools he first intended to get. His experience in the shop causes him to alter his mind, or he sees some machine, in the meantime, which takes his eye, or he finds out that the machine he had in his mind is not just what he thought it was.

* * * * When a new lathe, or planer, or drill, or slotter comes into the shop, there is always a worry about where to put it. Sometimes the thing is settled by putting it in the best-looking vacant spot in the shop; say in the middle of the setting-up floor. Again it will be put in among a lot of machines of an entirely different character. This often leads to small machines for light work being set in among heavy tools, whose big work can be got to them by cranes, tracks, &c. Sometimes the whole question is settled by the convenience of locating a countershaft.

The new tool calls for a certain amount of floor

room, and a certain amount of ceiling room, properly located with reference to the floor room. When the spots have been found, and the machines set up, it is often found that the question of daylight has been left out of consideration; that the daylight comes in the wrong direction, or that it don't come at all.

* * * * Some men, when a tool is added to the shop, are smart enough to look into all the requirements. This often leads to a total reorganization of the shop; a general twisting around of things; the moving of this lathe and that one, and that planer, and this shaper, and both those slotters, and maybe half a dozen more.

* * * * When the shop is run by such a man, the said shop is liable to get turned upside down every time a new tool is bought. He is probably reorganizing six months out of the year, and when a lathesman goes home at night, he don't know what part of the premises he will find his lathe in when he comes to work in the morning.

* * * * The shop under such management is almost always a nice appearing and convenient shop, if you can spy into it some day when it isn't being reorganized. * * * *

This kind of business don't pay very well, for it is my experience in machine shops that you can't get much work out while the line shaft is being moved, or lengthened out, or raised or slid endwise, or while half the countershafts are on the floor, or while the floor is half ripped up.

* * * * Aside from other inconveniences attending the arrival of the new machine, the floor work is enough to call for resolutions of reform.

If there is plenty of room for the new machine, both on the floor and on the ceiling, and if there is plenty of daylight coming from the right direction, and if the aforesaid spaces are in exactly the right location, still the job of putting the tool in place is a demoralizing one.

There must be scientific sighting, and measuring, and chalking on the floor, and the floor must be torn up, and diggers must excavate and pile the dirt out in the shop, and mules and drays find their way into the shop, hauling out the dirt and hauling in the stone. And then the masons work awhile, and then the floor gets put down, and then the machine gets set, and belted up, and started. Maybe there has been a slight mistake somewhere, and the machine does not stand on the foundation at all; but that makes no difference, of course. It is so desirable to get this job over, that a matter of a foot or so in the matching of things cannot be considered.

* * * * Some men point with pride to a floor which is foundation all over, so that they don't have to tear up, and dig, and build, etc. This is all very nice, but if it means a brick floor for a machine shop, I, for one, can stand the digging.

If anybody can show up some kind of decent floor, which rests directly on bottom, solid enough to carry heavy tools properly, I wish he would unfold himself.

* * * * I have seen floors built right in well-packed earth, and no foundations were needed for ordinary shop tools, but I have noticed that the floors are always rotting out and smelling bad.

If such floors would last and be healthy, they would be just the thing for ordinary shops.

The fact that once in a while some tools require a pit, need not detract from the virtues of the floor. Much better to dig two or three pits than forty or fifty.

* * * * I once worked with a genius who had put a common floor in his shop—an *awfully* common one, in fact. It was on 12" joists, and was open enough in some places to let a small monkey-wrench through. I don't suppose there was a square foot of that floor which, at some time, some workman had not torn up in order to recover a scale, or a pair of calipers, or a chisel, or a job, or something.

Under each machine there were two or three loose trap doors, and all the chips and other hard accumulations of the shop were shoveled into these holes.

This would be pretty expensive in some localities, but at that place this stuff had no value.

In course of time, there was a heavy stratum of hard iron under the floor in the neighborhood of the machines. Care was taken to flush all parts up nicely, and then the traps were nailed down. Then traps were put in other parts of the shop, the intention being to put solid iron under the entire floor. When a section was well filled and set, a good floor was laid, and it was able to stand up under any machine likely to be set upon it.

This all looked very well, but I should hardly fancy the job of excavating a pit in this floor for a long-spindled boring mill.

* * * * There may be some kind of a floor which will endure, and be neat and healthy, and which will do to set machine tools on without any underpinning or foundations. If there is, I should like to know what sort of thing it is.

* * * * I am informed that English law makes real estate out of anything attached to a building. Thus, if you rent an empty factory, and fill it with machinery which you bolt to the floor, the machinery so bolted becomes a contribution and a part and parcel of the premises, and is not to be removed by you when your lease is up. This condition of law has led to the contriving of a plan to get around it. Instead of bolting your machines to the floor, you bolt them to shoes previously bolted to the floor. When you buy a new machine, it comes with these shoes on its feet. You fix the shoes to the floor, and then fix the machine to the shoes. When you clear out, you take your machines, but leave the shoes as a souvenir of your respect for the law.

* * * * In European shops paved floors are common; so are steam engines and drilling machines attached to the walls of the building; and so is "laying off" on Saturday, and sobering up on Monday. The absence of all washing conveniences, too, is universal in English shops.

Europe has plenty of machine-shop ideas which we would do well to filch, but it is to be hoped that we will never import the above-mentioned features.

* * * * When I was out at the Millers' Exposition, I heard machinists talking about the nickel-plated work on the Wheelock and Brown engines. I did the same thing myself at the American Institute in 1876. The finish was so far beyond my own understanding of things, that I supposed, of course, it was plated. I afterwards satisfied myself, that what I saw was iron with a good finish on it.

Almost every lathesman understands that finish is simply a nice arrangement of scratches. He knows that he can file big scratches out of a job, if he is lucky enough not to file a few bigger ones in; and that he can use a finer file and get the scratches still finer; and that he can take emery clamps and grind the scratches still finer. Here he generally ends, and his finish is nothing to compare with the fine work stuck right under his nose every day. He sees work in which the scratches are so fine that he can't see them at all. He wants to know how the fellow who did this job managed to get big scratches out and to get such little scratches in. Such finish as this is real polish. It

I wish, for my special amusement, you would send an artist out into the world with instructions to bring back a good sketch of a common boiler front.—Page 299.

isn't a temporary polish put on top of a wretched finish.

* * * * Proprietors are interested in this question of finish. They want their work finished, but they have an idea that it costs too much money. The fact is, that it don't cost much, not as much, hardly, as common finish. It is a notorious fact, that high-finish shops can get away with other shops on prices. There are, of course, other reasons for this; but it shows that finish does not conflict directly with cheapness.

The real truth is, that in certain shops the men know how to put a finish on work and the expense is nothing. In other shops, doing tip-top work, the men don't seem to know anything about it, and any attempt that way may involve discouraging expense.

* * * * I wish, for my special amusement, you would send an artist out into the world with instructions to bring back a good sketch of a common boiler front. By common, I mean the kind one is most apt to see. I want to see a picture of an ordinary boiler front alongside one that you lately gave a view of. I know a lot of high-toned mechanics or engineers, or what not, who would take a fit if they should see that front.

* * * * These men have got it into their heads that every line and every pound of metal about anything made of iron, should serve some useful purpose. These are the men who make the outside of a machine the same shape as the inside of the core boxes; the same men who speak of polish as a thing of utility only; the same men who paint things lead colored and call it steel color; men who never find out how to do work economically, and find themselves compelled to leave all the nice things off in order to get the expensive product into the market.

* * * * The very appearance of this fancy boiler

front shows that care, thought, skill, knowledge and time have been expended in its design. A design thus treated is bound to be based on good, practical principles. If there is some peculiarly good point at which the grates should be set, I should look for a demonstration of the fact in a boiler front which looks as though it had been studied over. If there is a bad, warpy disposition in boiler fronts, this matured affair is apt to have been designed to avoid the defect.

* * * * Really nice things are seldom badly designed. It is in the coarser and more serviceable materials, purely "functional apparel," that we are apt to see misfits. Good looks tend to better every thing around. There is no nobler use for iron than that of ornamentation, and, like all good things, ornamentation costs money. Beautifying a boiler front is just as reasonable and proper and elevating as beautifying a pier glass, or a book case, or a cornice. I have known of an artist being called on to design a paper collar for a chimney stack, which, when done, was a thing of beauty, and real, honest, human utility, and, at the same time, the base of that beautiful stack stood near a boiler front so infernally ugly, that the furnace walls bulged out and staid bulged out. I can't imagine such a thing happening with a nice front.

* * * * The separation of beauty from utility in design has led to the entire separation of the arts, and now-a-days the designer is simply either an artist or, what is worse, an engineer. As a consequence, certain ugly things of real utility come from the engineer, and certain pretty things of no utility come from the artist.

* * * * I once negotiated at a good jewelry house for a pair of sleeve buttons. They were elegant, but a little investigation showed that the stems were not long enough to admit two thicknesses of cuff;

they were not worth five cents for the purpose intended. All the lines of these things had probably been fixed by some light-headed artist, who knew nothing of utility, and didn't want to mix it up in his occupation. He is as bad as the engineer or designer who leaves beauty out of his work.

* * * * Once upon a time I went into partnership with an artist. We had invented a draw handle or pull, which possessed functions not necessary to explain. It was a question of design and patterns. There is no art about me, and I simply measured my own paw, and thus determined the proper length of the handle. This dimension, embodied in a sketch of the mere essentials of the device, constituted my contribution to the design. I turned it over to my artistic partner to put it into good form. He said at once that the thing was too big to look well, and wanted to contract it for beauty's sake, and he stuck to it, too. We argued and fussed and quarreled over that miserable little drawer handle for a week, and then quit. The thing was never made.

* * * * I was attracted by that boiler front, because I have been brought up on ugly fronts of my own design. When I see pictures of old machinery, I am glad I was born after the Corinthian order of architecture was abandoned in design, and, when I look at my own work, I am sorry I was born before dead work and lead-colored paint were abandoned.

CHAPTER XXXV.

SACKETT'S EXPERIENCE WITH A TITLED ENGINEER.—PERSONAL IDENTITY OF BENNETT, SACKETT AND WYCOFF.—SHOP DRAWINGS AND SYMBOLISM.—TRAMPING JOURS.—STARTING NEW SHOPS.—CHORDAL AS A PILGRIM.

* * * * Sackett lately employed a new man; a man with testimonials; a man who had taken two or three degrees; a man who had a college's authority for writing C. E. after his name; a man who was no civil engineer after all. He was not smart; he was simply learned. He had no knowledge; he had simply education. Judgment cannot be based on education; it must be based on knowledge. This C. E. had no knowledge and no judgment. He was a nice man, and a learned one, and a C. E., but Sackett bid him good bye after three weeks' knowledge of him. I don't know who wants such men. Sackett says he don't, and I know for a certainty that Wycoff don't.

* * * * When Sackett told me of his experience with this man (he was no youth just out of college, mind you, but an old hand, if he was a weak one) our conversation naturally turned on titles. I mentioned that I had read, in several places, that C. E., &c., could be rightfully affixed to a name only atter permission had been conferred by some educational or similar body; and that others assuming such titles did it for the purpose of leading to the inference that they had such formal right to it; and that merit alone would seldom tempt a fair-minded man to appropriate such a title.

"Bosh!" said Sackett, "the writers of such stuff don't know exactly what they are talking about. An engineer is a man who has had the title conferred on him, whether he is an engineer or not; or he is a man who is an engineer, whether he has had the title conferred upon him or not. Both these men have a right to the title, and either should blush to take it if not properly endowed. Even if conferred by a college, the conferree should hesitate before he accepts such a vocative title as engineer. M. D. at the end of a man's name indicates that he is a doctor of medicine. Doctor is a word with a meaning not at all analogous to surgeon, or physician, even. No college, or course, can make a man a surgical man, even though they endow him with the title of surgeon.

"F. R. S. is not a vocative title. It can only be properly conferred by the Royal Society, and after they confer it, the man is a fellow of that society. Ph. D. means that a man has received the title, and not that he is in reality a doctor of philosophy. Engineer or C. E. at the end of a man's name, indicates that the man has an engineer's title, or an engineer's vocation.

"It is not a sure indication, because the man may be a fraud. He may not be an engineer at all, and he may never have taken a degree. I have got," continued Sackett, "two captains and one major working out in my foundry. They have no right to the title, because they never had it conferred by any proper authority, and they never fulfilled the functions the title would indicate. If they saw fit to write moulder, or sand rammer after their names, they would be right, even if there was such a courtesy title, because the word is vocative. I have a designer upstairs who has a right to put M. E. after his name, because he is a mechanical engineer and a good one, though he has no diploma; and he has a right to put M. D. after his name, because he has studied medicine, and has a diploma. He is a good engineer and no physician."

* * * * I tried to find out from Sackett what had been the trouble with his late C. E., but I failed to get anything but indefinite grumbling. I gravely suspect that the aforesaid C. E. had been trying to rush some "correct mechanical principle" into Sackett's work, without regard to the expense or propriety of it ; and that some of this "principle" had failed to operate, and has consequently got Sackett into trouble.

* * * * I got a letter yesterday from one of the best machine shop managers in the United States, asking who Sackett is, and stating that he would like to form his acquaintance. I could not give the party Mr. Sackett's post-office address, but gave him the address of one of his shops instead. Another gentleman wrote me, asking where Bennett's shop is. Few men enquire about Wycoff. I wish to take this occasion to answer all such inquiries.

If you want to see Bennett's shop, you will have to travel in several different directions, for his shop is scattered. His foundry is in one state, his machine shop in another, his line shaft in another, his pattern shop in another, and his excellent intention of doing something to keep castings from littering up the machine shop is in several states, principally in a state of uncertainty. When the elements of Bennett's shop are combined in one geographical section, I want to be on hand at the opening.

Sackett and Wycoff are men who are ubiquitous in different proportions. I would describe Wycoff as a good-looking gentleman of almost any age, a good and lively citizen, a man tolerably well fixed in the world, a pleasant man to meet, no specially bad social qualities, and a very numerous and short-sighted machine shop manager. I would describe Sackett as a good-looking gentleman of almost any age, a good and lively citizen, a man tolerably well fixed in the world, a pleasant man to meet, no specially bad social qualities, and a very long-sighted machine shop manager.

If I should show you their portraits, they would look much more alike than two pieces of some of the interchangeable machine work we often hear about. Outside the shop you can only distinguish them by the relative increase in their wealth, and that of their employes. Inside the shop they are readily distinguished.

The front of the shop tells whose shop it is. If you see any old, rusty, odd bevel gears half buried in the earth before the shop, or behind it, either, it is Wycoff's shop every time.

They come from different lines of ancestry, but have traveled the world together. Their ancestors discovered the new world as they sailed together. One furnished the reckless daring, the willing muscle, and the devil-may-care readiness to go I don't know where; while the other brought the cool head, the definite intention, the best attainable chart, the compass, the glass, and a brave, prudent energy.

* * * * I know little or nothing of drawing, but I have given much attention to the subject of drawings. This may look like a narrow point of difference, but it is as broad as the difference between product and process. My attention has been given to machine shop drawings; not to the art of making them, but to the desirable points in them after they are made and before they are made.

* * * * The machine shop drawing is simply a memorandum, showing what is to be produced. It is essentially an illustrated memorandum, or it would be no drawing. To be perfect, it should answer all questions which a workman can reasonably ask in regard to the piece of work; it should be durable enough to form a record for future use; it should be small enough to be easily preserved in a safe place, and it should be as low in cost as possible.

* * * * A drawing should be complete, for a

drawing which requires explanation from a draughtsman is no drawing at all. Instead of being the workman's memorandum, such a drawing is simply a draughtsman's memorandum, and if he is not present, the drawing fails in its mission.

Drawings for use in the shop, right at the draughtsman's elbow, should be so complete and self-explaining that they could be sent a thousand miles away without a word of explanation, and enable properly-skilled men to execute the work as well as the man who can confer with the man that made the drawing. It requires no more artistic skill to make a self-explaining drawing than it does to make a drawing of which the draughtsman is an essential part.

* * * * The mechanics of the shop, such as have to do with the drawings, are pattern-makers, blacksmiths, boiler-makers, wood-workers, painters and packers. The drawing is the record of results to be accomplished by all these men, and properly-made drawings should tell all these men what the ultimate result is to be, and should not contain any blank hints that will lead you to ask questions till you find out what is wanted.

* * * * Drawings are destroyed by being torn, broken, defaced, faded, or lost. Durability is secured by making them so they can't be torn, broken, defaced, faded, and so forming them that they are not liable to get lost.

A paper drawing, as a record for continued future use, has no place in a machine shop. It gets defaced in a short time, gets torn in a short time, and, fragment by fragment, it gets lost. They do not last long enough to fade. They should never be used in machine shops, except on such work as permit the drawing to be destroyed as soon as the job is finished.

Tracing cloth is but little better than paper. It gets

soiled and broken, and requires a clumsy process of unfolding or unrolling before it can be consulted, and even then, it will not lie flat. These tracings are expensive because they imply a total unnecessary duplication of the draughtsman's work. They cannot be distinguished or designated when rolled, and time is lost in going through a cord of them to find the right one. If rolled, they will not store away in some accessible and compact shape, and if folded, they are constantly liable to be mislaid or lost.

The machine-shop drawing should always be flat, and it should be made a penitentiary offense to roll or fold it.

* * * * If a paper drawing is glued on a board, it ceases, as we are speaking of it, to be a paper drawing. It then becomes a wooden drawing, and it has many superior virtues. You can't roll it; you can't fold it; it lies flat; it is always open : and some designating character, conspicuously placed upon it, will tell if it is the one wanted, and it is not liable to get lost. Numerous coats of hard varnish will secure durability of surface.

The objections to the wooden drawing are : It is thick, and a number of them composing a set will not pack closely ; if of any size, battens must be put on the back to prevent splitting, which makes them still bulkier, and prevents their being moved over each other in a search ; they are very heavy ; and are altogether so large and clumsy that no safe preservation can be given very many of them. They also cost too much money. The lumber, the building of the boards, the drawing paper, and the artistic gluing of the paper all count up.

* * * * As to size, little need be said. A draughtsman can't make a good drawing so small that a workman can't follow it. The scale of a drawing is immaterial. No one is called upon to *measure* a good shop drawing; and a scale of five inches, or two and a quarter inches, or seven-eighths of an inch, or three-sixteenths of an inch, to the foot, is far better than full size, because the men will then keep their rules off.

Wooden drawings are generally about twenty by thirty inches. This size is entirely too large for convenience, and is not called for by any class of work. Such big boards cannot be handled in sets; they take up too much room; it takes too much time to make such big drawings; the boards are too large to use around the lathes, the vises, or anywhere; they get used for tool boards and dinner tables, and trays, and tend to destroy each other by bulky contact. Boards half as big, say ten by twelve inches, are much more convenient, and are large enough for bridge work, locomotive work, steamship work, boiler work, and every other kind of work.

* * * * Sackett uses drawings which seem to combine all the virtues. They are made on cards about an eighth of an inch thick. The cards are good tarboard, with a peculiar quality of drawing paper pasted on one side. The edges of the paper are brought over the edges of the tarboard and pasted to the back. They are very light and strong; in fact, they seem indestructible. They cost $80 a thousand, or eight cents each, and are made by William Mann, stationer, Philadelphia. The size is 10 x 13½ inches. These cards are nice. A set of detail drawings for a common slide valve engine (the size of the engine makes no difference in the drawings), requires about twenty-five of these cards. The whole set can be carried in one hand. They slide over each other like a eucre deck; they are light; they are of convenient size to handle around the shop; they store nicely in a safe, and they are cheap.

* * * * Sackett uses these card drawings, and his whole drawing system has many tip-top points in it.

A panel drawing board is used with these cards. The card drops into the panel, so that its surface is flush with the stiles. In the edges of the panel, wood screws, with their heads half cut away, are fixed. A half turn of the screws brings the sharp heads around into the edge of the card. Nothing projects above the surface of the card, and a card may be returned to the board and nicely trued up.

* * * * When Sackett gets up a new machine, he has temporary detail drawings made on brown detail paper. The machine is given some short symbol like $G\,6$, which is used as the name of the machine. Patterns and drawings are marked with this symbol, and the time and cost books deal with this symbol. Of symbolism, more hereafter. After the first machine is made, corrections made, and the details all approved, the permanent drawings are made on these cards, and the temporary drawings are immediately destroyed. The drawings are made in detail, no two pieces being shown in contact; and the fewest possible number of lines are used in making the drawings. No dotted lines are used where not essential, and there is no hatch shading, shapes being brought out by pencil shading. Every confusing element is omitted, and everything is shown, past all misunderstanding. Then, before a figure is written on the drawing, it receives one coat of white shellac varnish. This is sand-papered, and on the hard surface thus presented all the figuring is done. A printed general instruction sheet is then pasted on the back of the card, together with a big symbol, so the drawing can be easily identified Three coats of white shellac varnish are then applied to the card, back and front. If errors should at any time be discovered in the figuring, it is only necessary to erase through the external varnish, correct the figure, and re-varnish. Were the figures put on the paper surface, some ugly digging would have to be done in correcting an error. If subsequent changes are made, it is a trifling matter to make one of these little cards new.

BENNETT'S DRAWING RACK.

* * * * This reminds me that Bennett uses these card drawings, and that he has got up a music-stand sort of rig, as a lathe attachment to hold the drawings. The rack attaches to the carriage of a lathe, to a planer rail, or to any such thing, and is really a good institution. Above is a sketch of it.

As previously stated, Bennett uses 10 x 13½ inch drawings exclusively.

This rack is simply a light casting, socketed loosely on a rod, which is arranged to fasten into the lathe carriage. On the same rod, just under the rack socket, a square cast iron arm is fitted. The upright rod is shouldered to receive the arm hub and the rack socket.

On the arm slides a light cast-iron cup, which will hold about a quart of water. The mortises, to fit the arm, are cast in the cup; in fact, the work is all gotten up cheaply, though it acts and looks well. A piece of one-eighth inch piping is screwed tightly into a base cast near the bottom of the cup. This pipe reaches out about four inches, and then bends downward with an easy curve. The bent end of this pipe is carefully faced, and provided with a long thread of very fine pitch. On this thread is loosely screwed a brass snoot, having a milled collar at its upper end. By a simple but peculiar arrangement of the inside of this snoot, the end of the pipe is adapted to seat against a shoulder and thus form a stop valve. Turning the snoot by the collar, regulates the flow of water. It is simply a cheap and substantial form of cock. Bennett puts these complete things on lathes, planers, shapers and slotters, and he uses a similar rig, minus the water works, for drill presses, vises, boring mills, gear cutters, pattern lathes, and all other machines. It is no slouch of an arrangement, and, being made in a lot, they are very much cheaper than the hap-hazard thing we usually see. Come to think of it, I don't remember ever having seen any other shop provided with any kind of water cans, except such as each lathesman seems to have conjured up himself.

* * * * I take Sackett's shop drawings as models, because he seems to have got things reduced to a smooth working system. I have noticed the system of drawings used in many of our finest shops, but in almost every case it looks as though little attention had been paid to any regular plan. This, of course, has no reference to the character of the work shown on the drawings, or to the character of the draughtsman's work. I am speaking of the drawings themselves, as drawings, and with reference to their functions in the shop.

* * * * I will first briefly refer to Sackett's symbolism. Nearly all good shops symbolize their work, but some do not, and ever so many bad shops do nothing which will save work. Symbolism saves in the drawing room, in the pattern shop, in the pattern store room, in the foundry, in the machine shop, and in the office. I do not believe it possible to keep stored patterns in come-atable shape, without some symbolical system of marking them.

* * * * Symbols are only of real value in shops which build something regularly. Take the case of a shop building threshing machines, fanning mills and sugar mills. It is almost impossible to stamp such a word as "Thresher" on little patterns, and they must be marked for identification to avoid a mix. Under a system of symbols, a single letter will be chosen to typify a *class* of machines, as A, for threshers; B, for fanning mills, and C for sugar mills. In this way, any pattern, piece of a pattern, core box, drawing, or casting, marked B, is at once known as belonging to a fanning mill. The shop may make two kinds or sizes of fanning mills. It thus becomes necessary to mark work in such a way that we may know just what style of fanning mill the thing belongs to.

This is effected by combining with the machine symbol, a style symbol. Thus fanning-mill patterns may be marked B 1 for one style, and B 2 for another style, and so on. The figure 2 in the last case doesn't show that B 2 is a larger machine than B 1, or that it is a smaller machine, or that it is a later style. It simply shows that it is a *different* fanning mill from B 1.

If, in course of time, B 1 is radically altered, it takes a new symbol like B 3, for instance, indicating that it is not B 1. B 3 is a machine made in conformity with B 3 drawings, cast from B 3 patterns, and run on the cost books as B 3. Under this system, the men in the shop will cease to speak of the little fanning mill or the big fanning mill, and will only talk of B 1, or B 2, etc.

A stranger don't know what the men are talking about in a symbol shop, and he don't need to care. A new workman drops into the thing very quickly.

* * * * Every piece of drawing or pattern referring to B 3 will be marked B 3. B 3 patterns will be kept in a space devoted to B 3, and if they get mislaid, their place is easily found. The men keep time on B 3, instead of on some kind of a fanning mill, and the time-keeper's book deals with B 3.

* * * * The machine not only has a symbol, but each piece has a designating number. The draughtsman puts the number on the drawing of the piece; the pattern maker stamps it on the pattern of that piece, and on all loose pieces of that pattern, and on all core boxes for that piece. Time is kept on that piece, and castings are ordered by the number as well as symbol. The draughtsman marks a certain gear No. 1, and another gear No. 2, and so on. If castings are wanted, it is not necessary to show the pattern, or to describe the shape of it. The order is simply made for B 3, No. 2, and this will be found stamped on the proper pattern. Time is kept by number as well as symbol. A lathesman's slate may read: "Boring 40 pcs. B 3, No. 28, 9 hours." This would cover a slate, if written in full, and would wear out a time-keeper.

* * * * Many shops use the piece numbers in such a way as to indicate the material the piece is to be made of.

Thus, a drawing marked No. 3, No. 22, No. 16, would mean that the pieces were to be of cast-iron. If marked No. 03, No. 022, No. 016, it means wrought-iron or steel, it don't make any difference which, as the blacksmith's drawings tell him which it is. Machinists know that any piece marked 02 is to be made of a forging. No. 003, No. 0022, etc., mean brass. No. 0003, No. 00022, mean wood. No. 00003, malleable iron, and so on, as may be adopted. It is customary to use the last kind of numbering for all rare materials, such as malleable iron, if rarely used, leather, rubber, and special metals, thus indicating that the piece is not made of common material, and the drawing will define what it is to be made of.

* * * * I do not intend to say much about Sackett's instruction to his draughtsmen, regarding the execution of the drawings, but, as part of the system, I should explain that no one but the pattern maker is ever to measure a drawing. He never has to do so but once, and he can measure closely to any scale. But if machinists ever measure drawings, there is no telling what will happen. No two men measure alike, and, as a consequence, the drawing would be subjected to a dozen different translations.

For this reason, a drawing should show *figured* dimensions wherever it is to be brought to a size. Parts which are not to be touched by machinists, have no dimensions given. Sometimes a place is to be turned or finished, and at the same time it may make no difference about its distance or dimension. If a dimension is marked on such a place, a man will use up as much time bringing the piece to figured size, as if it was very important. Figures are not put on such

H, 6.

6 x 10 Inch Portable Engine. March, 1880.

INSTRUCTIONS.

TO PATTERN MAKERS.

A plain number, as No. 7, means cast-iron. If preceded by a cipher, as No. 07, it means wrought work. If preceded by two ciphers, as No. 007, it means brass. If preceded by three ciphers, it means wood-work. Patterns are wanted for cast-iron and brass pieces.

Measure and make your own allowance for shrinkage and draft.
Holes with no sizes given are to be cored to size.
Do not measure where figures are given.
Always add for finish, when figures are given. Add for finish when you find the word "polish," or "face."
Where two views are shown, the size is generally marked in but one place; the same with holes of the same character. Look out for this.
Don't forget the fillets and rounds on all rough work.
Mark all patterns, core-boxes and pieces, with the symbol and number.
If one pattern makes two pieces with additions, put both numbers on the piece used for the two.

TO BLACKSMITHS.

If there are forging sheets, work to the figures and to the shapes shown by the red outlines. If there is no red outline, the piece is not to be finished and calls for a smoother forging. If there are no forging sheets, make forgings from working drawings to order only, and leave finish where figures are given.

TO MACHINISTS.

Do not finish where there are no figures, unless you find the word "finish," or "polish," or have special instructions.
Where nuts and boltheads come down on rough castings, you will counterbore the surface, so as to allow them to come down square.
Counter-sink the first thread out of all tapped holes, not with a drill, but a hand counter sink.
Touch all bolt holes lightly, with the same tool.
Chamfer the first thread off all screws before trying them in a hole.
Leave no ragged corners. Where a corner is formed by a rough surface and a finished one, round the corner nicely and boldly.
A hole marked "tap" is to have a thread in it, either tapped or chased.
All screws are standard thread and right hand V, unless otherwise mentioned.
All key seats are to be in depth one-half their width, and straight, unless otherwise stated.
Don't polish any work not marked polish, except on special instructions.
Don't touch a tool to any part not figured, unless you find the word "polish" or "face." If the word "polish" is placed after the number of the piece, it means polish all over the outside.
Where a hole to be drilled is shown and no distances are given, it is either to be scribed from some other piece, or is to be in the center of a boss.
Make all fits by varying the size of the internal piece. Let all holes be standard.

SHERMAN G. SACKETT, - - - Proprietor.

OHIO VALLEY IRON WORKS,

CINCINNATI, O.

(See page 316.)

places. The simple word "plane," or "face," or "polish," and the absence of figures, will show the dimensions or distance is immaterial. All this business looks like work, but there is no point where "save work" comes in to better advantage than in the arrangement of shop drawings; and a decided system of drawings will pay many times over for its cost.

* * * * As before stated, Sackett pastes a back on each drawing card. These backs are of such size as to meet and lap over the margin. On the preceding page I show the back work of one of Sackett's drawings. The upper section is printed separately, and if a machine requires but five or six drawing cards, the draughtsman makes this section himself. If ten or more are needed, printing is the nicest and cheapest. The symbol is brought out very boldly, as shown, so that drawings may be easily identified. The balance of this thing is printed in one piece, and all is pasted on before the drawing is varnished. * * * *

* * * * No machinist in this country has done himself justice until he has worked somewhat in railroad shops, but the lad so unfortunate as to learn his trade in one is to be pitied. No matter how good a workman he is on railroad work, which is almost always old repair work, he finds himself decidedly "off" when he gets out in the other shops. He finds he must stick to railroad shops, or else grit his teeth and learn his trade over again.

* * * * I may be accused of intimating that a machinist ought to tramp over the country and work around. That's just exactly what I mean. I hold that there is a time to commence sticking to one shop, and that too much sticking before that time tends to damage a man's future.

* * * * It is a knowledge of the experience and emotions of men that makes me firm in the belief that a workman does well to begin tramping early, after finishing his time, and to quit tramping soon after beginning. The idea is to get posted in the general ways of the trade—something which cannot possibly be done in any one shop—and, at the same time, the variety is not so great that its salient points cannot be absorbed in a short time spent in judiciously moving around.

* * * * My advice to a young chap, after serving out his time, is to start out, no matter what pay can be had by staying. Call your starting point your home, and never call it abandoned. Go so far from home that you can't get back, and don't go near any friends or men you have ever seen before. This will put you to the rack of self-reliance, but the thing must come before the boy changes to the man. You will march out into the world, confident that you know all about machine shops. You will get work where old stagers fail, and you will make friends where the old stager don't look for them. Every new shop will be a grand revelation.

Pick out different kinds of shops. Railroad, car, steam engine, locomotive, machine tools, woodworking machinery, mining machinery, agricultural implements, printing machinery, steam pumps, mill machinery, etc. Take in the whole variety in small doses, and then go home and settle down, or move your home to the place you like best.

* * * * This country is awfully big, and, with all respect for the thousands and thousands of lathes which this very minute are revolving while some chap leans over them with outside calipers; for the thousands of planers, which are at this instant knocking their dogs against their tumblers; for the thousands of drill presses, which this instant would show their spindles gradually descending; for the thousands of

vises, which this instant have a death grip on some piece of metal; for the shower of chips flying before the thousands of chipping chisels now creeping slowly forward before thousands of ball-pein hammers—with all respect for these many evidences of the existence of machine shops in this land, I venture the opinion that the machine shops haven't got started yet. There are lots of them yet to come. Not monster establishments with full lines of regular articles to make, with a routine business and printed catalogues, with stocks of patterns in regular use, with story after story full of fine tools and fine workmen; not such shops as these, but little shops which will some day, under the management of boys now sweeping the shop, grow up and find their place. These little shops wil have a certainty of nothing, and will do every thing.

* * * * Men with nothing have finally got shops of their own, and it will continue to happen that way. A man some day learns that if he can't ride, he can walk. If he is not born to move, he can stand still. There are riding shops, and there are walking shops; I know something about these walking shops; in fact I was raised in a shop that was too weak and puny to creep well, and I saw it in a full gallop before my term of apprenticeship was up.

I actually believe that the most successful owners are those who come from these good shops. The slouch from the rough little shop can start one of his own and feel at home, but if the business should grow in spite of him, it would probably get away with him, while the lordly chip from the big shop, if he can narrow his gauge to start on, is always ready for a healthful growth.

* * * * There are two ways of starting small shops. One is to depend on your superior skill and wit and mechanical reputation, and start right under the nose of the big shop you came out of. If you have luck, you may absorb the big shop in course of years. If you don't have luck, they will absorb you. Such shops generally start with the intention of making a certain thing, and depending on luck and management to bring other things into line.

The other way is to hunt around and find a place miles and miles and miles away from any other shop. The place must be located in the market center of some saw-mill country, or agricultural country, or sugar-mill country, or some machine-using section.

The intention is to get the repairs of the surrounding section, do such odd new work as can be picked up, and finally get into the manufacture of the very machines you repair. In proper hands this plan is the sure road to fortune. But it is hard, up-hill work, and takes lots of pluck and good judgment. Repair work in such a shop brings fabulous prices. There is no competition, and skill must be used to keep competition away. West of the Mississippi is the place for such shops to hunt for locations.

Such shops require more money than the little city shops, because you can't get supplies inside of three weeks, and you need them every instant. It might be thought that a railroad would be a convenience, but a railroad would spoil the whole game. It would bring your supplies quicker, but it would also bring them to your customer quicker, and would allow him to go to headquarters.

After a while you will get up a saw-mill or engine, no better than anybody else's, but a little different, so you can call it your own, and sell it for five prices. Your real estate is given to you with a cash bonus to encourage the enterprise, and you become a curiosity and a power in the neighborhood.

* * * * Can you imagine the enthusiastic artist admiring the rare creations of the masters, always alive to their points of excellence, and ever striving to give his own atmosphere the color of their bold superiority? And can you imagine the rare delight this artist would find in that reversal of time, which would allow him to touch these masters and see them at their work? If you can, you know something of my experience as I made my first pilgrimage, and set foot in the sacred premises, and found myself in contact with the men whose names have been always by me through my shop life.

I did do it, sure enough, and I hope to do it again. I put on my summer hat, stopped the mill, and made the grand rounds. I never saw these shops before, and for that reason am glad I didn't die last summer. If I should commence to make what I saw and was interested in the subject of these letters, I wouldn't have time to write them, and these pages wouldn't be big enough to hold them, so I won't do it. * * *

CHAPTER XXXVI.

THE MEN WHO DESIGN MILLS AND SHOPS.—CHARACTERISTICS OF PROFESSIONAL AND NON-PROFESSIONAL MEN.—ARCHITECTS WHO FAIL IN DESIGNING INDUSTRIAL WORKS.—INCONVENIENCES IN MACHINE SHOPS.—THE USUAL EXPERIENCE IN BUILDING AND EXTENDING THEM.

* * * * I am on the hunt for an architect who has made a study of industrial works. I know of lots of them who pretend to make a specialty of such business, and who can point with pride to many magnificent shops, mills, factories, etc., in which the exterior seems to indicate a special fitness within. But when we come to investigate these establishments, we find them full of architectural blunders. The utility of a thing seems to be entirely outside of the architect's range of comprehension. A canvas awning, or a business sign, put on a building, disarranges all the architect's calculations; in fact, I never heard of one of them showing a sign on an elevation. I suppose they would protest if asked to dot one in, just to see how it looked. It might spoil the looks of the drawing. The New York Post-office is a fair sample of functional architecture. It was, or was supposed to be, designed for the manipulation of mail matter and the transaction of postal business; but no proper calculation was made for light, and no means were provided for getting mail into the building, or for getting mail out. A wooden addition, with some common sense in it, had to be resorted to, before the place was at all fitted for the very work it was intended for.

* * * * Modern mill architecture has apparently fallen into the hands of mill operators, who, as a class, know as much about mill designing as a woman does about designing a kitchen. The modern mill is designed by a millwright, or an operative, and the modern machine-shop design springs from the brain of a machinist.

* * * * The mechanical engineer lives, and works and deals with machinery and machine work. He is a designing mechanic, with observation and executive faculties. He also works with drawing paper and T-squares and compasses and bow pens and dotted lines, and talks freely of elevation, section, plan, and detail.

It would look as though such a man was an engineer and architect combined in one machine; and that if he wanted to design a building for industrial purposes, in his line, all he had to do was simply to do it.

* * * * I have always divided men into two classes, professional and non-professional, to the disparagement of neither. Among non-professional men, I class those who carefully treasure every scrap of past experience, and who are guided by their accumulations of experience.

Among the professional men, I class those, who, without any special attempt to gain experience themselves, are constantly and forever absorbing the experience of others. If the non-professional never did a certain thing, he knows nothing about it. After he has done it, he gets one man's experience. The professional man, without ever intending to do a certain thing, may have thorough knowledge of the world's experience in that thing. To him the books bring the lifetime experience of ten thousand lives. Knowledge of others' failures will divert his thoughts and acts into original channels. The non-professional leaves on record the experience of one small life, and the professional man gathers in thousands of these. The non-professional man may grope alone a lifetime after one small fact, stored in a business-like way in the head of the professional man. The professional man's mind is a valuable text book in the school of experience, which the book itself may never attend.

It has taken all this philosophy to bring me to the conclusion that an architect ought to be able to tell me something useful about houses, especially as my sole ex-

I seek far and wide for the man who can measure me for a shop.—Page 325.

perience consists in a dissatisfaction with the last one I lived in.

* * * * When the machine man builds a shop, he botches it.

I don't know just why this should be so, but I have often noticed that new establishments, contrived with a definite purpose in view, have almost always proved the most awkward, and ill-fitted for their use.

Railroad shops, designed by some master mechanic with every possible point in view, are generally an abomination ; and I only know of one way to get them built worse, and that is to set an industrial architect at the job.

If some of our technical colleges will establish a chair of shopitecture, in which a knowledge of the ancient past forms a bar to approach, I believe the world would be a trifle advanced.

* * * * The fact is, Mr. Editor, that I want to build a shop. I am a mechanic myself. I know " how to set a slide valve," and how to cut a thread on chilled iron, and how to wash old waste, and how to unscrew a rusty nut, and lots of things ; and I know how to "draft," and how to figure up the weight of cast-iron, and all such ; but I have seen lots of shopmen far better and wiser than I, get up miserable shops. I don't want any such side issue to enter in on my life, and for that reason I seek far and wide for the man who can measure me for a shop as a shoemaker would for a boot.

* * * * With a full knowledge that I may have to be my own shoemaker, I am now looking at crack shops, and if you could set instantaneous pictures in type, I could send you a volume on modern shop architecture.

* * * * The best arrangements I have seen for handling heavy work have been in shops that never have made, and never intended to make, anything weighing a ton. I find heavy tools and heavy work done on sky floors, and tinkering work done in one-story shops. I find well-arranged cranes fixed where small tools run, and see the heavy lifting, around big planers and lathes, done by pure back muscle. I find raw stock in warehouses, and finished stock out-doors. I find monster elevators well arranged in shops whose delicate little work could be blown through a pneumatic tube; and in some shops doing heavy work, I notice that an open hatchway and a dollar's worth of rope, are the sole dependence.

* * * * A storeroom for castings is seldom met with, and when found, it is invariably so arranged that it is simply a casting pile under roof.

A casting storeroom systematically arranged and adapted to contain all the standard and wild castings of a concern; a place where the foundry's delivery ends; a place where the machine-shop's receipt of cast stock begins; a place where every stock casting belongs, and can be actually found, is a rare sight.

It is so useful a thing, so economical of valuable time, so convenient, and so absolutely void of expense that it is hardly to be looked upon as a refinement or a luxury.

* * * * The power of extension is the great architectural feature in a shop. The presiding genius may deliberate and dream over the new shop; may lay down on drawing paper every machine and area which the fairest and most prophetic anticipation can suggest, and when done he makes his estimates and finds that the cost of the brick exceeds the sum of all *present* intentions. All the deliberations and dreams are to be rubbed out, and the plan redrawn on a smaller scale. This thing figures up all right, and the new shop is built accordingly, and when done everything is satisfactory and the memory even of the big drawing fades away.

* * * * Two short years and prophecy asserts itself. Something is to be added, and a review of the old drawing shows that the very item was borne in mind but discarded on the final decision. The shop is built, however, and the new item *must* be added. A long planer, or a big lathe, or a crane, or another cupola, or room for more patterns, or a paint shop, or a sand shed, or a flask yard, or a wood shop, or a forge, or something must be wedged into a space already calculated with economy.

A few years show added buildings shutting out light from the original ones; floors with jumping-off places at the most unexpected points; little machines peppered in among big ones; cranes which either lap or fail to connect; line shafts at angles driven by belts turned over mule pulleys; crowded areas originally intended for setting up floors; castings piled wherever luck has left room for them; patterns piled where luck has left no room for them; vises at windows far from the setting-up spaces; shaving shops to leeward of foundry and blacksmith shops; and so many other things awry and disordered that the presiding genius, his own architect, wishes he was back in the old shop, so that he could build the new one to suit the present demands.

* * * * I honestly believe that the question of shop architecture will some day receive the attention of some of your readers who are willing to give their experiences; and that some one will suggest that elastic shop which can be built with present funds to suit present needs, and at the same time be capable of systematic extension in pursuance to a contrived plan. Making a new drawing on a smaller scale is wrong in principle. The scale of length only should be altered.

CHAPTER XXXVII.

THE ACQUISITION OF KNOWLEDGE.—EXPERIENCE OF THE COUNTRY BANKER'S SON IN A MACHINE SHOP.

* * * * We are told that a little learning is a dangerous thing, and also to drink deep or touch not the Pierian spring. This may be all right when applied to mental and moral philosophy, astronomy, or the square root of 2; but it is glaring fallacy when applied to the mechanic arts. As the scales of ignorance drop from the inquiring mechanic's eyes, he sees behind him paths of pleasant conjecture, and before him a somewhat negatively forbidding glare of certainty.

I take it to be the experience of every advanced mechanic, who is anything of an enthusiast, that his pleasures in his art have lessened as his special knowledge increased. Agathos says: "Not in knowledge is happiness, but in the acquisition of knowledge. In forever learning we are forever blessed; but to know all were the curse of a fiend."

All mechanics are not enthusiasts; all do not advance in knowledge; all do not conjecture, and all are not so situated as to have the spirit of conjecture aroused.

* * * * A country banker's son, in his school holidays, finds himself at the open door of a machine shop. It is the only shop for a hundred miles around. Like all such shops so situated, it is called the "foundry." The boy is, perhaps, fourteen: he has never seen a railroad nor a steamboat. He has seen two steam engines, perhaps, in dusty flour mills. Horse powers, and reapers, and treadle grindstones, and whirligig egg beaters have always possessed a charm for him. He has had an investigative eye for clock movements, and knows that they have a cog wheel and a fluttering arrangement inside. He has read papers and books, and has lots of pictures, and his mind is stored with mechanical matter for ten thousand questions, if he could find any one as intelligent as himself to put them to. He looks in at the "foundry" door, and becomes instantly aware that there is something inside which he never saw, nor read of, nor heard tell of, nor dreamed of. From the door sill he looks up and sees a revolving shaft, with pulleys and belts. His wondering eye follows these belts. He sees that they lead to counter shafts, which in their turn have pulleys and belts. His eye follows these belts down to various kinds of machines, and to a man standing by each machine. This is a vision to him. He dares go no further; he goes back to school with his mind full of the whirling glimpse. He asks himself, What were those things, and what were those men doing, and what were they doing it for? The next Saturday he finds the foundry door again; he ventures inside, and finds himself close to one of these men running one of these machines; he knows the man from the machine, but he doesn't know the machine from the work which it is doing.

It is a lathe, but he never heard the word. What is it for, and what is the man for? The machine doesn't seem to be grinding anything, and the man doesn't seem to be feeding anything to it. Parts of the machine seem to be simply turning around, and the man seems to be simply watching them turn around. His eye wanders around the shop wildly and wonderingly, but he sees only mysteries repeated. But the boy is a boy, if he is a puzzled one. His looks of wonder and inquiry touch the heart of the lathesman, as such looks always do touch the hearts of lathesmen. The latter beckons the boy to him, and bows him over the lathe, and shows him a revolving bar, mostly black and rough, and brightened part of the way. The boy can see that the bright part is a trifle smaller than the black part, and that a something or other is close up to it where the black part begins, and that dirt or something is continually falling from it. Still he does not comprehend, and the man has to explain. "That is a bar of iron, and

I am turning it off to make it smaller and round and nice. The lathe turns the bar around, and this tool does the cutting."

The boy sees it all and begins to explain it to the man:

"Oh! now I see it! This little thing is the thing you're turning, and this big thing is the thing that turns it; and this is the stuff it turns off, and you stand here to watch it. My! ain't that funny! I didn't know they could turn iron. What do they use such a big machine for? It's bigger than the piece of iron; but, say, what makes the thing keep cutting? I don't see the bar move up any."

Then the whole thing is explained, and he puts his finger on the carriage and feels it move. The man draws the tool out and lets him feel the point, and explains that iron is not hard, and he moves the carriage by hand and shows him the screw, and shows him the knob he turns to stop and start the feed, and he stops and starts the lathe, and throws the belt to show what the cone pulley is for.

The boy's active mind grasps the whole general idea, and he grows many years older in a few moments. Then he walks around the shop and sees other lathes on other kinds of work, and he sees a planer and a drilling machine, and a man chipping iron with a hammer and chisel, and then he goes out into the moulding room, and sees ugly men and pretty holes in the sand, but he doesn't know what they are for.

He goes home and tells wonderful tales, and dreams wonderful dreams.

Other holidays come, and he makes other visits and gains more knowledge of the shop and men.

* * * Vacation comes, and the foundry takes possession of him, and he takes possession of the foundry. He is always there; the first to come in the morning, the last to go at noon or night; finds out everything, noses around everywhere, seeks the dignity of standing by machines when no one else is by them, coats his clothes all over with grease, and is an over-willing, insistent, incorrigible, and, withal, a very happy, tolerable nuisance.

* * * * Vacation ends, and there is a row at home between the country banker and the country banker's son. In the battle both win. The boy goes back to school for one term, and then can go to the "foundry" as an apprentice.

* * * * This shop seems a poor, miserable institution to us. A couple of shackly lathes, one splendid new lathe, a little old chain planer, a wooden-frame bolt-cutter, a drill press, weighing 300 pounds, a six-by-ten steam engine, twenty feet of line shaft, three vises, ten flat drills, two die plates, about one set of taper taps, three or four home-made plug taps, a blacksmith's fire, a few files, a noisy old blower, a cupola, some sand, some patterns, some pattern lumber, a wood lathe, six pattern maker's clamps, handsome scrap iron—these make the sum and substance of the inventory.

* * * * The men in the shop consist of the owner, who has spent all his life in shops, but who never was, and never will be, a mechanic; one hired man, who used to be a machinist, but who has been twenty years farming; three younger men taken as learners, their muscle being their principal recommendation; an old, gray-headed chap, who may some day have been a moulder, and a lively carpenter, who may some day become a pattern maker. The old machinist gets $3 a day; the young ones, $8 a week; the old moulder and the young pattern maker $2.50 a day each. The owner is the hardest worker in the shop, and is making money, as his work is all repair work, and there is no competition.

* * * * Is it reasonable to hope that the banker's boy can go into this miserable shop and become a mechanic?

Anyhow, he goes in at $5 a week for three years. He has more natural sense than all the others in the institution combined, the young pattern maker being the only man with a mind beyond the crudeness of this little shop. The routine of the boy's life is known by all except those poor unfortunates whose first view of mechanical life was a view of the thing in its full completeness.

He chipped castings, wrestled with the old bolt cutter, cut bolts with the hand dies, run the drill press, and made himself generally useful. His hands got rough and bruised up, and cut, and dirt got into the cuts. He had really entered upon the sea of life and in a ship hardly seaworthy.

* * * * The boss runs the little lathe himself, and being called away frequently by other duties, gets into the habit of leaving the banker's boy John to watch it till he comes back. As a matter of fact the banker's boy John knows more about the lathe than the boss ever dreamed of, but the boss is no fool and soon finds it out, and the banker's boy John becomes the lathe hand Johnnie. He does his work well and leads a life of ambition and inquiry. He reads everything he can lay his hands on, and every day he tells the old machinist something about machine work or asks the old lathesman some reasonable question which he cannot answer. He reads of twist drills, but it is years before he sees one; he finds a picture of one and shows it to the old man. The old man doesn't know. The boy wants to know.

Nuts are tapped in the shop by running a blacksmith's taper tap into both sides. The boy reads of a nut tap and makes one for use in the bolt cutter on his own hook. Merit and conceit are so mixed in the act that it leaves his reputation as it was.

* * * * These blacksmith's taps are used to start plug taps; the boy reads up on the tap question, and on his own hook constructs starting taps with the outside only tapering; he organizes a set of tap wrenches. He also organizes a set of tap drills, and has many a row over them.

He does not use these drills himself, and he is not the owner nor boss of the shop; but he forges these drills himself at idle times, and sticks them in the board by the drill press, and insists on full benefits being derived from them. This brings on a fuss every time his watchful eye catches a man reducing or spreading one of these drills. His next piece of impertinence is to find fault with the square hole in the spindle of the drill press. He puts the spindle in the lathe, cuts a thread on it and screws on a nice socket with taper hole and slot, and he makes the shank of every drill in the shop to fit it. There is not work for him every day, so he finds time enough for this nonsense, about which there is no complaint; only indifference.

* * * * There are several things on this boy's

mind; he wants to know what a big lathe looks like, and whether a man uses a step ladder when running one. He wants to know what a boring mill is. He wants to know how the holes in the planer rail are counterbored from the inside, as it seems a physical impossibility. He wants to understand the working of a steam engine. He wants to see a planer that will feed downward and a lathe that will feed across. He wants to know how a lathe carriage can be fed along by a round rod with a key way in it. He wants to know what a cutter is, and what is meant by milling, and how gear teeth are cut, and what sort of a thing a chuck is, and what an open die bolt cutter is, and what is meant by scraping, and how they plane under the inside edge of a lathe bed, and how they turn the solid pin in a crosshead, and what a reamer is like, and a rosebit, and, above all, he just wants to try a twist drill once. He gets all the books he can and becomes well posted on the steam engine, and becomes anxious to see one larger than 12", or some of the peculiar forms he sees in the books.

* * * * The boy has, so far, never seen a machinist except those mentioned, and they are ignorant and inexperienced and have never given him an idea which he was incapable of originating. For a wonder, the idea of a large and extensive shop has never entered his head; he has never seen one, nor read of one, nor heard of one; and has never thought of the thing.

* * * * He becomes an expert workman on the little lathe and on such fitting as turns up. Owing to the poverty of tools, every day calls for some impossibility, and every day he manages to see some impossible job finished.

* * * * A new day dawns on the boy in his second year. The boss has made money and the business increases; the shop is enlarged, a new 20-inch lathe is purchased, and a new man is coming from a distant world where there are lots of machinists. The boy can't sleep o' nights; he wants to see the new man. What will he be like?

The lathe comes, and Johnnie starts it up, and goes all through it and takes it all in. There is a disappointment now that he has acquired new knowledge: one of the future pleasures of life has past. He has seen a lathe with a rod feed and cross feed and chuck.

He hears the man has come and will go to work tomorrow. In the evening he slips around and sees the man through a window. Another pleasure over. The man looks just like other men.

* * * * The new machinist is an intelligent young fellow whose entire experience has been in the Great Northern Railroad shops. He is disgusted with the little shop, but he has sense, and goes to work with a will. The little shop can afford to pay big wages. He takes at once to Johnnie, in a patronizing way, as the only tolerable element about the place. Johnnie takes to him, and pumps him for month after month till George has nothing to tell which Johnnie does not know.

* * * * Revelation has come to Johnnie. The Great Northern shops are big—sixteen lathes, several drill presses, several planers, etc., etc. He hears of locomotives and of compound planers, and hears machinists called finishers, and an engine a "stationary;" and this man has used twist drills, and can explain scraping on a valve seat.

* * * * But George never saw a boring mill, nor a gear cutter, nor any kind of an engine except stationary and locomotives, and cannot tell how the inside counter-boring was done in the planer rail. And Johnnie instructs George in the principles of the steam engine and in the scientific theories of the link motion, and in the general structure of beam engines, trunk engines, side-lever engines, Corliss engines and condensing engines—things which the boy has never seen except in his well-thumbed books.

* * * * When Johnnie's three years are up, his wages are put at $3 per day. Three months more and another lathe is got and three new men are sent for, for Johnnie to pump. They are drunken ignoramuses with nothing in them, but they excite in Johnnie an irresistible desire to see the land where machinists grow.

CHAPTER XXXVIII.

SHAPES AND STYLES OF CHIMNEYS.—MISTAKES IN BUILDING CHIMNEYS.—HOW THE LADIES SET OUT TO IMPROVE A DIRTY CITY.—MR. SINTON'S PRIDE IN HIS SMOKE CONSUMER.

* * * * You have published many useful drawings in the *American Machinist*, but I very much question whether you have ever shown anything more needed than Mr. Towne's chimney, illustrated in a late issue. A chimney is of course nothing but an expensive hole for smoke to go through. The books are full of formulas for ascertaining the proper area and length of the hole, but are generally silent as to the methods of production.

* * * * In constructing the hole, safety and cost are the elements to be considered. A sheet-iron chimney, put together on the ground, lifted and guyed by rods, is, of course, a perfect chimney. It can be raised on any kind of soil; it costs a mere trifle compared to a brick chimney; it can be lengthened if found too short; it can be moved in two days if wanted in a new position; and it is salable and available elsewhere if needed no longer. It is thus seen to possess some merits not found in brick chimneys. There are probably three hundred sheet-iron chimneys to one brick one in this country. I refer to furnace chimneys or smoke stacks, of course.

* * * * The main demerits of the sheet-iron chimneys are short life and the necessity of using guys. The necessity of frequent painting is no demerit, as the paint money goes for interest in brick chimneys. The short life of sheet-iron chimneys is due to the quick inside corrosion through the thin metal, and the strength of the metal is not sufficient to permit a base hold to take the place of guys. The sheet-iron chimney is almost universally made round and straight. The only decorative features ever seen are in the way of top beads and paper collars. Some of this top work is so infernally "sheety" and ugly that it should send the designer to the penitentiary.

* * * * The brick chimney needs no guys, the immobility of a heavy mass being the dependence for stability. When a designer, who is governed by perfunctoriness, goes at a brick chimney, he reasons after this manner: I want area of hole with the least surrounding material, and of course a circle is the thing. I want the least aggregate vertical section of entire chimney, whereby the effect of wind pressure is reduced. Of course the circle is the thing. Thus a round chimney is determined upon. By a perfectly proper analysis of the strains, our designer is led to construct the walls with a thickness decreasing towards the top; and, by a careful consideration of the relation of the volumes of gases to their temperatures, he arrives at the fact that the hole may be tapering towards the top.

* * * * This designer, holding to the rigid proprieties of things, will not entertain the idea of a shape more beautiful than the circular one, not even if the more beautiful one costs less.

But after all he will ornament the top of this ugly but perfectly proper chimney. The ornamentation may be a simple ring formed of projecting halves of bricks, or it may be a gorgeous capital taken from the ancients, but it will be something ornamental. Our chimney designer is much like a certain class of machine tool designers, who shape everything about the lathe with a view to its proper uses, strains, etc., and then concentrate their æstheticism in the legs of the lathe. I honor all these men for their inability to make a thing ugly all over.

* * * * The square chimney comes from a desire to cheapen a round hole by constructing it of common square bricks with common labor. The polygonal chimney with from six to a hundred flats is an approach to the circular form in the matter of economy of material; it approaches the square one in the simplicity of form of brick required, and in the grade of labor. They possess inherent qualities of beauty which do the heart good and don't interfere with the draft.

* * * * The fluted brick chimney, having sundry ribs and buttresses, is designed in view of the fact that a tube is stronger, against flexion, if it is crimped or corrugated. Such chimneys have a capacity for beauty not found in the round or square shapes, but the top ornamentation must be carefully attended to or the eye becomes offended.

* * * * The Pennsylvania Railroad, which has, by the way, furnished many good models of things and precious few poor ones, builds a standard chimney of brick. They have an elegant taper, a fluted or buttressed section, and a flaring top of the most dignified beauty. They have lots of these chimneys, and all are alike.

* * * * A few miles from Philadelphia, near Germantown Junction, I think, some man has built a chimney patterned after the Pennsylvania Railroad chimney, but may the Lord have mercy on him for the errors committed! Few men could ever see the top of this chimney and forget it.

I believe the courts have decided that the owner of real estate has title from the earth's center to the uttermost limits of space. This being true, he can build such a cellar as he likes; he can build such a chimney as he likes; and he can put such a top on the chimney as he likes.

But I question his right to abuse the privilege by erecting in high heaven such a chimney top as the one spoken of. If it leaned towards Sawyer's the law would declare it unsafe and command its destruction or correction.

It does seem that the law could have some effect on a chimney leaning so far towards ugliness as to endanger the artistic morals of a neighborhood.

* * * * Tall chimneys require much care and judgment in the construction of their foundations. On more than one occasion such structures have been built on the solid rock, and after years have shown that the rock, while solid, was not big enough to keep them from tipping.

* * * * Chimney straightening is a simple art, requiring simply a cool judgment. The operation consists in taking a course of brick out of the long side of the chimney and substituting a thinner course, or in wedging up the short side and putting in a thicker course. The work at the Washington monument is one of the finest examples of chimney straightening on record.

* * * * A brick chimney one hundred and seventy-five feet high will swing from two to six feet at the top. The elasticity of the structure should be properly proportioned from bottom to top, else bottom strains may be imposed through too rigid a lever.

* * * * The man who builds a tall slim chimney alongside a big tall building, and takes occasion to guy the top of his chimney to the building, generally makes a mistake. The building and chimney, not being tuned to the same pitch, or having different swings, will cause trouble. The chimney will become subject to short flexions below the guy. Much better to let the chimney swing as it wants to and distribute the swing from bottom to top.

* * * * There is another kind of chimney, better and more costly than a sheet-iron one, and as good and cheaper than a brick one, and—it is handsome, or may be. I refer to a chimney made of plate iron, and stiff enough to hang by its bottom hold. These chimneys are made of plate iron varying in bottom thickness from a quarter to a half an inch, and the top iron is best about an eighth. A bottom plate with a nose on it is well belted to the foundation, and the first course of iron starts from the nose. These chimneys are heavy to start on, and are lined with brick, so that they possess certain of the stable features of brick chimneys due to their weight. As a mobile mass which will whip around in the wind, it must have the elastic strength to whip itself back. Its base hold must be rigid.

* * * * I have written to an experienced builder of these chimneys, for drawings of one lately erected on the shore of a lake where the winds blow, and I can probably soon send you sketches showing all details.

* * * * There are two ways of erecting these plate-iron chimneys. One is to start at the bottom course and rivet in place each successive course, using an inside scaffold only. The other plan is to start with the top course, jack it up, and rivet the next course under it, and so on till finally the bottom course is put in place and riveted at top and bottom. Guys are used during the operation. This is the common method of erecting electric light towers or masts, which are simply poles built of plate-iron rings.

* * * * Once upon a time a dirty city built in a hollow got art upon its social and municipal brain. This city was and is an important manufacturing place, and burnt and still burns green coal. Industry and soft coal and art, when mixed and allowed to settle, will generally precipitate the art. In the said city elegant cornices, with brackets, modillions, and dentils of light colored material, danced in the delight of high light and shadow and beauty. But the dance stopped the second week after the cornices were up. Smoke blackened everything, and bracket and modillion and soffit and spandrel and volute and abacus all lost their projections and high lights, and sank into the dead flat of sombreness.

* * * * The æsthetes protested and argued. The smoke makers claimed that the smoke made the living of the town and paid the decorative bills, and simply soiled its own riches. Nothing could be done so long as argument lasted.

* * * * There is a sex which substitutes pleading for argument. The ladies organized a society for the prevention of smoke.. They set to work right womanfully, not to prevent the smoke they made themselves, but to plead

Mr. Sinton is very proud of his device, and has almost paralyzed his forefinger.—Page 344.

with other smoke makers. They captured the town. They talked art and chemistry, chiaroscuro and carbonic oxide, Neapolitan sunsets and the smokeless chimneys of Liverpool. They worshiped at the shrine of the smoke-consuming god.

* * * * Mr. Sinton was one of the most wealthy, cultured, and foremost men of the town. He went over to the ladies' side, and pledged his wealth and numberless beautiful buildings and his business abilities to the cause of the prevention of smoke. He did more than talk about smoke prevention—he set to work to prevent the smoke from his own buildings. In short, he invented a smoke consumer, and spared no trouble or expense in applying them, and in getting good firemen to operate them.

* * * * At last the municipal government itself became inspired with an indefinable yearning after a something clean and smokeless.

The chimneys had become a bore, and the city powers decided to muzzle the entire smoke nuisance with an ordinance. Charged with this duty they vented their artistic feelings in an ordinance which made it a breach of the peace for any big chimney to smoke. Dire penalties attached to a violation of the law. A smoke inspector was appointed. All the inventors of smoke-consuming devices on earth, or in the waters under the earth, moved their headquarters to this utopian city. The ordinance did not say that all smoke should be consumed, but it said that all good citizens would have to put some sort of a machine at their furnaces looking toward that end.

* * * * The music has just commenced. More than one of the brass knobs has already seen the inside of the police courts, and the smoke inspector has not yet got warmed up to his business. The line of action mapped out by this city is a novel one in this country, and will result in many good things if such results are possible, and when the battle gets a little warmer I will try and get you

some valuable information on means and methods of burning soft coal without smoke.

* * * * Mr. Sinton is very proud of his device, and has almost paralyzed his forefinger pointing, with pride, to the top of one of his chimneys.

He got hold of one of the smoke makers, and gave him a sidewalk view of the chimney tip, and the two steadied their eyes and concentrated their gaze on the chimney. But the smoke could hardly be perceived. They went below decks to see how it worked, but there had been no fire built that day, so the investigation had to be deferred.

CHAPTER XXXIX.

MR. BAKER BUILDS A MILL WITH DOORS AND A LEAN-TO.—A REFORMED CONSUMPTIVE PERSUADES HIM TO INVEST IN A HYPHEN.—HOW THINGS TURNED OUT.

* * * * A certain Mr. Baker, within the range of my acquaintance, has a mill, and grinds up wheat for a living.

Mr. Baker is a progressive man in his section of the world, but elsewhere he might be looked upon as a fogy. We look upon all men as fogies, who fail to act upon the suggestions of well-established, economical principles and practices. May it not be true that many of these fogies are really men of progress, who for some "reasonable" reason cannot accept many of these same principles and practices as "established"? May there not be something in the atmosphere surrounding some men, which perverts the ordinary established laws of economy?

* * * I know Mr. Baker to be a man who thinks for himself and for others, and a man alive to the general advance of human affairs. But when you see his mill, you see an old-fashioned mill, with a roof having just enough of mansard qualities to be ugly without and awkward within—robbing the universe of space, without giving it to the mill. Such a roof was put on Mr. Baker's mill, because Mr. Baker had seen profitable mills with such roofs on them. The front door is a double-barreled affair, so fixed that the top section can be opened and the bottom left shut, or the bottom can be opened and the top left shut, or both be opened, or both be left shut. This door is certainly a very ingenious and wonderfully contrived thing, and I have no doubt that it is a very useful thing to have about a mill, but not being a miller, I am not able to explain its special utility with reference to mills. I only know, that when the two several doors are properly adjusted with reference to each other, and to the mill, and to the miller, the contrivance is very handy for the miller to lean over when he looks out upon the world from within the mill. I furthermore know, that many paying mills have front doors constructed and arranged to operate substantially as set forth.

Mr. Baker knew this also, and probably saw no reason for putting in any other kind of a door. Mr. Baker is keen to act on established certainty, but is slow in matters of risk.

* * * * When Mr. Baker built his mill he built a lean-to behind it. This was for an engine and boiler room. I regret being unable to set forth the advantages of the lean-to in industrial architecture. It may be that a lean-to is suggestive of growth. I think it must be. Certainly a mill or any other sort of factory building which is self-contained, may be said to be in an experimental stage. The thing may succeed and grow, and it may not. But when the lean-to begins to develop, we may safely judge that the business has grown beyond original anticipations. If this is a reasonable theory, is it not also reasonable for a miller to build the lean-to when he builds the mill? Does it not, in a way, show confidence in the expectation that the mill business will exceed present anticipations? Millers are supposed to have good reasons for what they do, and Mr. Baker built a lean-to when he built his mill. Mr. Baker was not a miller then, but he intended to be, or he would not have built the mill.

* * * * Within Mr. Baker's lean-to was a steam engine of a popular form, designed on well-established principles of construction—that is to say, many of the engines had been used with satisfaction in paying mills.

The engine was a plain, long-stroke, slide-valve, rockshaft affair, and there were few peculiarities about it.

In those few disparities from common practice, the designer seemed very careful not to tread on delicate ground.

The exhaust passage all round and all over the cylinder, to form a jacket to prevent loss of heat, while not common on such engines, was an arrangement whose expediency was obvious, of course. So also was the small cross-head friction surface. Anybody could appreciate the importance of so proportioning wearing surface, that the engine would not eat all its power up in its own friction. The little cross-head brasses were of brass, as all brasses should be; and there were set screws to set these brasses up with. Anybody could see that this set-screw arrangement had established merit. If the cross-head got out of line it could be got back by means of these set screws, and when the brasses wore away, the set screws were always ready to set them up.

Another merit of having an adjustment on the cross-head was this: If the engineer set the brasses so tight as to heat and cut, he could loosen up by these features of adjustment. Can anything be plainer?

If there were no means of adjustment, how in the world could he loosen up things that would in some manner get too tight? There being take-ups all over the engine, it is only to be expected that sometimes something would be left so loose as to pound. In such cases an adjustable cross-head is of incalculable value, because the engineer can tighten up the cross-head, and thus see if that is where the knocking comes from. An important function is thus seen to be added to a common cross-head, for it may become the seat of a knock, and, having features of adjustment, the knock can be stopped; while, if the cross-head was not adjustable, the knocks would probably be concentrated in those parts of the engine which were adjustable. What engine could stand this for any length of time? Imagine an engine adjustable only at the crank brasses. Would not all the knocking occur at this point, and would not these brasses soon knock themselves to pieces, and would not the engineer have to devote himself and his wrench solely to those brasses? How much better, then, to put set screws in the cross-head, and in the eccentric strap, and in the outer pillow block, and in the piston packing? By this simple means it is possible for a knock to be stopped without really touching the cross-head, for the knock may be elsewhere.

* * * * Mr. Baker's engine had a long stroke and a slow motion, and it had them bad. But the engine was simply an element in the mill, and its duty, in its small way, was to produce rotary motion of certain mill machinery by methods whose utility had been established.

This engine not only had a long stroke, but it had also a short valve, by means of which the steam could be utilized during the entire stroke. What would be the use of having a good long-stroke engine, and then only using the steam port (where all the power *must* come from) a part of the time? No, sir! No cutting off in this engine—not this stroke, anyhow. Maybe, when the engine was built, it was intended to cut off a little; but it had deferred doing so from one stroke to another till the desire had passed away.

* * * * Mr. Baker's smoke-stack pointed to perpetually sunny skies. The invigorating influence of contrasting seasons was lacking in Mr. Baker's latitude. Mr. Baker's mind was always progressive, as hereinbefore stated, but I have noticed that Mr. Baker's progressive actions of body partook of the nature of impulsive spurts after certain visits to lands of snow.

* * * * The consumption of coal per horse power per hour does not depend so much upon the geological conditions of a locality, as upon the geographical location. A high price for coal does not insure that means for economy in its use will be applied. Statistics of energy, applied to observations for latitude, will furnish data for getting at the geographical efficiency of the steam engine.

* * * * In Mr. Baker's lean-to there was a door,

through which the fireman carried his coal. . It was a very ordinary door, such as becomes the lean-to of a mill. In the front of the mill there was, as stated, a proper and becoming form of double door, out of which went the barrels of flour. Here we have another example of the inscrutable ways of the mill: a double door to let flour out, and only a single door to let coal in—and a full-stroke slow-motion engine at that!

* * * * Many years ago, while lots of coal was being crowded through the little door in Mr. Baker's lean-to, and while a little flour was finding exit without wire-drawing through Mr. Baker's big double door, and while Mr. Baker was making money on the operation of these doors, a young man walked out of the front door of a Northern technical college with a thesis, a sheepskin, and a title. He was an M. E., and knew about logarithms, densities, and things. He settled by a lakeside, took a sneezing fit, tore something inside of him, commenced to spit blood, and was told to "drop all hard work," and journey to a sunny land to save his life. He took his indicators and density tables, and in a week became an invalid loafer in the office of Mr. Baker's Southern mill. His name was McCann.

* * * McCann had never seen the inside of a mill before, and had only seen about a dozen engines, but he gathered in books the experience of men who had seen lots of engines and mills. He was good company for Mr. Baker, and he employed himself by applying mathematical constants to the things in the mill. He counted the speed of a big pulley, and then figured how fast the little one was driven by it. Then he counted the little one, and found that things didn't agree. He kept on figuring, and maybe he is figuring yet.

* * * He figured out something awful in Mr. Baker's engine room, and with blanched face he told Mr. Baker that he was using a hundred and fifty pounds of coal to the barrel of flour. Mr. Baker said he didn't care if it took a ton—he was making money.

McCann tried to contract for Mr. Baker's power, and offered to go to the expense of a lean-to and a good engine, in consideration of a yearly sum equal to the present coal bills. Mr. Baker would listen to nothing of this kind; he told of many such mill outfits doing well financially, and pointed to his own case, which was entirely satisfactory; the trick of successful milling being to buy wheat low and sell flour high.

* * * * In course of time, argument upon productive economy and a showing of facts prevailed, and Mr. Baker built a new lean-to and ordered a Hyphen-Corliss engine. The machine was set up, and McCann, to keep himself from dying of inactivity, assumed charge as engineer, a position of pride in his case, for he refused pay. He was in good circumstances; and if he should accept pay he might be charged with doing the hard work forbidden by the doctors.

* * * * After a week's run, McCann informed Baker that he was running on forty pounds of coal to the barrel of flour. Mr. Baker didn't seem to care if he was, but was proud of the engine because it was nice. McCann said he would get things into shape to do better still. Baker didn't care. He might be glad if McCann succeeded, but would not waste any unnecessary effort in getting sorry if he failed.

* * * * McCann stood by his engine like a man, kept his indicators on all the time, and got results out of the thing which would startle Hyphen himself. The forbidden work restored his health, and he went again to the lake side. Mr. Baker was sorry to see him go, for he had thoroughly appreciated the companionship of the young man. As to the changes wrought in the mill he cared nothing.

* * * * The old engineer took the new engine and

McCann informs Baker that he is running on forty pounds of coal to the barrel of flour.—Page 350.

liked it. As defects developed in the engine he remedied them the best he could, without much work or much knowledge. A claw block wore out in course of time, and he put a new one in. This one wore out quickly, and, to avoid the labor of replacing them, he invented a slight change in the claw device which prevented the let-go, and thus saved the blocks from all wear. From this brilliant step he was naturally led to an investigation into the governor, which seemed to be useless and in the wrong place. The miller was complaining, in a languid sort of a way, about the irregular speed. Finally, the governor of the old engine was put on the new engine, and then the speed began to behave itself.

* * * * A gentleman wrote to Mr. Baker asking for information regarding his experience with this engine. He replied that it was a very good engine, and, with some trifling changes made by the engineer, was giving perfect satisfaction. Said he did not see why it was not every bit as good as the old engine, and he knew it to be very much better looking. Said he was making money in the business.

CHAPTER XL.

MR. MARLING THE MOULDER.—HIS INDUSTRIAL AND SOCIAL HABITS.—HIS EFFORTS TO MAKE HIS CO-WORKERS MISERABLE.—HOW THEY APPRECIATED HIS EFFORTS.

* * * * Mr. William Marling is a moulder. He is a very common moulder, and does only the commonest kind of work. It cannot be charged that he has a soul above his business. Somebody might raise the question whether it could be proven that he has a soul at all, or that he has any idea that he has a business. I think he confines himself to the idea that he is a moulder.

Mr. Marling is not the kind of a man to make anything but a moulder out of—anything but the very commonest kind of a moulder, I mean. It was a happy thought which suggested to Mr. Marling the choice of a vocation, supposing, of course, that he thought some before choosing. With a full knowledge of Mr. Marling's intellectual, moral, and social qualities, in case I had been appealed to to select his vocation, I should have set him to work in the moulding shop, provided I could see plenty of very common moulding to do, so that his energy would not outrun his supply of work, and providing I cared nothing for the other moulders, who would thus be favored with Mr. Marling's company.

With such a grade of moulding as would call for special skill, or special anything, in view, or with a care for the moulders already at work, I hardly think I would have recommended the foundry to Mr. Marling, or Mr. Marling to the foundry, rather.

* * * * Mr. Marling is not only the commonest kind of a moulder, but is also a painfully common kind of a man.

As a moulder there is but little in Mr. Marling which draws him toward, or appeals to, the warm and sympathetic feelings of other moulders. When Mr. Marling gets burnt in the foundry the other moulders seem to feel just about as they would if Mr. Marling had not been burnt. When Mr. Marling mashed his nose by stumbling over a shank ladle, no one seemed called upon to think of arnica till the owner of the shop came in and saw the nose; no moulder thought of going after arnica till the owner went himself, and when the owner and arnica came back, no moulder thought of rubbing the arnica on the nose till they saw the owner doing it. They thought Mr. Marling would rub the arnica on his nose himself; that is if they thought anything about Mr. Marling at all.

The owner of the shop was a moulder, and might have many reasons for ministering to Mr. Marling's mashed nose, but I think he had no reasons which the other moulders didn't have. Maybe the owner was a little warmer, or a little quicker, or a little smarter, or a little broader in the mind than the other moulders. Maybe that would also account for his, instead of the other moulders, owning the shop. Who knows? It don't make any difference anyhow. Somebody had to own the shop, or else there wouldn't be any shop: and if there were no moulding shops what would the moulders do, and what particular trade would Mr. Marling have been forced to choose?

* * * * Mr. Marling is about forty years old. He has been working, or occupied rather, at his trade of common moulding for about twenty-five years. During that long twenty-five years he has never brought into the moulding shop a single idea which would tend to advance the moulder's trade, or an idea which would tend to advance the joys and pleasures of a moulder's life, or an idea which would in any degree add to the happiness of a moulder's wife or a moulder's children. I know moulders who go to work in a moulding shop, and give a new tone to the sandy atmosphere around them. Moulders change in life and character when these men come into contact with them.

When they go there is real hand shaking with something in the touch of it, and there are thoughts remaining. Mr. Marling is not that kind of a moulder.

* * * * If an association with Mr. Marling has any effect at all on his fellow moulders, it is to make them less happy. If a moulder has hopes in life; if he finds a certain pleasure in labor; if he goes home nightly to a home of his own, and has his fun with his wife and babies; if he sees the comfort and pleasures of these gradually increasing as the accumulation of his labor increases; if the little wrinkles in his face are all wrinkles of general good will to all who live; these things are not bettered one whit after contact with Mr. Marling.

If he has hopes, Mr. Marling tells him to give them up. If he can be pleasant while he works, Mr. Marling tells him never to be gay at a funeral. If he steps lightly toward his front gate, Mr. Marling sours him by pointing to somebody else's gate, which is a bigger gate. Mr. Marling changes the wrinkles in moulders' faces.

* * * * Notwithstanding nobody cares for Mr. Marling, Mr. Marling has an effect wherever he goes.

Mr. Marling carries his sole possessions in a very poor sort of a satchel.

Mr. Marling has worked twenty-five years, but he has no nice moulding tools. He has no nice clothes. He has no nice home. He has no family. He has no books, no watch, no fiddle, no nothing. He has no parents, or brothers, or sisters, or close warm friends. He has never been troubled with sickness.

It seems sad to work in a dirty moulding shop for twenty-five years, and then only own a trowel, two slicks, and two ratty suits of clothes. It seems sad not to have any ties or hopes in the world. But this is the case with Mr. Marling. Mr. Marling's efforts to make himself a miserable man, a serf, a slave, a specimen of all that is unpleasant, seem successful in themselves, but Mr. Marling has

Mr. Marling takes an inventory—a trowel, two slicks, and two ratty suits of clothes.—Page 356.

a mission which extends beyond himself. Mr. Marling's effort to produce certain conditions seems to take in all the moulders. Mr. Marling is generous with his misery. He has had experience in turning human life to nothing, and he proposes to have all other moulders understand the art. In this transfusion of ideas Mr. Marling is more successful than he is in common moulding. He seems to have devoted more of his mind to the former work. True, he gets paid for his common moulding, and gets no thanks even for his earnest efforts in making moulders sick of life. His is a labor of love.

Love of what? It's hard to tell. If Mr. Marling sees a moulder with a home and pleasures and worldly goods and hopes, Mr. Marling tells him that he should have everything in an ugly satchel so he could growl at fate.

Mr. Marling thinks his own condition the normal condition of a true moulder, and when he sees a moulder who seems to have been born into the world to live, he proceeds at once to treat his abnormal case.

* * * * When Mr. Marling goes to work in a moulding shop he at once assumes charge of the miseries of all the moulders. If he finds a foolish moulder with no miseries, he lends him a stake and shows him how to increase it. He lays out all the work for the men. Before he has been in a shop three days he has told every man just how much work he should put up per day. The men don't care for Marling, but there is something about him which stays by them and goes home with them and mixes into their home life.

They can wash facing dust off their bodies, but at home they find a marling kind of a something about their persons which won't rub off. It is unpleasant to wife and children, but it stays. Besides portioning out the work for the men, Mr. Marling sometimes undertakes the adjustment of wages. Long as I have known Mr. Marling, I have never known him to increase a moulder's pay. He devotes himself to reductions. If a moulder earns a little too much money, Mr. Marling will commence on the matter at once. The generous Mr. Marling wants all moulders to partake of his own miseries and to work for his own pay.

* * * * The idea of Mr. Marling making an individual effort to increase his own pay would seem queer to any one who knows him. An underpaid moulder is Mr. Marling's delight. A well paid man is his abomination.

Point out to Mr. Marling a moulder earning good wages, and you will see pain pictured on the face of misery. Soon, however, the pain will give way to pleasure, for he has labor before him—a labor of love. Love for what?

* * * * On several occasions Mr. Marling has made efforts to raise the pay of moulders, but when he found out that certain moulders took advantage of such increase of pay to surround themselves and their homes with more of the good things and good feelings of life, he saw that he was working in the wrong direction. Mr. Marling talks "live and let live," but a moulder must be very careful how he lives in Mr. Marling's view. Once Mr. Marling struck a shop where every moulder in it owned a house and lot, and had it all paid for. Then Mr. Marling was in real pain, but he set to work manfully. He pointed to these moulders pictures of the most finished misery and discontentment. He commenced to regulate the amount of work each should do. He found one man getting a nickel a day too much, and he tried to fix it.

He pointed to his own example, and invited them to follow it by heeding his words.

But it was all no good. These foolish prosperous moulders not only would not be taught by the experienced Mr. Marling, but they incontinently kicked him out of the shop and out of the town, and hustled his satchel and his trowel and his two slicks after him.

Mr. Marling thinks there are some queer moulders in this world.

CHAPTER XLI.

LOOKING FOR A COAL VASE WITH TRUNNIONS.—THE CONFUSION AMONG CATALOGUES.— A HARDWARE CLERK'S SYSTEM.—BENNETT'S SYSTEM OF KEEPING CATALOGUES. —CHORDAL'S OWN SYSTEM.

* * * * A short time ago I wanted a fancy coal vase to set alongside a fireplace. I went to a hardware store and was shown some. They didn't suit me. I said I wanted one hung on trunnions, so it would tip down. Hardware man said he never heard of such a thing. I told him to bring out his catalogues, find the thing and order one for me. He led me back to the office, and pulled out a drawer which contained about half a bushel of mixed-up trade catalogues, some in fair shape, some "busted" and separated into fragments, some sheet pieces crumpled up, and all in a state of chaos. The subject of catalogues drove the coal vase out of my mind, and I watched the search.

* * * The first catalogue picked out was a gorgeous volume on plated ware. Dealer fumbled over it aimlessly, and then laid it aside decisively. Of course, he knew that firm didn't make things for coal.

The next was an illustrated dissertation on chandeliers and lamp hangings. This received the same fumbling before being laid aside. The next was a stove catalogue, and called for a careful inspection from preface to finis. The next was a barn-door sized sheet of artificial wood ornaments. It was opened, scanned, and laid aside. Next, a small folder listing numerous night latches; then a note sheet in solid text, which was read entire to see if it said anything about coal vases hung on trunnions; next, a catalogue of stamped tinware. This was getting hot, and I saw the librarian scanning closely each cut of a bread box, or a cake pan, or match safe. Next came a piece of a catalogue commencing and ending with coal scuttles. Thinks

I, if this man has the luck to find one of the other pieces to that scrap, he may find what we want.

Then came a general hardware catalogue, whose index failed to show the proper thing. Then came more silverware, and more locks, and more hardware, and more stoves and moulds, and chandeliers, and screws, and tinware, and stamped and japanned ware, and wire work, and folders and price sheets without number, and then came the bottom of the drawer, and then bang went the litter back into the drawer, and then the hardware man said, "I can't find it."

* * * * He didn't find it, and he could not have found it if it had been in that drawer, as no doubt it was. He didn't seem to know how to find anything except by a random search among everything.

* * * * I did not care much about the coal vase, but I had got interested in the catalogue business. I went to another hardware store, and was met by a youth about eighteen years old.

Told him I wanted a coal vase. He showed me some. I said I wanted one on trunnions so it would tip down. Youth bit his lip and said he never had heard of such a thing, but if I would step back in the office he would investigate. We went, and before I could count ten this young man laid four catalogues on the desk; before I could count ten more he looked through certain pages in each of the four, and said to me, "I find no such thing, and can only get further information by writing to the parties."

* * * * This chap was "business" when it came to a question of catalogues, and I proposed to see more of him. The following conversation took place:

Chordal.—How do you know that coal vase isn't in some of your catalogues?

Clerk.—Because we only have four catalogues from houses handling that class of goods. Here they are, and I see nothing of it.

Chordal.—How do you know that you have not had half a dozen extra sheets or slips from Winchell since you got that catalogue of him?

Clerk.—I don't know it. I know I have, and I know the contents of every such sheet is noted here in the catalogue. See here. See this spittoon scratched out. That shows that its manufacture is discontinued. We got notice to that effect. See this cash box with its pencil note. "No tray in this size." We got notice to that effect. See this note, "See circular in back;" that was too long to write in. Here is an illustrated sheet pasted in the book, and forms part of the catalogue, and here in the front is pasted the last discount sheet. Some houses get up their catalogues and extra sheets so as to be added to catalogue in nice style, and I wish they would all do it. Sometimes we get a notice of change of price or style, which don't mean anything till we trace it back through half a dozen previous amendments. This forces us to keep all the circulars, though their effect is obsolete.

Chordal.—There's Sidney Shepard & Co.'s catalogue. How do you know that is the last one, or that my swiveling coal vase isn't in a previous one?

Clerk.—This is Sidney Shepard & Co.'s catalogue to date and complete. We get the new ones as soon as issued. If the new one is a supplement to the old one, I fasten it to the old one, or write "See our supplement" on the title of the old one. If the new one is a substitutive catalogue, I burn the old one up. We have not a full line of catalogues by any means, but I can quickly get at anything in what we have got.

Chordal.—How do you keep them in shape for quick reference?

Clerk.—Easily enough. I pencil a number on each one, and pile them up in consecutive order. This list pasted on the wall gives the number of any firm's catalogue, and tells whether it is in the bottom of the pile or in the top.

That's about all there is of it, except that they are put back in place each time they are used.

Chordal.—How about little sheets, circulars, folders, card notices, etc.? They are not stuck in that pile, are they?

Clerk.—Yes, they are. See here: The list says, "Yale locks, 26, and En. 17." That means that there is a Yale catalogue, which is number 26, and also some Yale stuff in one of those big envelopes marked number 17. Here it is now. You see this little thing is a catalogue by itself, and should not be pasted in the main catalogue. You see it marked "En. 17," so we will know where to put it when done with it.

* * * * I arranged about the future of the coal vase on trunnions, so it would tip, and went off admiring the evidence of system, small as it was, which this clerk in a retail hardware store had seen fit to produce.

* * * * If catalogues are much to the hardware store, they are more to the machine shop. The item from a catalogue stands on its own value and profit in a store, but in the shop it may be a key note and turning point on a heavy job.

* * * * Queer things happen in regard to printed matter. I knew Walker to tumble over his printed matter for three days to find the price of a three-inch tube expander. He had the list, and should have been able to find it in three minutes. Rockwell held a customer around all day while he tried to find out if Judson's governor, fitted as a Sawyer's cut off, was in the market. He finally telegraphed, and ten minutes later uncovered the identical circular searched for. A two-dollar safety valve or check valve will often call for a three-dollar search in drawers, pigeon holes, boxes, barrels, and what not. Inch and three-quarter gas pipe must be ordered at least once before it is discovered that there is no such thing, when the papers in the case are inevitably on hand—*i. e.*, somewhere, if we only knew where to look for them. Pipe fittings, such as crosses, odd tees and manifolds, are always a puzzle. Some office men settle this thing at once and forever by pasting a long-searched-for circular on the wall, and then they sink into ignorance of all the things not so pasted.

* * * * I was in Bennett's office, and had an eye for his plan of dealing with printed matter. He has a case containing fifty drawers, numbered plainly.

An index book hangs beside this case. I examined this index under the letter H, and found entries like this:

Harrison Boiler Works, 12.
Hall, Thomas, 24.
Halteman, A. K., & Co., 6.
Hammers, Steam, 44.
Hangers, etc., 31.
Head Blocks, 16.
Heaters, 29.
Holly Manufacturing Co., 16.
Horse Powers, 46.
Hoisting Engines, 24.
Hoisting Machinery, 24.
Hydrants, 8.

I saw at once that firm names and general classes of goods were entered, so that a thing could certainly be found under some head. I also noticed that there was no attempt to classify the different catalogues. They were all simply put somewhere, and a record made so they could be found. I liked this negative feature, because it showed a disposition not to undertake so much as to deter the undertaking altogether. One little defect rendered this whole thing valueless. I wanted J. A. Fay & Co.'s catalogue, and looking in the index under F, I found Fay, J. A. & Co., 32. I looked all through drawer number 32, but couldn't find a sign of J. A. Fay & Co. I called on Bennett for help. He repeated the process, and then commenced to go for the unknown party who had put that thing in the wrong drawer. A general search among numerous drawers developed the catalogue. There was no number on it to show which drawer it belonged in, and memory had failed the party last using the catalogue.

I mentioned the hardware youth's plan of numbering each circular so as to show where each one belonged, and Bennett at once set a boy at work to straighten every drawer by the index, and to mark the drawer number on every separate scrap therein. I have no doubt, should I call on Mr. Bennett now, that before proceeding to business he would first index me under my appropriate number and shove me into a pigeon-hole marked C.

* * * * For my own part I have a sort of literary pride in preserving catalogues, price lists, photographs, etc., and have gone to a trouble and expense in the matter which I hardly think many will care to incur. As fast as catalogues, etc., accumulate I sort them into uniform sizes and have them bound in volumes. In each volume I put an index, which refers to every individual article of subject or person. At the end of fifteen volumes I have a general index of the same careful construction. In looking over one of these indexes, I find Slate's taper-turning arrangement referred to under the heads : Slate—Taper—Turning—Lathe—Former, and Pratt & Whitney.

* * * * Such a plan as this is a marvelous convenience, and I should feel helpless without it, as it enables me to hunt up a thing belonging to no special class of goods, and not known to be in any particular manufacturer's list. Thus I want to get on the track of a charcoal filter for sugar works ; I find it referred to as being in the catalogue of a concern popularly supposed to be builders of woolen machinery exclusively. Nothing but such a specific index as I refer to could ever unearth the thing—a search through a ton of catalogues being altogether out of the question.

The indexing must be done thoroughly or it is not worth

Bennett's office—indexing Chordal under his proper number, and shoving him into a pigeon-hole marked C.—Page 366.

having. Reference must be made under every possible name a thing may have. A man may want a " Monte Jus," without knowing there is such a thing as a Monte Jus. In the index spoken of I find it referred to under Monte Jus —Pressure Pump—Sugar—Beet Sugar—Distilling, etc., etc.

* * * * It seems to me that simply numbering the article, let it be book or sheet or card, and putting it into a numbered drawer, or filing case with one index, is about as convenient and accessible a plan as need be followed in most shops, and its expense is practically nothing. It also permits of a periodical weeding out of obsolete price lists, etc.

CHAPTER XLII.

ALTERING THE FORM OF A MECHANICAL PRODUCT TO SUIT CUSTOMERS.—SOME OPINIONS AND EXPERIENCES.—HOW THE PUBLIC SCHOOL PRINCIPALS LIKED THE INK.—HOW MACHINE-SHOP PRINCIPALS MAY TAKE A HINT.

* * * * In one of my very earliest letters to you, I referred to the question of altering the form of a product to please the present customer. I gave the views of the leaders of two classes, Mr. Sackett and Mr. Wyckoff. Mr. Wyckoff said he would do anything a customer wanted him to, and that he did not care whether the want was right or wrong. Mr. Sackett said he would make no changes, except such as would add permanently to the value of things. He would lose a sale before he would gratify the unwise whim of a customer.

* * * * Later experiences of my own have caused me to often think of my interviews with Wyckoff and Sackett. I have talked with and gathered the opinions of others on this subject, and I feel that I am doing a service in presenting to you the various views of various men.

* * * * Mr. G—— was many years ago a leading manufacturer; I need not say of what. He is now on the dwindle. In a conversation with me lately, he expressed himself about as follows: "When I was in good business I seldom looked around for causes. I exerted myself; the people bought my product; it satisfied them, and I made money. Young competitors sprang up around me, and my business began to fall off. Then I began to look into the science of the thing. I compared the products with a just judgment, and saw no merit in the competing articles superior to my own. Still, the articles were driving me from the market. I compared business processes, and found that my own exertions, under the decline, were far more energetic than those of my competitors, whose trade seemed almost to seek them. I then did what few men of my age and experience would do. I sought the advice of younger men. I got it in the opinion that my competitors made what the people wanted. I decided to do likewise. I investigated the form of competing products, and found that with unchanged functions they had been given meretricious shapes of novelty. I further found that the shapes, etc., were originated without an express demand from the market, and that the market welcomed the pleasing changes. All I had to do was to anticipate the wants of the people, and design my product accordingly. That was all. I soon found, however, that I could not take the first step in that direction. It required a genius of prophecy and perception far less attainable to my mind than the spirit of useful invention. I might add to the position, utility, or capacity, or convenience of a thing; but to deliberately entertain the idea of an Eastlake wheelbarrow, or a hand-painted crowbar was beyond my ability. I cleaned out my old corps of talent, and substituted men of the new school—prophets, artists, inventors, gods of taste and genius.

"They produced forms of seductive grace and wondrous suitability. I found that qualities which I had considered meretricious were qualities of real merit.

"What I had called a fancy, trifling, weak thing, proved under my own tests to be the clumsy thing of old, properly proportioned, and better suited for its strains. The wheelbarrow was half as heavy and cost half as much as the old one, but it ran twice as easily, held twice as much, was twice as strong, and a thousand times as handsome. The crowbar had what looked like artistic swells and tapers, but which I found to be simply a scientific leaving off of metal where not needed. The things had really been too pretty to look useful to an old man like me.

"I now had my samples of things which my young advisers told me would sell, but I could not make them. My outfit, though very extensive and complete, was old style, and unsuited to the modern work. My chief men in the shops were of my own unmodern stamp, and not adaptable to the new way, and, above all, there was within me the feeling of inability to properly direct a business so much at variance with the past business of my life.

"Evidently my proper course was to abdicate in favor of a salaried manager of the modern type, and give him power to alter the plant and get new men. I am getting old now. I am rich. Life has few rough corners for me, and but few ambitions. Commercial ambition was the only prompter of what I have done in the matter so far, and when I see that before these promptings all the old men, who have been my lieutenants for years and years, must enter a new apprenticeship, and find themselves ignorant children or sour old men, as the case may be, I think seriously of quitting altogether, and throwing the onus of the change upon some one else. Either this or let the thing run back in its old channel. This will lead to a downward course, while if I quit, and quit soon enough, I can say I was one of the most useful and successful in my line."

* * * * So much for old Mr. G——, who never sees his customers. He sells to the trade. Mr. W—— builds something larger, and sees most of his customers. Here is what he says: "I always change when ordered and paid for it, except where I see that the change would do damage to my standing as a manufacturer. I didn't use to do it at all; and now I do it all the time with everything. It is having a bad effect on me and my business. The form of my product becomes uncertain and unrecognizable. If I send out a certain thing in good form and am praised for it, I immediately offset the matter by showing a defective shape in the next shipment. I find that my 'standing of product' account is generally on a balance with an ever-present tendency to run behind. I consider this such an important asset that the matter worries me. I think it better to sacrifice present profit to permanent future reputation for merit, than to sacrifice the immense future for the present profit. Still, I don't do what I think best. The effect of the erratic-production system on my own personality is bothering me also. Some years ago I had my business in my own hand. I was a king among my patrons. On my judgment and knowledge of what the majority needed my patrons depended; and in this position I had my own pride and reliance. As it is now, I yield to every wind that brings a sale. Instead of a king, I am the creature of my customer, who uses, not my judgment, but my ability to execute his will. I have begun to look upon myself as a mere moneyed workman. I no longer read up on things; I no longer contrive; I no longer look into requirements; I idly wait for instructions."

* * * * Mr. Morgan is still another kind. He builds big machines originated on his premises. Said he: "There never was a step taken in my line which I did not inaugurate myself. For years the trivial whims of customers had no effect on me; but finally, not from principle or policy, but from pure laziness, I began to doctor my machines at the suggestion of every buyer. I have never looked into the philosophy or policy or result of the thing, but I know it to be an infernal nuisance. Of two customers for a machine for exactly the same purpose, one will want something made larger so it will be better, and the other man will want the same part made smaller so it will be better. That's the way the thing goes. Of course I know better than any one customer, or any half-dozen of them, what is correct. It is my business to know. I sometimes, on my own account, sacrifice a thing which I know to be superior, for a thing which I know will give most universal satisfaction to the crotchets of buyers. The changes sometimes ordered in my machines are annoying and exasperating. That is what a man gets for being in the machine business anyhow. If I was to choose a new business I would make molasses, or something which customers would not ask to have changed in form every day."

* * * * I find on my desk an advertising circular from a certain manufacturer of ink in New York. The circular will do Mr. Morgan a service, and will also illustrate a valuable and rare feature in advertising. The circular says:

"To 175 Public School Principals of New York we sent circular inquiries regarding our ink, as follows:

Do you use it? Do you like it?

We summarize the answers as follows:

22 Use it; like it exceedingly.
92 Use it; like it.
18 Use it, and use no other.
12 Will order it.
4 Use it, but think it a little too thick.
1 Uses it, but thinks it a little too thin.
2 Use it; best ever used.
4 Don't like it.
2 Say it is too black.
6 Say it is too pale.
3 Went back to Davids'.
1 Likes Davids' color.
3 Not satisfied; will try it again."

Eastlake Wheelbarrow.

CHAPTER XLIII.

PERSONAL HISTORY OF A YOUNG MACHINIST.

* * * * A young machinist named John stepped from a train in a large city. He went to a hotel, cleaned the travel dust off, had a good breakfast, and started out upon what he considered the most important expedition of his life. He proposed to see the inside of some extensive machine shops.

* * * * This man John was a quick-witted fellow, son of a country banker, the graduate of a two-cent machine shop. This shop and his home were located far from navigable water and rail. He had worked five years at his trade; and had stuffed himself with things from the books, and with ambitions natural to an active mechanical mind. Up to the time that we speak of he had never seen but five machinists. He never saw but one planer, three or four lathes, one drill press, and he had never seen a twist drill. Until he was well started on his long trip he had never seen a locomotive. He had not yet seen a steamboat, nor a broad river by daylight, nor any form of steam engine, except simple horizontal ones, and the locomotive lately revealed to him.

This young fellow was bursting with inexperience. He had good sense and was as sharp as tacks. He had been palpitating for years with the thought of some day seeing things. Now the day had come; here was a large city full of everything pertaining to industry, and all those things on the most extensive scale. A circle of a day's journey would encompass every ambitious view. A mighty river rolled past the city and could show every type of inland steam craft. Only fifty miles to the ocean, with its massive vessels of sail and steam. Only one hundred miles to an immense locomotive-building establishment. There was a large machine-tool-building-shop in the city. There was immense water-works machinery, and a rolling mill, and nail works, and fabric mills, and shoe factories—such things, world without end!

This young man proposed to go and work at his trade, if such an ignoramus as he could get work, but he proposed to see something first. He knew not where to begin. He began to doubt his pleasures, as they seemed within reach. He had seen a locomotive, and had been disappointed, because it did not astonish him; it was exactly what he had expected, and nothing more. What would the other things be?

* * * * He visits the water works, and sees one of the most gigantic beam engines in the world. He is not a bit surprised at the size of the engine, but his breath is taken away at the size of the machine work. The books which had familiarized him with monstrous engines had never, for some reason, led him to think of the massive jobs of which such engines are composed. Here were connecting rods which would weigh as much as any lathe he had ever seen. Here was a cylinder near ten-foot bore, with cylinder heads, etc., to match. Up there was a walking-beam, and John could not bring himself to believe that all the cast iron which he had ever seen in his life, if put together, would make this beam. Here was a shaft eighteen inches in diameter, and John never dreamed that bar iron was made over four inches. What an immense thing a rolling mill must be! And what immense lathes and planers they must have to do such work!

Then he tried to imagine the lathe that had turned these thirty-foot fly-wheels. In his mind, he sees the lathe bed on legs, with a pile of chips under it; with its head-stock and tail-stock, and carriage, and tool post, and cone, and back gears, and change gears, and brass plate on the head-stock to tell what gears to use, and a belt shifter over the lathe, and a board on the lathe with tools on it. And then he thinks of the three feet from the floor to the top of the lathe bed, and of the fifteen feet from the top of the lathe bed to the centers—eighteen feet in all; and then he thinks of the little latheman only six feet long. How in the world does he work it? Does he use a ladder to look at the tool?

John examines the engine critically, but sees no workmanship to puzzle him; he sees nothing which he has not done himself on a very small scale. He understands the engine perfectly, for he knows the books by heart.

* * * * John visits a big marine shop—the very shop, in fact, that built the big engine he saw at the waterworks. The first thing he notices is that this high-toned shop is a very much worse shop than the one he was brought up in, and that the only apparent difference is that this one is about five thousand times as big. He recognizes the floor, with its multitudinous heaps of scrap, finished work and litter.

He recognizes the dirty vise benches, the dirty walls, the rickety trestles, the odd blocks, and the greasy, blue workmen. He finds a big planer, and it is a huge one, twelve feet between housings. "But what makes this big planer look so small?" He ponders and scrutinizes, and finally discovers that it is the shortness of the planer which so affects its dignity. He thinks of the little two-foot planer at home, and expected to see here the same proportions on a grander scale. It seems to him this big planer is no longer than the little one. The big planer, in fact, planes thirty feet long—as long as six of his little planers; but this thirty feet, when compared with the twelve feet between the housings, seems to be nothing at all. The thing seems to be the longest the short way. He sees that it is all right, but is fearfully disappointed. For years he has been hoping to see a big planer, but he never hoped to see it look like that. He finally comes to the big lathe at work on a fly-wheel like the ones he saw at the water works. "Great guns! is this a lathe?"

A hole in the ground, stone walls, a few odd reckless pieces of casting, and a belt! "How have the mighty fallen!" The man doesn't need a ladder, unless it is to get down in a pit. He sees many kinds of machines, but nothing to surprise him, nothing to please. He sees no twist drills. Between the two shops he would rather have the little one at home, which strikes him as being more complete for its work. He looks among the men, but sees few faces to make him proud of his trade.

* * * * He goes to another shop and walks in. He hears the foreman talking "German," and it makes him sick and he walks right out. He goes to another shop, and here he finds a boring mill which he studies on for some time. Then he sees a man using a twist drill, and his spirits drop at the complete fulfillment of his hope. He inspects the river craft and thinks the machinery more slouchy than saw-mill work. He goes out to the locomotive town, but fails to discover anything new. He goes to the ocean and sees the heaviest marine work. What most surprises and pleases him is the consummate skill with which the traps have been gotten into the cramped spaces.

* * * * As in years gone by, our young man, John, again trembles before the door of a machine shop. He is going to ask for employment. He has never done so before and doesn't know how. If he was an old stager he would hunt up the foreman and say, "What's the chance for a job to-day?" But he is not an old stager and never heard that expression in his life.

He goes to the office and asks for the owner of the shop. The president of the company is pointed out to him, and he quickly introduces himself to him by name. He gives the president his history; tells him of the little shop out home; of his experience; of his vast ignorance; and concludes by asking him if he can go to work in the shop on any sort of terms which will enable him to learn something. The president picks his teeth and says in a decent sort of

He hears the foreman talking " German," and it makes him sick.—
Page 378.

a way, "I think we need some men out in the shop, but we want good men, and I don't see what use you can be to us just now, as we can get plenty of learners. You would be the same to us as an apprentice, exactly; but still I will turn you over to the foreman and you can see what can be done."

* * * * The foreman gave him less hope than the president; the shop was full of boys, and he wanted men. John went and looked around the shop some and examined the operation of things closely. A new idea struck him, based on what he had seen of the shop. He went to the foreman and wanted to hire out as a first-class man. He took the old man's breath away, and the matter finally ended in his being set to work. He was to receive the best of pay if he did the best of work.

* * * * At the end of the week he found his wages set at \$2.25 per day. This disgusted him.

* * * * Monday he devoted to business, and learned a great deal more of the machine business than he thought there was in it. He called at the office of the president of the company and was well received, and asked to state his business. He opened as follows: "I would like to ask why you don't pay better wages?"

"Young man," said the president, "if you think we set these wages you are mistaken. The machinist fixes his own wages at such a figure that other machinists will not out-bid him. Those wages we have to pay. When a man asks us what we are paying, we simply give the figure which our men are charging us. If you were in search of work, and I should tell you that we were paying a certain man \$4 per day, you would agree to take that man's place at \$3 per day, if \$3 seemed high enough to you; is that true or not?"

"Of course it is," said John, "but what will keep the next applicant from under-bidding me; and so on, and so on, till the wages were 10 cents a day?"

"The result of such a course," said the president, "would be, that the lower the wages got the less men would care for the places, and as a consequence, few new men would enter the uninviting trade. Men want the places were the wages are desirable, and as a consequence the under-bidding always ceases when undesirable figures are reached. If I should allow men to set their own prices, they would always set them a few cents below what other men are getting, so as to get a place. Every man in search of a place is auctioneering wages downward. If employers would listen to these bids the trade would soon invite no smart learners into it, and soon we could get no good men at all.

"The policy of the employers is to protect the trade against destructive cutting by the workmen. It makes no difference to me how high the wages in my shop are so long as the other shops have to pay the same. That new engine now being built I contracted to deliver for $2,000, and there were over twenty shops bidding on the job. If I had been paying my men $5 per day, some other shop paying only $2 would have got the job, and so with every job on which we would bid, until, finally, of course, I would have to shut up the shop, and my men would have to seek work in the $2 shops, and in order to get places they would bid slightly under $2. In this way you will see that high wages in one shop will finally reduce the wages all over. If all the shops had been paying $5 this could not happen, because all the bids on the engine would be based on the same cost of machine work. It is not high wages which does the harm in this way, but it is a difference in wages which plays the deuce. Every shop makes the most money during the time they can keep the men at work at the highest wages; this has never failed to be true since the trade was started. You had better cut that out and paste it in your hat."

"Then tell me," said John, "why in the world can't

some arrangement be made by which machinists all over the country can get high wages and keep getting them without any bother at all? This would pay the machinists better, and you say the shops would make more money."

"Well," said the president, "I wish that could be; but it cannot. You will see that low wages would chase learners out of the trade and bidders would become scarce, and in a like manner, high wages would bring learners into the trade, and the surplus number of bidders would auction wages down and spoil the whole thing. Another thing is this: That engine you worked on we now sell for $800, and we have a good trade in them. I have sold over 500 of those engines at that price, and as you see we keep about 30 men working on them all the time. Lots of men can afford to buy these engines and so there is plenty to do on them. Ten years ago we never dreamed of selling one of these engines for less than $1,200, and at that figure I never succeeded in selling more than a dozen of them altogether. Few people can afford to buy such expensive engines, and our 30 men would soon have had to go fishing. Instead of going fishing and getting no wages they work for less wages and cut the price of the engines way down, and now, behold, every Tom, Dick and Harry wants one of those engines, and I have no doubt but that these 30 men will be building these engines ten years from now. Let me double their wages, and thus double the price of the engine, and very soon nobody could afford to buy these engines, and we would all have to quit business. I give you this merely as an example, but it will hold good for everything made in machine shops. What would the farmers do if the machinists who build their reapers should charge $5 a day for building them?"

"It is easy to tell," said John; "they would have to cut their grain by hand."

"Well," said the president, "do you know how many hands are now employed on reapers?"

"I should judge," said John, "from what I have read of the reaper business that there must by five or six thousand men at it." (This was many years ago.)

"Now," said the president, "do you know of any shorter way for those five thousand men to kill their business of reaper building than simply to raise their price?"

"I don't see any other way," said John, "by which they can kill it at all."

* * * * "Now," said the president, "I have given you the views of a man who has worked 30 years in the shop, and I ask you these questions: First, what will keep wages up?"

"Why," said John, "lots of men to buy machine work and very few workmen to underbid on doing it."

"Second question," said the president, "what will keep wages down?"

"Why," said John, "very little to do and lots of men wanting to do it."

"Next question," said the president, "at what point do wages stop going down?"

"When they are down so low that they are not worth the having if any lower," said John.

"Last question," said the president, "where is the desirable point to have wages stick?"

John studied awhile and finally answered, "at the highest point at which purchasers will buy all of the work that all of the men will do."

* * * * It was fifteen years ago that I met John as I happened to be working in this same shop. I lost sight of him soon after, but I now have his full history up to date. It is full of interest, and his name is well known.

CHAPTER XLIV.

DIFFERENT KINDS OF FOREMEN.

* * * * I actually believe that all the immense amount of rushing work now being done is done by fifty per cent. of the men employed on the work. Certain elastic workmen feel every change in times. When things are dull and but few hands working, the special ones of the few will do less in a given time than the balance. When things boom and the shop fills up, these chaps get enthusiastic and pitch in and do the work, and they keep doing it. Their rise in spirits is the only thing tending to keep up the average performance.

* * * * Priceless is the enthusiastic boss who can keep his hands off things. The temptation to take a dull-headed man's work out of his blundering hands is a strong one, but it must be resisted, or the boss sinks into a mere improver of a single blunderer's work, and as such is worth per day just the increase effected in one man's work, and no more.

* * * * John Paul was a foreman in a machine shop, and had charge of about a dozen men. Wherever you would find this foreman, John Paul, you would find a machinist standing close by watching John Paul do the work.

John Paul was a splendid workman and a good worker, but he did not know how to pick out good men, or how to make good men out of indifferent ones.

An extra heavy job had to go into a lathe. John sends Jim, a laborer, after a sixteen-foot ladder. In comes the end of the ladder, ubiquitously hitting everything in the shop, followed at half stroke by Jim, the clumsy, who carries it. Why should not Jim be as able as any one to engineer a ladder into and through a machine shop? He has been superintendent of that ladder for months, but has never been able to improve its running time. John Paul, with an impatient mutter, with eye and mind on the spot where he wants the top of the ladder to go, takes two quick strides, snatches the ladder from Jim, and, with one free, perfect, thoughtless movement, plants it exactly in the right place. I question if he thought of the process or of the ladder. He saw only the place up there. There is an eyebolt, close up to the flooring, between two joists. He tells Sam, the big lathesman, to go up the ladder with the chain block. Sam fusses with the hook and strains himself, works clumsily at arm's length, and runs his tongue out of the corner of his mouth, blows the dust out of his eyes, and wears himself out and gets shaky. John Paul twitches impatiently, for the thing is tiring him as much as Sam. He calls Sam down, takes the block up the ladder, hooks it in place and comes down again. Why could not Sam do a little thing like that as well as John Paul? Then there's a sling to rig up, and a chuck to take off at the eleventh hour, and a dog to get, and a tail stock to set, and a carriage to be run out of the way, and a tug on the chain, and a steering of things, and an oil can to get, and a center to oil, and a final and finishing screwing up of the center when the job is in place. Who does most of all this? The six men standing around? John Paul does it.

* * * * Do the men shirk? Not a bit of it. They pester John Paul by their abortive willingness. Then why does John Paul do this work? Another question too hard for me.

* * * * John Paul's brother-in-law, Paul Johnson, is a boss, too, and works fifty men. No ladders, or blocks, or chucks, or oil cans in his labor. He gives his orders, and behold, the work is done as though he had an army composed of John Pauls working for him.

John Paul can only push one thing at a time. Paul Johnson waves his hand and a dozen ladders move to place, a dozen chain blocks work themselves up, chucks

John Paul on the ladder.—Page 386.

unscrew themselves, tail stocks retreat, carriages get out of the way, jobs rise into place, and oil cans squirt. What share has Paul Johnson in these things going on all around him? What magic is there in that wave of his hand? What kind of clay is Paul Johnson made of, and where was the error in mixing it when John Paul was made? I give it up.

* * * * John Paul's soul was in a constant revolt against awkwardness, clumsiness, ignorance and stupidity. He appeased his revolted soul by doing the work himself with active, intelligent dexterity. What will become of a shop full of men while a too nervous foreman is appeasing a revolted soul with a key drift, or a file, or a lathe, or a hand reamer, or a pipe die, or a crowbar? John Paul never seems to have struck on any successful plan for transferring some of his excellent qualities to his men. He can simply substitute his own excellent labor for theirs.

Considering the fact that John Paul will do about five men's work without knowing it, his mode of operation is not so very bad when he is working only eight or ten men. The smart men do their own work, and John Paul does the work of the dull ones. It takes just so much pay roll to get so much work done.

* * * * But with fifty men is John Paul long enough to reach? Won't there be more pay roll than work? With Paul Johnson it is different. Ten men, forty men, a hundred men, all are the same to him, except that he has trouble keeping engaged when he has but a few men to attend to. Two more men means two more days' work per day to Paul Johnson, and he doesn't do this extra work himself either. I wish I knew how he managed it.

* * * * Paul Johnson is no machinist himself. He don't know how to file anything flat, but he knows how to get flat filing done. If he undertook to file a piece of brass he would not know what was the matter with the slippery thing, and would call for new files indefinitely. But he don't undertake to file brass. If he should screw up a pipe joint it would leak. But he has other men screw up pipe joints and there must be no leaks. If he tried to waltz a ladder through a crowded shop the ladder would get away with him. If he should attempt to reach up and hook a chain block in place, he would break his neck. But there is no danger. He is not a member of the hook and ladder company. He is the chief.

* * * * Another thing Paul Johnson don't do is to be eternally belittling the skill of his men by going over their work. He may test the work, but you can't catch him at it, and the shop turns out accurate work.

* * * * A man working for John Paul puts a line through an engine; along comes John Paul and tests the line with calipers. The man puts a marked stick in the crank pin; John Paul measures the stick. The man rotates the main shaft and squares it by the line; he must rotate it some more, so that John Paul can see if it is square.

A good blacksmith has just hardened a big tap; John Paul will sandpaper it and draw the temper properly. A big shaft is to have shoulders turned at certain spots; John Paul measures and prick-punches, and when the shoulders are turned he measures again to see that no mistake has been made by the lathesman. A shrinking fit is to be made. This is John Paul's sole prerogative of course. John Paul puts on the big belts; John Paul cuts and laces such belts; John Paul has the biggest crowbar when something is to be pried, and he has the heaviest strain when there is a lift. John Paul's mind centers on the thing to be done and neglects all else. A heavy job is to be shifted under a radial drill; John Paul is of course on hand as one of the main shifters. With intent mind, and dexterous bar, and horizontal back, he is doing the work of the entire gang, to the total neglect of his minor end, which the revolving twist drill delights to seize.

Whatever John Paul does, he does properly. He does it properly because he is honestly anxious to see it properly done. What don't he do? What would be done if he didn't do it?

Paul Johnson does no such business as this, and the work is all done, and properly. How does he manage it, anyhow?

* * * * A few weeks ago I stood in the top gallant crosstrees of a big beam engine. The cylinder head was to come off, and Hanlon, the chief engineer, had sent three men up to do the work. Hanlon had half a dozen of these engines under his charge, and plenty of men, but he did nine-tenths of the work done around the engines. He stood by me as his men unscrewed at the thousand-and-one nuts which held the cylinder head on. The work proceeded very slowly, as things were hot, positions awkward, and the men a trifle clumsy. I saw Hanlon was itching to go at it himself, but by idle conversation I held him back till about ten nuts had been removed by the three men. I turned my head and when I turned it back again Hanlon had possession of the field. He had cleared all the men away except one to follow him up to remove the loose nuts, and in a jiffy was done with the job. I asked him why he couldn't keep his fingers off, and he said "It hurts me to see things drag." Even so with John Paul.

* * * * One bad thing about John Paul and Hanlon is, that by degrees their men become untrustworthy and absolutely worthless in the absence of their chief.

Certain air valves of Hanlon's engines are articles of consumption. They are bound to give out, and duplicates are always held. Putting new ones in is a somewhat tedious, dirty and undesirable job, but Hanlon is the man who always does the job.

I looked at this as a fault, and Hanlon said, "I have had men put these valves in, but they never did it right. There is too much at stake, and I will never trust a man to put one in again as long as I have charge of these engines."

* * * * I asked Hanlon what provision he had made against his absence by sickness or otherwise. He said he couldn't get sick. Had to stay and tend to those valves, or fancied he did. He thought it might be a fancy, but, if so, it was a very troublesome one. Is John Paul a man of mere fancies? If he is, there are many such. Do not let me be understood as denying the potency of a master's eye. There must be one head to everything, but if that head, who should direct the general policy of the business, fritters away his time on trivial details, the great matters of the concern are liable to be overlooked; the manager is worn out, and the men, finding they are not trusted, become indifferent and in time untrustworthy. I know of a large establishment where the proprietor wished to know about and check the smallest detail of his business. He is always in a stew, and runs from one thing to another and yet never accomplishes anything. You can't be with him ten minutes but you feel nervous and irritated. He had a good foreman, one capable of taking all this matter off his hands, but the foreman became discouraged, for he could not give any instructions, not even "jaw an apprentice," but the proprietor asked for an explanation. The result was that another firm marked the foreman as a rising man, and it took but little inducement to get him away. Since he left, the business steadily declined; the proprietor still frets and worries; he has grown through his hair and now parts it in the middle with a nice coarse towel.

The servants of the machinist.—Page 395.

CHAPTER XLV.

A SHOP WITH SERVANTS FOR THE WORKMEN.

* * * * The Niles Tool Works had, and still has, one of those long shops running the whole length of a city block, with a tool room located in the center. Probably no better form of shop has ever been devised, but the form has one demerit. The men and the foreman and the laborers have to walk long distances in the ordinary working of things, and the long trips to the tool room are well calculated to wear the average machinist out in the leg part, even before noon. An ordinary machinist doesn't object to walking his legs off going to and from the machine shop, where he makes his living working at the trade, but he is justified in growling at a ten-mile tramp between meals.

* * * * The Niles Works have lately added three new shops to their long establishment, and the result is that the distances have increased, and the tool room is no longer in the center. It is an easier matter to build machine shops than it is to move a tool room to the spot where the center of gyration will be supposed to exist. In the shop referred to a plan has been inaugurated which, so far as I know, is new and worthy of investigation. They have put in an electric call system, with an annunciator at the tool room, and have numbered push buttons at every vise and machine, and scattered around generally. Bell boys are stationed at the tool-room bar. Tom, Dick or Harry wants a drill, or a reamer, or some waste, or his oil can filled. He touches his button and a boy dances up to him for instructions. These boys are to black their boots and keep their faces clean, and sleeves rolled down. They are not apprentices, nor cubs, nor laborers. They are the servants of the workmen. This arrangement is not yet completed, but will be in a week or two, and I will make inquiries and post you as to its workings.

* * * * If I, in my days, had been lucky enough to find myself working in a shop with a slave of the ring to answer the bell, I should certainly have insisted on the thing's being done up brown with a man at the grindstone to do the heavy sharpening.

* * * * At one time I dumped all the fancy tools out of my tool box, and provided myself with a tip-top set of lathe tools. This was to prevent borrowing. I always hated a grindstone, and it finally occurred to me that, if I had a double set of tools, I would be happier. I doubled up and then had a pair of side tools, a pair of diamond points, three or four cutting-off tools, a patent screw-cutting tool with removable cutters, and two pairs of broad, square-ended tools. These latter were always favorites with me, as I could use them for almost anything, especially for all chuck work. I never found anything so good for boring out big work, like packing rings, etc., and they could be used for all manner of big turning and facing. But the double set of tools didn't help me any on the grinding question. I got to putting off the operation of grinding till everything got dull, and then I had to go and stay by the grindstone till meal time. I always preferred a lathe to a grindstone, and my objections to having my lathe stand still an hour or two were not entirely disinterested on my part.

No one ever offered to grind any tools for me, and no boy ever came around to see if I didn't want something done.

www.ingramcontent.com/pod-product-compliance
Lightning Source LLC
Chambersburg PA
CBHW030427300426
44112CB00009B/889